# GREAT FRENCH
# DETECTIVE STORIES

# Great French Detective Stories

## Edited by T. J. Hale

NEW YORK
THE VANGUARD PRESS

First American Edition 1984

**Library of Congress Cataloging in Publication Data**

Main entry under title:
Great French detective stories.

Bibliography: p.
1. Detective and mystery stories, French—Translations into
English. 2. Detective and mystery stories, English—Translations
from French. I. Hale, T. J.
PQ637.D4G7   1984       843'.0872'08       84–13062
ISBN 0-8149-0892-6

Manufactured in the United States of America

To Natacha

'. . . and the muse who presides over the police romance, a lady presumably of French extraction . . .'

*Robert Louis Stevenson*

# ACKNOWLEDGMENTS

Thanks are due to the following copyright holders for permission to reprint the stories:

*The Mysterious Railway-Passenger* by Maurice Leblanc reprinted with permission of Macmillan Publishing Co, Inc from *The Seven of Hearts* by Maurice Leblanc, translated by Alexander Teixeira de Mattos; Victor Gollancz Ltd for *The Mystery of the Four Husbands* by Gaston Leroux, translated by Mildred Gleason Prochet, from *The Gaston Leroux Bedside Companion* edited by Peter Haining (1980); Georges Simenon for *Storm over the Channel* by Georges Simenon from *Les Nouvelles Enquêtes de Maigret* (Editions Gallimard, 1944); Mme Faure-Biguet for *The Amethyst Fly* by Jacques Decrest from *Six Bras en L'Air* (No. 1 *Le Labyrinthe*, 1943); Productions Saint-Clair for *Watch the Red Balloons* and *The Lady of the Museums* by Pierre Véry from *Cinéma, Cyanure et Compagnie*; Léo Malet for *The Haulage Company* by Léo Malet from Ellery Queen's *Mystère-Magazine*, April 1952.

Every effort has been made to trace the owners of copyright material but in some cases we have not been successful. We apologise to anyone our enquiries didn't reach and invite them to apply to The Bodley Head for appropriate acknowledgment if it is due.

# CONTENTS

# INTRODUCTION

The intention of this anthology is partly historical, but partly too to introduce an English audience to some Continental writers of detective stories who have been unfairly neglected in this country since before the Second World War. The reason for this will become apparent. With a few exceptions, there has been little good detective fiction which has not been written in English or French. All the authors gathered here are either French or Belgian, but they have more in common than the fact that they share the same language. They have all been highly original innovators of their chosen genre. They are the representatives of a century of French detective writers.

Some years before Sherlock Holmes made his first appearance, in *A Study in Scarlet* (1887), Emile Gaboriau, a Frenchman, had been writing lengthy serials for the Parisian popular press in which his detective, Monsieur Lecoq, made the same sort of oracular pronouncements as Holmes was to become known for later. In *Monsieur Lecoq* (1869), for example, he examines the snow-covered ground outside an inn, and describes the man who had walked across it half an hour before: 'He is middle-aged and very tall, wearing a soft cap and a chestnut-coloured overcoat with a fleecy surface. He is very probably married.'

Edgar Allan Poe's Chevalier Dupin was pulling a similar sort of trick a quarter of a century before him. It was Poe, an American, who wrote the first clearly recognizable detective stories which he set, appropriately, in Paris. He synthesized ideas he had gained from the memoirs of the first real-life French detective, Eugène-François Vidocq, with the narrative technique developed by the English anarchist William Godwin in his novel *Caleb Williams* (1794). As with most syntheses, the end result bore little resemblance to what had gone into it.

In the early days, then, the impetus of the detective story shifted from England to France, then to America and back to France, from whence back to England. Today, the only Continental writer of detective stories who is read to any significant extent in England is Georges Simenon, creator of Maigret. But it has not always been so. In his day, Emile Gaboriau was well subscribed to in this country. As well as his newspaper serializations, he also wrote the first French detective short story, *The Little Old Man of Batignolles*, which was published in 1876, three years after his death. After the Holmes phenomenon, Maurice Leblanc and Gaston Leroux both enjoyed enormous popularity in the 1920s in Britain, and the latter exerted a not inconsiderable influence on the overall development of the genre.

By the 1930s England and America were producing enough home-grown talent not to be dependent any longer on France, and consequently the many fine Continental writers of that epoch and after are unknown—or virtually unknown—in translation. It was the decade of Ellery Queen and John Dickson Carr, of Margery Allingham, Ngaio Marsh, Agatha Christie and Dorothy Sayers, of Nicholas Blake and Michael Innes. On the other side of the Channel, the French detective story underwent a process of renewal under the impact of translated English and American material. Authors such as Pierre Véry, Jacques Decrest and, later, Léo Malet, all of whom are to be found in this anthology, rapidly established themselves in this period, as did others, such as Noël Vindry and Pierre Nord, who unfortunately are not included, for the very good reason that they did not write any short stories. Yet for all their considerable talent, only one of their contemporaries, Georges Simenon, has won recognition beyond the Continent, and even he was poorly received initially.

## Godwin and Vidocq

Some historians of the detective novel, confusing its genesis with its explanation, seek to find its origins in ancient history: in Herodotus, Greek legends, the Bible, *The Thousand and One Nights*, and so on. In a seminal study, *Le 'Detective Novel' et l'influence de la pensée scientifique* (1929), Régis Messac analysed all these various sources thoroughly without ever realizing this distinction. For although examples of deductive reasoning can be found in most ancient writings, they serve as indications of the universality of logical thought, not as instances of detective stories.

William Godwin's *Caleb Williams* (1794), although a remarkable novel of criminal detection and pursuit, must likewise be considered as generally outside the critical canon of the detective story. It was intended as a political novel, and we must not lose sight of the original title of the book, *Things As They Are.* The author of an *Enquiry Concerning Political Justice* (1793) was anxious to show the extent to which human motives depend on social conditions; he was not concerned with writing a detective story.

It was Godwin's method of construction in *Caleb Williams* which was significant for the development of the detective story. In a later account of the novel's composition,[1] which Poe was certainly aware of since he obliquely refers to it in his essay *The Philosophy of Composition* (1846), Godwin states that he 'formed a conception of a book of fictitious adventure, that should in some way be distinguished by a very powerful interest'. This interest would be provided by 'a series of adventures of flight and pursuit; the fugitive in perpetual apprehension of being overwhelmed with the worst calamities, and the pursuer, by his ingenuity and resources, keeping his victim in a state of the most fearful alarm'. From this point, Godwin followed his theme backwards. First, it was necessary to project the motive responsible for such a persecution. 'This I apprehended could best be effected by a secret murder, to the investigation of which the innocent victim should be impelled by an unconquerable spirit of curiosity.' And lastly, Godwin had to excite our sympathy for the persecutor as well as for his victim.

This process of regression from effect to cause, from solution to problem, lies at the very heart of detective fiction. It is the basis of the achievement of Poe, Gaboriau and Doyle. Nearly a century later Holmes could say:

Most people, if you describe a train of events to them, will tell you what the result would be. They can put those events together in their minds, and argue from them that something will come to pass. There are few people, however, who, if

II

you told them a result, would be able to evolve from their own inner consciousness what the steps were which led up to that result. This power is what I mean when I talk of reasoning backwards, or analytically.[2]

Caleb is the victim of his own insatiable curiosity and of his unrelenting pursuer. At first, Caleb is the pursuer of his employer, the rich landowner, Falkland, but once Falkland admits the murder to him, Caleb becomes his victim's victim. 'Do you know what you have done?' Falkland asks him. 'To gratify a foolish inquisitive humour, you have sold yourself. You shall continue in my service, but never share my affection.' When Williams attempts to escape, he is hounded across England and Wales by Falkland's agent, Gines.

Gines, who 'had fluctuated during the last years of his life, between the two professions of violator of the laws and a retainer to their administration', was not an uncommon figure in that century. There was considerable hostility to the idea of a police force, lest it be staffed by government spies, and the standard practice was to offer rewards for 'information leading to arrest'. The system was open to considerable abuse. Rogues like Jonathan Wild, the self-styled 'Thief-Taker General of Great Britain and Ireland', were able to recover stolen goods, taking a large cut from the reward offered and letting the thief go free, merely by developing their connections with the underworld. There was a code: 'Among the honourable fraternity of thief-takers it is a rule never to bring one of their own brethren to a reckoning, when it can with any decency be avoided.'[3] Unfortunately, Caleb's case 'did not fall within the laws of honour he [Gines] acknowledged'. Occasionally, Wild would organize robberies in order to earn the reward. He was hanged in 1725, but did not lack imitators. Gines was in this tradition.

Godwin anticipated the logic of the detective story and, as a further mark of his genius, in Gines he anticipated Vidocq.

Although *Caleb Williams* was translated into French in the same year which saw its publication in England, it is doubtful whether Eugène-François Vidocq (1775–1857), the son of a poor Arras baker, ever read it.

There cannot have been much opportunity for reading in his early life; he was, in rapid succession, thief, circus performer, vagabond, foot-soldier (fighting fifteen duels in six months), deserter, smuggler, corsair and gaol-breaker. Above all, he was a gaol-breaker. But by 1809 he was tired of life on the run and decided to become an honest man by the simple expedient of turning police informer. After twenty-one months as a prison spy, his escape was engineered by the authorities and in the same year, 1811, he was appointed Chief of the Sûreté, the detective force that he had created under the aegis of Monsieur Henry, head of the criminal department of the Paris police. It was not a large force; at first Vidocq was allowed only two agents, though later he commanded twenty-eight.

Vidocq continued as Chief of the Sûreté for the next sixteen years. Nearly all the men he employed were ex-convicts, and he seems to have been pleased with them. But despite the phenomenal number of arrests they effected, or perhaps because of it, there was mounting criticism that they acted as *agents provocateurs*. Moreover, their probity, and that of their chief, came increasingly under attack—mostly, it seems, from orthodox police officers, jealous of their successes, and disgruntled politicians.

It is unlikely that Vidocq would have resigned, all the same, unless it suited him to do so. When he left, in 1827, there were two projects which he had in mind. One was the partly philanthropic venture of starting a paper factory, recruiting the work-force from amongst ex-convicts, many of whom returned to crime because they were unable to find jobs; the other was to write his memoirs.

The first half of Vidocq's *Mémoires* contains an account of his adventures set against the background of Revolutionary Europe; only the second part relates his career as a detective. But, like most amateur manuscripts, Vidocq's was too short. To recoup his generous advance, his publisher, Tenon, required a lengthy *succès de scandale*.

The first volume was 'revised' by a literary hack, Emile Morice. Vidocq insisted on him being sacked, but he would have done better to have left him well alone, for he was succeeded by an even greater literary villain, L. F. L'Héritier. L'Héritier produced another three volumes of progressive supplementations, culminating in the last volume in which he interpolated a poor novel of his own.

Although Vidocq's original writings are devoid of any literary pretensions, the story he tells is a good one, not least because of his sympathetic characterization of the small-time crooks he knew so well. Vidocq's version is, in every way, superior to the excesses of his 'revisers'. But it is by the Morice and L'Héritier edition that he has been judged. In his invaluable history of the detective story, *Murder for Pleasure* (1942), Howard Haycraft remarks with some justice: 'If Vidocq was the colourful liar that this work indicates—if the work itself, as seems only too likely, contained vastly more romance than fact—then perhaps he, rather than Poe, was the actual if fortuitous inventor of the detective story!' The Appendix of this anthology consists of an excerpt chosen from Vidocq's *own* writing (though the title is taken from a sub-heading in the 1859 edition of the L'Héritier version) which has been edited by the Napoleonic scholar, Jean Savant.[4]

When Vidocq's *Mémoires* were published in 1828–9, the book was a sensation. It was the first time that a professional detective had appeared as a hero in literature. Unfortunately, though, there was little of the *deductive* detective about Vidocq. He was a thoroughgoing empiricist, whose methods were directly opposed to those of Sherlock Holmes. Each time he was entrusted with a case, Vidocq would dress up as a felon and sit around in the wine-shops until he overheard some talk of the theft. Once he had identified the criminal, Vidocq set about winning his confidence and so obtaining a confession or gathering information tantamount to a confession, such as the name of a receiver. Then Vidocq would arrest him, the criminal usually exhibiting suitable signs of surprise. There are, however, very occasional glimpses of the analytical detective, as in the story (see Appendix) where Vidocq recognizes the importance of footprints in criminal pursuit.

The duality of the criminal as hero was to become a fashionable theme. This ambiguity of role was highlighted in Vidocq by his skill in disguise: cook, cabinet-maker, German valet, thief. Gaboriau's M. Lecoq would also be a master of disguise, so would Holmes. In France, the criminal as hero would be a theme more exploited than in England (though we must not

14

forget Raffles). Vidocq would become Rocambole, Chéri-Bibi, Arsène Lupin, Fantômas.

In later years, Vidocq returned briefly to his old position, but was again forced to resign. He established a private detective agency in Paris, *Le Bureau des Renseignements*, some twenty years before Allan Pinkerton's *National Detective Agency* in Chicago. His friends included Victor Hugo and Balzac, and Vidocq is clearly to be seen in the pages of *Les Misérables:* a lasting tribute to one of the most remarkable figures of the age.

## Poe, Gaboriau and Doyle

Between 1840 and 1845, Edgar Allan Poe wrote five tales which were to establish the principal conventions of the detective story in the West. Of these, the three featuring the Chevalier C. Auguste Dupin and set in Paris, *The Murders in the Rue Morgue, The Mystery of Marie Roget* and *The Purloined Letter*, are pure detective stories. Two others, *The Gold-Bug* and *Thou Art the Man*, are also important forerunners. Poe's twofold achievement—first, in the delineation of his detective's character and, secondly, in the evolution of plot—have been too well chronicled to make it worthwhile attempting more than a few short remarks here.

It might be surprising that Poe, even briefly, should have relinquished writing his intense, melodramatic tales to adopt the logical complexities of detective stories; it is not surprising that he should have looked to France for a background. The French, ever since Descartes, have had the reputation of being a nation of philosophers—at least, for the Anglo-Saxon world. Moreover, Poe had read Vidocq, and had been impressed, even if literature's first fictional detective, his Dupin, could say, dismissively, of history's first real-life detective, 'Vidocq, for example, was a good guesser, and a persevering man. But, without educated thought . . .' Régis Messac has seen the origins of *The Purloined Letter* in a remark of Vidocq's: 'If you were obliged to be away from home for some time, where would you hide whatever you valued most except in the place most exposed; it is the only place no one would ever think of looking.' In Poe's story, a compromising document is left on the mantelpiece while the Prefect, Vidocq-style, has the thief waylaid twice and searched. The hiding-place hardly presents Dupin a problem.

The first of his tales of ratiocination, as Poe called them, was *The Murders in the Rue Morgue*. It opens, significantly, with an essay on the philosophy of analysis. Eventually Poe introduces his hero, the brilliant but eccentric Dupin, the first of a long line of purely cerebral detectives, whose keen amateur mind seems all the more sharply set against the comparative dullness of that of his, in this case, anonymous friend and narrator. This was to be the way of things for nearly a century: Holmes and Watson, Rouletabille and Sinclair, Hanaud and M. Ricardo, Poirot and Captain Hastings, Gaboriau's Méchinet and Godeuil in *The Little Old Man of Batignolles*.

Dupin finds the opportunity for putting his theories to the test after reading a newspaper account of a particularly atrocious double murder committed, apparently, in a locked room. (The hermetically sealed room would become a favourite theme of detective writers.) He deduces that the murderer must have come in through a window secured by a nail. On examination he finds that the nail is broken, and the window is held by a concealed spring. By certain other deductions, Dupin comes to the conclusion that the murder was committed by an escaped orang-outang.

Poe gave the detective story the concentration it needed to emerge from the confused realms of the popular novel: he recognized the need for brevity, and he saw that it needed to be constructed in a special manner: With Poe, the impetus for detective fiction passed from France to America. From America, it would return to France again because, if Poe was the father of the detective *story*, Emile Gaboriau was the father of the detective *novel*.

Another twenty years were to pass before the detective story again tried to throw off the shackles of popular literature. In the meantime, in France, the newspapers were boosting their circulation by printing sensational novels in serial form. Authors such as Eugène Sue, Alexandre Dumas the elder, and Paul Féval were writing against the clock to produce their daily episode of thrills and surprises. The rules were simple: each instalment had to be of a specific length and leave the reader in suspense at the end. *The door opened, and a blood-stained hand appeared! (To be continued . . .)* But, although they habitually used criminal elements, neither Sue, nor Dumas nor Féval understood what Poe had done.

To be fair, the structure of the French press, though suited to a continual series of melodramatic pauses, was quite un-suited to the needs of a logical detective story. There are two reasons for this. First, it was not fatal to the story as a whole if the reader, for some reason or other, missed one or two episodes; after twenty-four or forty-eight hours it was still fresh in his mind and he could easily supply for himself from his own imagination anything which had occurred. The detective story depends on a chain of deductions, however. If the chain is broken, the story becomes meaningless. Even if the reader didn't miss any instalments, after thirty or so episodes he might have begun to lose sight of the object of the inquiry. Secondly, it demanded too much of the writer to expect him to produce an almost endless series of logical *coups de théâtre*.

It is a mark of the genius of Emile Gaboriau that, in spite of these obstacles, he managed to engineer the next significant advance for detective fiction, in France.

Emile Gaboriau fled from the countryside to Paris to avoid following his father as a lawyer. He had already published seven novels of military and fashionable life when, in 1863, the editor of a dying newspaper, *Le Pays*, accepted *L'Affaire Lerouge* (translated as *The Widow Lerouge*, 1873) from him. It attracted little attention until it was reprinted in another moribund paper, *Le Soleil*, in 1866. Eleven weeks later, encouraged by this success—the story had saved *Le Soleil* from extinction—Gaboriau started on *Le Crime d'Orcival*, 1867 (*The Mystery of Orcival*, 1871), still in serial form. *Le Dossier No. 113*, 1867 (*File No. 113*, 1875) was followed by *Les Esclaves de Paris*, 1867 (*The Slaves of Paris*, 1882) and *Monsieur Lecoq*, 1869 (1880 in translation). He published another nine novels, few of any interest, before dying of exhaustion in 1873. He was thirty-nine. *Le Petit Vieux de Batignolles* (*The Little Old Man of Batignolles*), which has been newly translated for this volume, was possibly intended as the first of a series of short stories which the author never realized.

It appeared posthumously but was probably completed in the 1860s. Julian Symons, in his account of the detective story, *Bloody Murder*, considers it Gaboriau's best work, and Valentine Williams has described it as 'in some respects the best detective story ever written.'[5] One of Gaboriau's most important contributions to the genre was the introduction of the red-herring, and *The Little Old Man of Batignolles* is possibly the earliest example of this ploy.

The distinction which has to be drawn is between the *detective novel* and the novel concerned with detection as one of several themes. There are extraneous elements in Gaboriau's best *feuilletons*, but there is no difficulty in affirming that *The Widow Lerouge* is the first European novel in which the principal action derives more or less from a series of logical deductions aimed at solving a crime. (I shall not consider the case here of Wilkie Collins, whose *The Woman in White*, 1860, slightly preceded *The Widow Lerouge*, since I consider him as primarily a writer of mysteries.)

*The Widow Lerouge* still corresponded to the old formula of the sensational novel yet introduced a new exotic element: the scientific vocabulary and mathematical metaphors of the elderly eccentric who solves crimes by a purely deductive process. This is the world of Père Tabaret, the retired pawnbroker turned amateur detective. For the first time, the world of the detective is portrayed as more interesting than that of the criminal he pursues.

Gaboriau possibly intended to project a character called M. Lecoq into a sort of Vidocq. He appears in an early chapter where he is described as 'an old offender reconciled with the law'; but Gaboriau failed to develop him. Instead, he returns to lead his own inquiries in the next four *romans judiciaires*; he is given a new family history, and Gaboriau takes pains to point out that he was not an ex-convict at all: that was the result of a silly misunderstanding. In France, prejudice against the police ran deeper than in England. It was important that neither M. Méchinet nor M. Lecoq should be like the hated detectives of reality. Lecoq is as smart and honest and arrogant as Holmes himself—and with good cause, for his abilities are in no manner inferior to those of the Englishman. Neither are the talents of Père Tabaret. At an early stage of *The Widow Lerouge*, he examines the scene of the crime, and says: 'He is a young man, below average height, elegantly dressed and wearing a top hat. He carried an umbrella, and was smoking a Havana cigar in a holder.' Could Holmes have done any better?

Gaboriau was a prisoner of the *feuilleton*; he never really escaped. *Monsieur Lecoq* illustrates the compromise he made. The first volume, complete in itself, is a story of pure ratiocination but, as soon as the denouement is in sight, he throws us back a quarter of a century and, in the second volume, recounts a tiresome family history which he could have provided (and indeed did) in six lines at the end of the first.

The first part of *Monsieur Lecoq*, however, is perhaps one of the most brilliantly sustained pieces of detective fiction ever written. Furthermore, it should be said that none of his detective stories present insurmountable structural problems for the modern reader, given a little judicious skipping.

'Have you read Gaboriau's works?' I asked. 'Does Lecoq come up to your idea of a detective?'

Sherlock Holmes sniffed sardonically. 'Lecoq was a miserable bungler,' he said, in an angry voice; 'he had only one thing to recommend him, and that was his energy. That book [*Monsieur Lecoq*] made me positively ill. . . . It might be made a text-book for detectives to teach them what to avoid.'[6]

Holmes' criticism of Lecoq is not essentially different from Dupin's criticism of Vidocq. Vidocq has perseverance; Lecoq is energetic. Lecoq is a bungler; Vidocq is a good guesser. Holmes is the disciple of Dupin: 'I never guess. It is a shocking habit destructive to the logical faculty,' he says in *The Sign of Four*. But if he had been less conceited he might have acknowledged his debt to Dupin. From Dupin he learnt to think; from Dupin he borrowed some of his most distinctive characteristics, the lectures on reason, the habit of turning the conversation to futile subjects pending the theatrical climax; from Dupin he gained his interest in ciphers.

But although Holmes was to call Dupin 'a very inferior fellow' in his autobiography, his creator was more generous. Neither Poe nor Gaboriau merited the brunt of Holmes' sarcasms. 'Gaboriau had rather attracted me by the neat dovetailing of his plots, and Poe's masterful detective, M. Dupin, had from boyhood been one of my heroes. But could I bring an addition of my own? I thought of my old teacher Joe Bell, of his eagle face, of his curious ways, of his eerie trick of spotting details. If he were a detective he would surely reduce this fascinating but unorganized business to something nearer to an exact science.' Doyle's contribution was to reconcile the genre with the numerous monthly magazines appearing at the time—notably, of course, *The Strand*. He rediscovered the detective *story*, and structured the Holmes cycle accordingly. The ordinary serial was clearly not feasible for a monthly publication, yet a disconnected hotch-potch of short stories did little to establish the reader's loyalty. 'Clearly the ideal compromise was a character which carried through, and yet instalments which were each complete in themselves, so that the purchaser was always sure that he could relish the whole contents of the magazine.' Doyle believed himself the first to realize this, and *The Strand* the first to put it into practice. There was no corresponding expansion of the market for monthly magazines in France, with the result that the short story has been largely ignored by French detective writers.

Holmes made his first appearance in *A Study in Scarlet*, published in the unlikely *Beeton's Christmas Annual* for 1887. Just as in Gaboriau's novels, there are two distinct parts. The first part is a reprint of Watson's *Reminiscences* of his life in the army and his first meeting with Holmes. At length, the crime is introduced—the murder of a certain Enoch Drebber in mysterious circumstances. Drebber's secretary, Joseph Stangerson, is later murdered as well, but by the half-way stage Holmes has got his man. Part two brusquely transports us from London to the Plains of Utah twenty years before, and the murderer recounts his strange tale of revenge.

*Monsieur Lecoq* might have served Doyle as a textbook of what to avoid in the matter of construction—but Doyle didn't learn from it. Instead, Doyle remarks that he admired Gaboriau's 'neat dovetailing' of his plots. For this reason, one editor described *A Study in Scarlet* as, at the same time, too long and too short. *The Sign of Four*, *The Hound of the Baskervilles* and especially *The Valley of Fear* (which is also by far the most inferior piece Doyle wrote) exhibit a similar structural weakness.

In *Monsieur Lecoq*, the detective breaks a code of a series of numbers: 235, 15, 3, 8, etc.; in *The Valley of Fear*, Holmes does likewise with a message: 534, C2, 13, 127, etc. The solution is the same in both cases—the numbers indicate the words on the page of a book decided on in advance, *Whitaker's Almanack* in Doyle's novel and Beranger's *Chansons* in that of Gaboriau. One could multiply incidences where the reasoning of Lecoq and Holmes are not dissimilar. Gaboriau was certainly not the inventor of this cipher, but Dupin, Lecoq and Holmes do belong to the same tradition. Lecoq and Holmes, for example, are equally penetrating in their analyses of print. In *File No. 113*, M. Lecoq examines a letter composed of printed words cut out and pasted on a sheet of paper. He deduces, from certain words it contains, that it was written by a woman. Furthermore, he even knows from which book or magazine the author clipped out the words. 'Small type, slender, clean, careful; the paper is thin and glossy. Consequently, these words have not been cut from a newspaper, magazine or popular novel. But I've seen this type-face before, I know it . . . Why did I not see it at once? All these words have been cut from a prayer-book.' He detaches one and, conveniently, the Latin word, *Deus*, is printed on the other side. Holmes works similar prodigies in *The Hound of the Baskervilles*, with if anything even greater panache. 'The detection of types,' he concludes, 'is one of the most elementary branches of knowledge to the special expert in crime, though I confess that once when I was very young I confused the *Leeds Mercury* with the *Western Morning News*.'

Whatever Doyle borrowed, he made something new of. Something brilliant and original. Gaboriau's achievement was his point of departure. It is a pity all the same that while Sir Arthur Conan Doyle is read and re-read, Emile Gaboriau is hardly read at all.

## Maurice Leblanc

'Upon one occasion, as I was entering the hall to take part in an amateur billiard competition, I was handed by the attendant a small packet which had been left for me. Upon opening it I found a piece of ordinary green chalk such as is used in billiards . . . I continued to use it until one day, some months later, as I rubbed the tip of my cue the face of the chalk crumbled in, and I found it was hollow. From the recess thus exposed I drew out a small slip of paper with the words "From Arsène Lupin to Sherlock Holmes." '[7]

In 1870, the Franco-Prussian War broke out. The conflict failed to develop into a wider European war and France was soundly defeated. She ceded Alsace and Lorraine and undertook to pay five billion francs in reparations. German troops remained in occupation of the northern provinces until the debt was paid.

Emile Gaboriau died in 1873 and although another *feuilletoniste*, Fortuné du Boisgobey, revived his most famous character in France, no new detective fiction of any importance was written for more than thirty years until, in 1906, the editor of a new monthly journal called *Je Sais Tout* had a space to fill and asked a hack journalist by the name of Maurice Leblanc for a crime story. In this manner was the extraordinary career of Arsène Lupin launched, though in those days he was still known as Arsène Lopin!

Jean-Paul Sartre, as a young boy, read the exploits of Lupin. Later he wrote: 'In 1912 . . . I adored the Cyrano of the Underworld, Arsène Lupin, without realizing that he owed his herculean strength, his shrewd courage, his typically French intelligence to our being caught with our pants down in 1870.'[8] Lupin would play for high stakes—the honour of France, the recovery of Alsace and Lorraine, the conquest of Mauritania.

*Arsène Lupin, gentleman-cambrioleur*[9] (1907) was the first collection of Lupin stories to appear in book form. The descriptive title is strongly suggestive of E. W. Hornung's 'amateur cracksman', Raffles. Indeed, the two have much in common. Both are handsome buccaneers living off their wits. Both are remarkable patriots (Raffles can say, without any embarrassment, things like, 'My dear Bunny, we have been reigned over for sixty years by infinitely the finest monarch the world has ever seen.'). Both can atone for their pasts by fighting for their country: Raffles by falling gloriously in the Boer War, Lupin by enlisting in the Foreign Legion.

Lupin, because he is quintessentially French, is more a reincarnation of an earlier Parisian rogue, Rocambole. Ponson du Terrail wrote his extravagant romances at about the same time as Gaboriau, but although they are composed of all the themes later to be exploited by the detective story—murder, blackmail, revenge, kidnapping, disguise, reviving corpses—they lacked that concentration fundamental to the detective story. Like Rocambole, Lupin is a master thief and the adventurous leader of a gang of crooks. The gang is large, and well organized. Lupin can tell the police inspector, Ganimard: 'I have such heavy expenses! Yes, you shall know my budget, it is the budget of a large town.' Like Rocambole, Lupin can juggle with his identity without regard to the laws of reality. Maurice Richardson remarked with some pertinency in an introduction to an English edition of *Arsène-Lupin, gentleman-cambrioleur*, 'Part of the suspense which he generated was due to the reader's not knowing which of the characters at the beginning of the story would turn out to be Lupin in disguise.'[10]

Hornung discussed his Raffles project with his brother-in-law, Sir Arthur Conan Doyle. Doyle was shocked. 'I told him so before he put pen to paper, and the result has, I fear, borne me out. You must not make the criminal a hero.' The morality of Raffles and that of Lupin are not dissimilar. Neither will commit murder willingly and neither seems to think that stealing is wrong. Raffles says on one occasion, 'The distribution of property is all wrong anyway'; and I have read reports, which I am unable to confirm, that Leblanc was sympathetic to the anarchist movement. In any case, Lupin's crimes have the idea of redistribution as their starting point. He will steal from rich collectors and those with excessive wealth, and from murderers and thieves, and he will also steal from institutions such as banks, insurance companies, and churches. In *Victor de la Brigade Mondaine*,[11] he justifies his theft of a valuable stamp album in a letter to the press: '. . . Seeing that M. Seriphos is a very wealthy man and that he kept all this money locked up in the form of a useless stamp collection, I consider it my duty to put the whole ten million francs into circulation down to the last centime.'

The letters to the newspapers in which Arsène Lupin chronicles his adventures and misadventures are just one side of his fantastic and paradoxical nature. In *813*,[12] he has posed as Lenormand, Chef de la Sûreté, for four years, and conducts the search for himself; as Victor of the Special Branch he even manages to arrest . . . Arsène Lupin! Lupin finds himself in a similar position in the first of his two adventures in this anthology.

'By a sort of Socratic paradox,' wrote Ronald Knox, 'we might say that the best detective can only catch the best thief. A single blunder on the part of the guilty man would have thrown all Holmes's deductions out of joint.'[13] Leblanc explored this insight in his second Lupin book, a loosely episodic novel, *Arsène Lupin contre Herlock Sholmès*[14] (1908), in which Lupin goes out of his way to make a monkey out of Holmlock Shears (the name has changed in translation). Shears has a bad time of it. 'Ah! My dear Wilson,' he says, 'Arsène Lupin is a sort of game we are not accustomed to hunt. He leaves nothing behind him, you see . . .' Leblanc had ingeniously hit upon Holmes's stumbling block. Unfortunately, Shears, slow and indecisive, and Wilson, pugnacious and prone to the whisky bottle, are cardboard Englishmen from the stage of the French Théâtre des Variétés. But from 1906 until 1939 Lupin twisted and turned through a fabulous world of ruined castles and secret passages where ratiocination had but little part to play. And in his best work, in *813*, in *Les huits coups de l'horloge*,[15] in *L'agence Barnett et Cie*,[16] and a few others, the enigma of Arsène Lupin is still enough to enthral us. Readers who would like more Lupin stories but find them difficult to come by (though there have been sporadic reprints since the twenties and thirties) are recommended to turn to Hugh Greene's *More Rivals of Sherlock Holmes* which contains two fine examples of Lupin at his best.

The public outcry that was caused by Doyle's attempt to kill off Holmes is well known. And just like Holmes, Arsène Lupin became more real than his creator. 'It is hard,' admitted Leblanc. 'He follows me everywhere. He is not my shadow. I am his shadow.'[17] Maurice Leblanc continued to write about Lupin almost up to his death in 1941, at which time, by one of life's bitter ironies, France was once again occupied by the Germans.

# Gaston Leroux

If the contents page of this anthology is seen as a roll-call of the great French detectives of literature, there is one name missing: that of Joseph Rouletabille. The omission is explained by the fact that Rouletabille's creator, Gaston Leroux, was a writer in the best—and the worst—tradition of Gaboriau, a *feuilletoniste* by temperament rather than a novelist. He wrote few short stories and none, apparently, featuring his finest creation. *Weird Tales*, however, published the translations of some mystery stories by Leroux in the late 1920s which are certainly amongst his best work.[18] They have recently been issued in book form in France under the title *Histoires épouvantables*. They are tales told by the old salts who gather around Captain Michel every evening in the Café of the Old Wet-Dock in Toulon, and whatever they lack by way of deductive display is more than compensated for by the weird, creepy atmosphere which Leroux evokes. From Poe down to Leroux, the detective story still retained its links with the thriller or Gothic mystery. The detective story was still about *atmosphere*. With the 1920s came Agatha Christie and her ilk; the atmosphere was dispelled and the puzzle was all that was left.

Although Rouletabille cannot be with us, *Le mystère de la chambre jaune*, 1907 (translated a year later as *The Mystery of the Yellow Room*), the first and by far the most adroit of the Rouletabille novels, must not be allowed to go unmentioned. Here Leroux combined meticulous logic with *feuilleton* sensationalism to produce a classic statement on the 'least-likely-person' theme, popularizing the methods of Sherlock Holmes to challenge the reader directly to find the solution—a clear anticipation of the direction in which the genre would develop in the golden age of the detective novel in Britain and America in the twenties.

The locked-room mystery was not new when Leroux came to it: Edgar Allan Poe was the probable inventor in *The Murders in the Rue Morgue*; more recently, it had been used by Israel Zangwill in *The Big Bow Mystery* (1892). But in Poe's story, the room was not completely sealed—there was a chimney, and there was a window through which the orang-outang, the perpetrator of the murders, could escape; in Leroux's novel, no such issues exist. What distinguishes *The Mystery of the Yellow Room* is the manner in which the reader's attention is constantly brought into play. The clues fall thick and fast, each one more perplexing than the last, a large red-herring is temptingly offered for the reader to swallow, and the solution shows that Leroux has more or less conscientiously played fairly. Even if the motive—family scandal—had been found by Leroux at the back of a very old closet, even if the plot depends a little too heavily on coincidence, the pace is so quick and the explanation so ingenious that the reader scarcely notices any shortcomings.

Rouletabille has been described as remarkable for his ordinariness: it was as if Leroux was consciously rebelling against the eccentricities of Dupin and Holmes. But as Dupin and Holmes have their narrators, Rouletabille has his admiring friend, Sainclair. And even if Rouletabille is the very opposite of an intellectual, his pronouncements often resemble those of Holmes. 'None of the evidence supplied only by the senses is capable of being a proof. I, too, am stooping over superficial clues but only to see if they will fit into the circle drawn by my reason.'[19] Shortly before saying this he has gone through the motions of making the traditional slighting references to his spiritual predecessors. 'I find myself more absurd—lower in the scale of intelligence—even than those detectives imagined by modern novelists, detectives who have learnt their methods by reading the stories of Edgar Poe or Conan Doyle. Storybook detectives! They build mountains of nonsense out of a single footprint in the sand, or the mark of a hand on a wall . . .'

The sequel, *Le parfum de la dame en noir*, 1907 (*The Perfume of the Lady in Black*), makes laboured use of a superficial parallel between Rouletabille's origins and those of Oedipus. With its spectacle of endless disguises, family scandal, outrageous coincidences, weak characterization, and exclamatory dialogue, it could have been written thirty years before *The Mystery of the Yellow Room*. Between writing a large variety of novels of pure sensation with charged Gothic atmospheres such as those concerning Chèri-Bibi, the magician turned criminal to clear himself of a charge of parricide, and *Le Fantôme de l'Opéra*, 1910

26

(*The Phantom of the Opera*, 1911), which must certainly be one of the most famous horror stories ever written even though most people will know it from one of the four film versions, Leroux went on to write another five Rouletabille novels, none approaching the quality of the initial volume.

Gaston Leroux's life was an exciting and, at times, dangerous one. He became a full-time journalist in 1890 and sought out international incidents in Europe and North Africa. One frequently told anecdote concerns how he burgled Joseph Chamberlain's private study during the South African War in order to obtain an interview. Unfortunately, a secretary came in first and he was asked to leave. But Leroux had got his 'copy' and wrote up a three-column article, 'How I Failed to See Chamberlain'.

The name of Gaston Leroux (1868–1927) is often coupled with that of another journalist who wrote detective stories, Maurice Leblanc (1864–1941). This is presumably because they were both writing in the same period and were both endowed with a considerable sense of atmosphere. Strictly speaking, as G. K. Chesterton pointed out, Gaston Leroux was a writer of mysteries while Maurice Leblanc wrote adventures—the former concerned, as in *The Mystery of the Yellow Room*, with complex enigmas; the latter concentrating on the resolution of a rapid succession of immediate difficulties. Of the two, Gaston Leroux was probably the more influential—his greatest novel becoming a model for the next generation of Anglo-Saxon crime writers.

## Georges Simenon

Born at Liège in Belgium in 1903, Georges Simenon has been the only Continental writer of detective stories to have had any widespread recognition outside his own country in the last fifty years. The detective story in Belgium and France was just beginning to organize itself again under the impact of British and American authors when Simenon, after a careful apprenticeship in popular fiction, launched his Maigret series in 1931; but Maigret owes little to how the detective story was developing elsewhere. Simenon, after a phenomenally prolific career, gave up writing novels in 1972—by which time his tally was well over the two hundred mark, eighty or so about Maigret. Although untiringly devoted to the shorter forms of fiction (most of the Maigret stories are what we might tend to think of as novellas), there is the easy fecundity of the *feuilletoniste* about his work. Maigret has become the most celebrated occupant of the 'P. J.', the Police Judiciaire which was formerly the Préfecture where Vidocq's Brigade of the Sûreté would report. And Maigret, if he is like anyone, has more in common with Vidocq than with any of the fictitious sleuths since then.

Simenon tells the story of how his publisher, Fayard, received the first three Maigret novels: 'He was a big man and he looked at me and said, "It's no good. These stories have no mathematical problems, no love story, no good and bad characters and no happy endings." And then he gave me a contract for eighteen novels.'[20] Fayard's impressions were quite accurate.

Down until the twenties, the detective novel was bound up with atmosphere (Gaboriau, Dickens, Wilkie Collins, Doyle, Leroux); then came the age of Agatha Christie, Anthony Berkeley, Dorothy Sayers and Ellery Queen, whose books began to appear in translation at the end of that decade. Later French writers would to a greater or lesser degree accept the conventions of the Anglo-Saxon murder story, but Simenon remained true to the older style. 'He finds the logic of events tedious since they are opposed to the logic of feeling,' wrote Thomas Narcejac in a perceptive study on Simenon.[21] Simenon never aims to present intellectual crossword puzzles although, since his readers demanded mysteries, he supplied them with mysteries. But the resolution is never dependent on the discovery of footprints in the snow or discarded cigarette ends; Maigret solves the crime through recognizing the moment of crisis which resulted in the crime.

Simenon does not believe there is such a person as a criminal. Murderers in his books are often better people than their victims. The first Maigret novel, *Pietr-le-Letton* (1931), translated as *Maigret and the Enigmatic Lett*, involves a schizophrenic twin who shoots his brother. Maigret solves the crime by studying old photographs, probing childhood secrets, and establishing a close relationship with his suspect by following him. When the whole story has been revealed to him, he doesn't bring the criminal to justice but allows him the dignity of suicide.

Vidocq had a crude notion of the intimacy which grows up between detective and criminal; William Godwin had a clearer idea. Since the criminal's first reaction is often flight, many of the Maigret stories are novels of pursuit. The pursuit may be a long drawn-out affair as in *Le Pendu de Saint-Pholien* of 1931 (*Maigret and the Hundred Gibbets*), in which Maigret harries a man across northern Europe merely because he is shabbily dressed and Maigret has seen him with a considerable sum of money, or it might be a momentary, involuntary reaction as in *Le Fou de Bergerac* of 1932 (*The Madman of Bergerac*), in which Maigret is disturbed by a restless man in the couchette above him in a train and, by accident, sees him preparing to jump out: 'Maigret did not stop to think what he was about. He simply made a dash for the door and jumped out after him.' In both cases, Maigret is lured on, like Caleb Williams, by his curiosity, and in both cases, a relationship has established itself, however slight. 'Excuse me, monsieur, but would you please try to keep still?' says Maigret to the stranger above him in the train, more gruffly than he intended. Then it occurs to him that it might not be a man at all, but a woman. Or someone who had just been to a funeral in Paris. Or someone on his way to a funeral in the provinces . . .

Another relationship between Maigret and the criminal is provided by the environment. Maigret has immense faith in the impressions he gathers, and one of the ways in which he tries to share the life of his suspect is by absorbing the weather and surroundings of the place he happens to be in—which could be anywhere between Antibes in the summer to a canal at the frontier between Belgium and France in the winter. All these impressions are presented to the reader through Maigret's eyes, not because any rational deductions can be drawn from them, but because they too represent part of man's character.

Simenon has probably written more important books than those about Maigret, but the Maigret novels, unlike most other detective stories, may be re-read. Maigret's great humanity and simplicity render him one of the most sympathetic characters in literature and Simenon's admirers consider him to be one of the most important writers since Balzac.

# Jacques Decrest

Jacques Decrest is the pseudonym of the historian J. N. Faure-Biguet. He was born in Paris on 1 October 1893 and lived until 1954. He wrote several historical works under his real name and, as Decrest, some twenty novels featuring Superintendent Gilles. The idea of writing a detective story did not occur to him until 1931, and he has taken the trouble to point out that he wrote about Gilles under a pseudonym to indicate a change in the orientation of a part of his work and not because he thought the genre was inferior or that he attached less importance to it.

The first Gilles story, *Hasard*, appeared in 1933 but was not translated, as *Meet a Body*, until 1953. It established Superintendent Gilles, unlike Inspector Maigret, as an elegant, cultivated man: the sort of man who had seen *Metropolis* and would recognize the *Tannhäuser* overture. The distinction is important though the nature of the insights which occur to Gilles and Maigret are similar in many ways.

Maigret does not understand the strange power of insight he has into the mentalities of other men. It can be explained by us only if we call it empathy . . . the 'changing of one's skin' which, as Thomas Narcejac observes, is so characteristic of all Simenon's psychology. Maigret gets on well with criminals and professional men such as doctors and lawyers, he is at home with the middle and working classes—but there are other types of people with whom he is less sure of himself. He is ill at ease with aristocrats and politicians, and his understanding of artists and scientists is definitely imperfect. It is with this latter group that Superintendent Gilles comes into his own. In *Les trois jeunes filles de Vienne* (1934), translated as *The Missing Formula* (1956), Gilles follows a Hungarian sculptress across Europe in a train to recover a stolen scientific document. At an early stage of the novel he reveals something of the nature of intuition when he interviews the scientist from whom the papers have been taken: 'The solution to the problem lies in yourself, hidden somewhere, in a corner of your memory or, if you like, in your unconscious mind.' Gilles goes on to discuss Freud which Maigret would never have done. Maigret, like his creator, is not a high-brow.

The only other novel by Decrest to appear in translation is *Le rendezvous du dimanche soir*, 1935 (*Body on the Bench*, 1953). The husband of an opera singer is discovered shot on a park bench opposite his home and Gilles is called in to take control of the investigation after the Minister of Fine Arts starts to become worried by the way in which the inquiry is being conducted.

The originality of Decrest was to give the detective novel a psychological subtlety and a culture not inherent in the genre. In England at this time a sort of 'don's delight' book was beginning to appear—marked by a very studiously literary flavour which would turn the detective story into an over-civilized joke. But there are few points of comparison between Decrest's Superintendent Gilles and, for example, Michael Innes' Inspector Appleby, except that they are both distinctly dilettantish.

The Maigret stories took France by storm in the 1930s but did not catch on in England and America until an enterprising American publisher hit upon the idea of issuing them two to a volume in the 1940s. It is probably too late now for Decrest to gain the recognition in this country that he deserves, but *Les trois jeunes filles de Vienne* and a few other Gilles novels deserve to rank amongst the classics of the genre.

## Pierre Véry

Pierre Véry was born in 1900 on a farm in the Charente in south-west France—a region which provides the setting for one of the two stories by him in this anthology, *Watch the Red Balloons*. His mother was from the Périgord, a neighbouring *département*, and his father Charentais. The young Véry followed his father, a mathematics teacher, in his successive posts in the area until he was promoted to the cadres of the *éducation nationale* and Pierre, aged twelve, was sent to a boarding-school at Meaux near Paris. Here, with two other pupils, he created a secret society with the objective of getting to the USA. They read avidly the catalogue of the *Manufacture Française d'Armes et Cycles de Saint-Etienne* and endlessly compiled lists of indispensable equipment for the trip. Later Pierre Véry would transform this anecdote into one of his most memorable novels, *Les Disparus de Saint-Agil.*

He came to live in Paris in 1915 where he met Pierre Béarn. After training to become racing cyclists and working in a variety of jobs, the two friends decided to go to India. They set off in 1922, but only got as far as the Hôtel des Hommes in Marseilles. Pierre Véry found a job in the kitchen of a cargo boat bound for Casablanca; Pierre Béarn signed up for three years with the merchant navy.

When he returned to Paris in 1925, Pierre Véry opened a second-hand bookshop which, after launching his literary career, he sold to Pierre Béarn. His first novel, *Pont égaré* (1929), was favourably received by the critics. André Maurois wrote in the *New York Times Book Review* of 27 October 1929:

> The peasant novel is a very old tradition in French letters . . . [*Pont égaré*] infuses the genre with new life through its unusual and true sense for the eternal paganism of the country. Fairies and demons still live in the fogs of the Périgord, where the action is laid. On some enchanted nights the beasts regain their power of speech. *Pont égaré* is a grotesque *Midsummer Night's Dream*, playing in a village peopled by monsters . . .

The following year, Pierre Véry published his first detective novel under the pseudonym Toussaint Juge, *Le Testament de Basil Crookes* (1930), an elegant satire of the Anglo-Saxon detective story. In 1927, Albert Pigasse had launched his collection, *Le Masque*, with the publication of the translation of Agatha Christie's *The Murder of Roger Ackroyd*. *Le Masque* was an enormous success: by the mid 1970s, publishing four new titles a month and three reprints, one hundred and thirty million *Masques* had been sold, including fifty million copies of novels by Agatha Christie (*The Murder of Roger Ackroyd* has sold one and a half million copies alone). At the same time Alexandre Ralli founded *L'Empreinte*, which also introduced the best English and American writers to a French audience: Earl Derr Biggers (creator of Charlie Chan), Freeman Wills Crofts, Austin Freeman, Anthony Berkeley, Ellery Queen, etc. Véry's *Le Testament de Basil Crookes* (No. 60 in the series *Le Masque*) was the first winner of the Grand Prix du Roman d'Aventures organized by Albert Pigasse with the intention of encouraging unknown French writers to pit themselves against their well-known foreign rivals.

There has been a tendency to treat this novel as inferior to the rest of his work. Véry himself spoke slightingly of it at times, and he certainly wrote it with his eye on the prize of 10,000 francs. The fact is that after its publication his work took a different direction. The plot of *Le Testament de Basil Crookes* is just as intriguing as that of *The Murder of Roger Ackroyd* (acknowledged by many of Agatha Christie's fans as being her *chef-d'oeuvre*), and Véry is infinitely the more stylish and amusing writer, but it is also open to the same criticisms: woodenness of characters, a nauseous sentimental affair, litres of blood and masses of deductions. In other words, Pierre Véry set out to produce an imitation of the English detective story and ended by surpassing what he intended merely to copy, because all these defects are redeemed by his tremendous comic sense.

'My dream is to renew detective fiction by rendering it poetic and humorous,' Pierre Véry later wrote to Pierre Béarn, 'hence my decision to write a series of mystery stories, forty or so, in the tradition of Chesterton's *chef-d'oeuvre*, *The Man Who Was Thursday*, with characters who will no longer be mere puppets in the service of an enigma to resolve, but human beings fighting towards their truth.' His dream was accomplished, even though Pierre Véry did not publish quite the number he had hoped. Between 1930 and 1949, he wrote twenty-eight *romans de mystère*, which can only be described as a sort of 'Thousand and One Nights' of the detective story. It is difficult to communicate Pierre Véry's uniqueness to an audience which has never been favoured with translations of his work —briefly, they are detective stories but they are also fairy tales for grown-ups.

Véry contracted with his publishers, Gallimard, for a series. During these years immediately before the war Gallimard also published the investigations of Noël Vindry's M. Allou, *Juge d'instruction* (in brown covers), and Jacques Decrest's Superintendent Gilles (in red covers). Pierre Véry (in blue covers) came out in 1934 with *Meurtre Quai des Orfèvres* (a rare case of a police inspector murdered in his office) and introduced the owl-like Prosper Lepicq, the perpetually financially embarrassed barrister who turns detective in order to find clients to defend.

33

This was followed by *M. Marcel des pompes funèbres* (1934), in which an undertaker's is twice plunged into mourning in a space of twenty-four hours, *l'Assassinat du Père Noël* (1934), in which Santa Claus is discovered strangled in the snow at night on Christmas Eve in a village whose livelihood consists in the manufacture of toys, and *Le Réglo* (1935), in which Prosper Lepicq solves out of curiosity the problem of a mysterious vandal who is attacking the foundations of science by destroying weights and measures. A second series (in white covers) continued with *Les Disparus de Saint-Agil* (1935), *Le Gentleman des antipodes* (1936), in which the drama unrolls in the shop of a taxidermist frequented by a bizarre society of men possessing a strange resemblance to animals, and *Le Thé des vieilles dames* (1937), a murder story pervaded with astrology.

Prosper Lepicq was not, properly speaking, a detective. In his other *romans de mystère*, Pierre Véry moved even further away from the 'golden age' detective story. In the bald outlines for which there is space here it is not possible to convey the poetic, childlike marvel and humour which is at the heart of all his writing. But the reader is soon to meet the barrister himself in two of the three short stories which complete the Lepicq canon.

After the war, Pierre Véry became absorbed in the cinema. He had already participated in the filming of one of his novels, *Groupi Mains Rouge* (1937), which had been an enormous success, and he rapidly established a reputation as a writer of scenarios.

In 1960, after several years of silence, he published two *romans de mystère* (an expression he always preferred to the term *detective stories*) for children which appropriately reconciled the themes of his work in the year of his death. Pierre Véry was a real original and if he has left less mark on the detective novel than Gaboriau or Doyle it is because his style is totally inimitable.

## *Jypé Carraud*

In England, the first golden age of the detective novel was the decade just after the First World War; in France, it was the

34

decade just before the Second World War. The celebrity of Pierre Véry, Stanislas Steeman, Georges Simenon, Jacques Decrest, Noël Vindry and Pierre Boileau dates from the thirties. All these authors continued writing after the hostilities, and were joined by Léo Malet and Thomas Narcejac.

Between the two wars, one could count a dozen or so collections of detective stories in France, the most notable of these being *Le Masque* and *L'Empreinte*. In the years after the Second World War this number doubled and then trebled.

These publishing enterprises were often meteoric due to insufficient capital, but even if, on average, they only published two titles a month, over the years they produced a considerable number of detective stories. The authors whose names appeared on the covers of these books were soon eclipsed. But a few are worthy of more attention, and one of these was Jypé Carraud.

Stanislas Perceneige (whose name I have taken the liberty of translating as Stanislas Snowdrop) started life as the magistrate of the title of his first investigation, *Le cabinet du juge 50* (1948). Because one of his old customers empties a love potion into his drink after a game of tennis, he falls in love with the principal accused, a young actress called Dolly Honeymoon, in a murder case which is before him. He turns private detective to prove her innocence. The intrigue centres around the typewritten letter which the deceased had on him at the time of his murder inviting him to a rendezvous in an isolated park an hour after closing time. It is established that the letter was written on a machine which Dolly Honeymoon had been using on the set of her latest film where she played the part of a secretary. The typewriter was new, given by the manufacturers to gain some free publicity, and unpacked just before the filming began, still with the maker's lead seals on it. She had been the only person to use it, and then only while the cameras were turning. Stanislas Snowdrop ingeniously proves with the aid of the 'takes' and a typewriting expert that she could not have typed the note. Despite the strange device of the love phial, it is a rather good whodunit.

Jypé Carraud wrote only three Stanislas Snowdrop novels and a collection of short stories. The enthusiastic reviewer in the French edition of *Ellery Queen's Mystery Magazine* compared his second novel in the series, *L'Ecuyère de Daumier* (1949), favourably with Pierre Véry's *Madame et le mort*. Any comparison between the works of Carraud and Véry is bound, I feel, to be further removed than the reviewer would have us believe, and is perhaps only to be found in the fact that Stanislas Snowdrop and Prosper Lepicq resolve mysteries of the most extravagant nature.

*For Piano and Vocal Accompaniment* comes from a collection of short stories drawn together by a loose geographical theme, *Les 5 plages de Stanislas Perceneige* (1949). In these stories, Carraud gives full range to his ingenuity and comic talent to create some memorable characters, such as the shy film director who wounds his leading lady to prevent her from acting in his film, and the entomologist who raises chickens on cantharides.

Stanislas Snowdrop's last inquiry is in *Le squelette cuit* (1950), in which he saves Dolly Honeymoon from being eaten by a club of ex-colonial cannibals. The story, apparently, abounds in cannibalistic reference and is highly sought after by collectors. Jypé Carraud wrote two other detective stories without Snowdrop, neither particularly memorable, it seems. I have been unable to find any biographical details, which appear to be as elusive as his novels have become.

## Léo Malet

Léo Malet was born in 1909 in Montpellier, a large city to the west of Marseilles. Self-taught, he had all kinds of jobs including casual labourer, diver, newsboy, literary critic and vagabond. He was attracted by the Surrealist movement and wrote poetry before turning to a more commercial form of literature and, under the pseudonym of Frank Harding, writing American-style thrillers featuring the journalist Johnny Metal.

When he launched the career of Nestor Burma with *120, Rue de la Gare* (1943), the first novel he published under his real name, he was both behind and ahead of his times. Behind them because Dashiell Hammett's first stories had appeared in the magazine *Black Mask* in the USA twenty years before; ahead of them because although Hammett's brief writing life was over, it fell to Malet to pioneer the *hard-boiled* detective story in France.

'Hammett gave murder back to the kind of people that commit it for reasons, not just to provide a corpse . . . He put these people down on paper as they are, and he made them talk and think in the language they customarily used for these purposes,' wrote Raymond Chandler in his essay, *The Simple Art of Murder* (1944). Hammett too had a restless early life, and perhaps it was their experience of both the high and the low moments of life that unite Hammett and Malet rather than the fact that they were both taking the detective story in similar directions. They both retain a central puzzle, not as the be-all and end-all of their writing, but in Raymond Chandler's phrase, 'dropped in like the olive in a martini'. There is a theme of personal integrity running through Malet's best novels as through those of Hammett and Chandler. Nestor Burma, with his downbeat sense of humour, would be the first to mock such values, but they are nonetheless real.

Prohibition America and France after the liberation had similar sorts of problems of political and social corruption, cruelty and violence. The *roman noir* could have been invented in the France of that epoch. As it was, *Série Noire* appeared in 1945, under the direction of Marcel Duhamel, modelling itself on the American thriller. Ironically, two English authors of ersatz American thrillers, Peter Cheyney and James Hadley Chase, were the first writers published. The great success the collection enjoyed in the 1950s all but eclipsed Léo Malet.

In many ways, the thriller looks back to the sensational *feuilleton* of the nineteenth century. In *Les mystères de Paris* (1842), Eugene Sue had used the Parisian criminal *milieu* to introduce his readers to some of his ideas for social reform. There was the same emphasis on slang, violence, action. There was the same perfunctory mystery. In the mid-fifties, Léo Malet had the idea of writing a cycle entitled *Les nouveaux mystères de Paris*. Each one of these novels is set in a different *arrondissement* of the capital, scrupulously observed again through the sardonic eyes of Nestor Burma. The series estab-

37

lished Malet as one of the most important figures in French detective fiction. Among the best of the cycle are *Brouillard au pont de Tolbiac* and *Les rats de Montsouris*.

# *I*

# *EMILE GABORIAU*
## *The Little Old Man of Batignolles*

### A Chapter of a Detective's Memoirs

#### J. B. CASIMIR GODEUIL

Some three or four months ago, a man in his early forties, correctly dressed in black, called at the offices of the editor of *Le Petit Journal.* He brought with him a handwritten manuscript of such exquisite penmanship that it would have inspired the jealousy of even a professional calligrapher.

'I will call again in a fortnight,' he said, 'to find out what you think of my work.'

Since no one was curious enough to untie the ribbon holding it together, the manuscript was stored away as usual in the box labelled: 'MSS to be read'.

And time went by . . .

I ought to add that a great many manuscripts are offered to *Le Petit Journal*, and that the reader's job is no sinecure.

The author, however, failed to return, and everyone had forgotten him when, one morning, the head reader arrived tremendously excited.

''Pon my word,' he exclaimed as he came in, 'I have just read something extraordinary.'

'Well, what is it?' we asked him.

'The manuscript of the gentleman, you remember, dressed all in black . . . I make no reservations, I was gripped by it.'

And as we made fun of his enthusiasm—for he was, as a rule, very rarely enthusiastic—he threw the manuscript on the table, saying, 'Read it for yourselves.'

This was enough to intrigue us seriously. One of us picked up the manuscript, and by the end of the week it had made the

39

round of all the editorial staff. The verdict was unanimous: *Le Petit Journal* must publish the story.

But now an unforeseen difficulty arose: the manuscript did not bear the name of its author. Only a visiting-card, inscribed 'J. B. Casimir Godeuil', was attached to it. There was no address.

What was to be done? Publish the manuscript anonymously? That was hardly possible at a time when the French press laws required someone to accept responsibility for every printed line.

It was agreed, therefore, that the only course was to search for this more than modest author, and for several days the management of *Le Petit Journal* instituted inquiries in all directions.

But without result. No one had ever heard of J. B. Casimir Godeuil.

At this point, as a last resort, the streets were placarded with the mysterious posters which so intrigued Paris and also, to some extent, the provinces.

'Who can this man Godeuil possibly be,' people wondered, 'that he is advertised for like this?'

Some took him for a prodigal son fled from under the parental roof, others for a missing heir, but most for an absconded cashier.

This time we were successful.

Scarcely were the first bills posted, when J. B. Casimir Godeuil hastened to our offices and *Le Petit Journal* contracted to publish his narrative, *The Little Old Man of Batignolles*, which constituted the first part of his memoirs.*

Having said this, we leave the rest to the words of J. B. Casimir Godeuil. The following short preface—which we have decided to retain because of the light it throws on the author's character and the worthy objective he pursued in writing his memoirs—precedes his narrative.

* Unfortunately, J. B. Casimir Godeuil, who promised us the conclusion of his manuscript, has completely disappeared, and all efforts made to find him have been unsuccessful. The following narrative (complete in itself), which constitutes an extremely moving drama, is therefore his only published work. (*Editor's note*)

# PREFACE

A prisoner who was brought before the magistrates was convicted of both forgery and aggravated theft, despite all his tricks and denials and an alleged alibi.

Overwhelmed by the evidence I had collected against him, he confessed his crime and exclaimed:

'Ah! If I had only known the methods used by the police, and how impossible it is to escape from them, I would have remained an honest man.'

It was these words which inspired me to write my memoirs. 'If I had only known . . .'

And I publish my recollections today in the hope, no, I will go further, in the firm conviction that I have accomplished a highly moral task and one of exceptional value.

Is it not desirable to strip crime of her sinister poetry, to show her as she really is: cowardly, ignoble, abject and repulsive?

Is it not desirable to prove that the most wretched beings in the world are those madmen who have declared war on society?

This is what I claim to do.

I shall establish beyond all doubt that it is to everyone's advantage to remain honest—an advantage which is immediate, positive, mathematical. You can depend on it!

I will demonstrate so that it is as clear as daylight that with our present social organization, with the railways and the electric telegraph, impunity is impossible.

Punishment may be deferred, but it is not to be escaped.

And without doubt there will be many misguided beings who will profit from my words by reflecting before they abandon themselves to crime.

And many who were not held back by the weak murmurings of their consciences will be arrested by the voice of fear . . .

Do I need to explain the nature of these memoirs any further?

I attempt to describe the struggles, the successes and the defeats of a handful of loyal men to whom the security of Paris is entrusted.

How many are they to hold in check all the criminals of a capital which, with her suburbs, counts more than three million inhabitants?

They number two hundred.
It is to them that I dedicate this book.

# I

Whilst I was pursing my studies to become a doctor—I was but twenty-three at the time—I lived in the Rue Monsieur-le-Prince, almost at the corner of the Rue Racine.

For thirty francs a month, service included, I rented a furnished room there which would easily cost a hundred today; a room which was large enough to allow me to stretch out my arms without having to open the windows when I put on my overcoat.

Leaving very early in the mornings to make my rounds at the hospital, and returning as late at night due to the irresistible attraction that the Café Leroy held for me, it happened that I hardly knew my neighbours – who were for the most part quiet people living either by their trade or off their incomes – even by sight.

There was one, however, with whom I gained, little by little, acquaintance.

He was a man of medium height, with unexceptional features, always clean shaven, and called, respectfully, Monsieur Méchinet.

The doorkeeper treated him with a special consideration, and never missed the courtesy of taking off his cap when he passed in front of his lodge.

M. Méchinet's apartment opened on to the same landing as my own, in fact his door was exactly opposite mine, and from time to time we would pass each other on the stairs. On these occasions we were in the habit of saluting each other.

One night he would knock on my door to ask me to oblige him with some lucifers; another night, I would borrow some tobacco from him; and one morning we chanced to leave the building at the same time and walked together to the end of the road, talking . . .

Such were our first points of contact.

Without being either curious or suspicious—one is not at the age I was then—I was eager to discover with what sort of person I was forming an acquaintance. Naturally, I did not start to spy on my neighbour's life, but I did take note of his movements and behaviour.

He was married, and Madame Caroline Méchinet—a small, fair-haired, plump, jovial woman—appeared to worship her husband. He, however, seemed to be a man of most irregular habits. Frequently, he left home before daybreak and I often heard him coming in after being out all night. Occasionally, he would disappear for whole weeks at a time . . .

Intrigued, I thought that our doorkeeper, usually a most garrulous fellow, would provide me with some information.

Error! . . . Scarcely had I mentioned the name Méchinet before he sent me about my business, rolling his great eyes and saying at the same time that he was not accustomed to spying on the tenants.

This reception so fanned my curiosity that, oblivious to all restraint, I applied myself to watching my neighbour.

I soon made certain discoveries which seemed most ominous. One day, I saw him come home dressed in the latest fashion, the ribbons of five or six medals displayed in his button-hole; the next day, I glimpsed him on the staircase wearing a dirty blouse and a ragged cap which lent him a sinister appearance.

And this was not all. One afternoon, just as he was going out, I saw his wife taking leave of him on the landing; she hugged him fondly and said: 'Be careful, Méchinet, I beg of you. Think of your poor little wife.'

Be careful! . . . Why? . . . With regard to what danger? What did this mean? . . . Was his wife his accomplice then?

I was fairly astonished, yet there was more to come.

I was soundly asleep one night when there was an urgent knocking at my door. I rose and opened it. M. Méchinet came in, or rather, burst in, his clothes dishevelled and torn, his cravat and the front of his shirt ripped open, his head bare, and his face covered with blood.

'What has happened?' I exclaimed, terrified.

'Speak lower!' he said. 'You might be heard . . . It's probably only a scratch but it hurts like the devil . . . I thought that as you are a medical student you might have a look at it for me.'

Without saying a word, I made him sit down and examined his wound.

Although it had bled profusely, the wound was not deep. To tell the truth, it was only a graze, running from his left ear to the corner of his mouth.

'Well, I've managed to escape safe and sound this time,' said M. Méchinet to me when I had finished dressing his wound. 'Many thanks, my dear M. Godeuil. Above all, though, I'd be grateful if you didn't breathe a word of my little accident to anyone and . . . well, good night.'

Good night! As if I would be able to sleep after that!

When I think of the absurd theories and the flights of fancy which passed through my head that night, I can hardly prevent myself from laughing.

In my imagination, M. Méchinet began to take on fantastic proportions.

He, however, called quietly on me the next day to thank me once again and invite me to dinner.

As you might have supposed, on entering my neighbour's rooms, I was all eyes and ears, but despite my closest attentions I discovered nothing to dispel the mystery which I found so absorbing.

Still, from the time of this dinner, our acquaintanceship flourished. M. Méchinet definitely seemed to regard me with favour. Hardly a week went by without him inviting me to take 'pot-luck', as he called it, at his table; and practically every day he would come to join me towards four o'clock at the Café Leroy for the customary vermouth, and we would play a hand of dominoes.

It was in this way that one afternoon in July, a Friday, at the stroke of five, when he was on the brink of catching me with the double-six in my hand, that a shifty-looking, badly dressed character came brusquely in and whispered into his ear a few words that I didn't catch.

M. Méchinet's face suddenly became animated, and he sprang from his chair.

'I'm coming,' he said. 'Run and tell them that I'm coming.'

The man made off in a hurry, and M. Méchinet held out his hand.

'You must excuse me, but business before pleasure, you know . . . we can resume tomorrow.'

Consumed with curiosity as I was, I dare say I showed a good

44

deal of ill-humour; in any case I said that I regretted that I could not accompany him now.

'Indeed,' he muttered, 'why not? Would you care to come? You might find it not without interest . . .'

My only reply was to pick up my hat and leave with him.

## II

Certainly I was far from thinking, at that moment, that such an apparently insignificant exercise as this would have a profound effect on my whole life.

And as I trotted along beside M. Méchinet I was full of stupid, puerile satisfaction. 'This time,' I thought, 'I will know everything.'

I use the word 'trotted' advisedly, for I had great difficulty in keeping up with my companion. Pushing through the passers-by, he rushed on all the way down the Rue Racine as if his life depended on it.

In the Place de l'Odéon, a cab luckily drove by.

M. Méchinet stopped it and, opening the door for me, shouted up imperatively to the coachman:

'Thirty-nine Rue Lécluse, at Batignolles . . . and don't spare the horses.'

The distance of the fare produced a string of oaths from the driver. All the same, he whipped up the horses and we lurched off.

'So we are going to Batignolles?' I asked with the false smile of a courtesan on my face.

But M. Méchinet did not reply; I doubt if he even heard me.

A complete transformation had come over him. He did not appear excited exactly, but his pursed lips and the manner with which his bushy eyebrows were drawn together in a frown betrayed his preoccupation. His gaze, staring into space, seemed to indicate that he was studying some mysterious unfathomable problem. He had taken out his snuff-box, and he incessantly extracted enormous pinches which, after rolling between his forefinger and his thumb, he held up to his nose without, however, inhaling.

I had observed this little idiosyncrasy before and it greatly amused me. The worthy man had a horror of snuff, yet he

45

always went out equipped with this snuff-box in the manner of a musical-hall villain. Whenever anything unforeseen occurred, whether it pleased or irritated him, he invariably drew it from his pocket and pretended to provide himself with pinch after pinch. He made the same gestures even when the box was empty.

Later, I learnt that it was part of an act he had deliberately created to divert the attention of those around him, and so conceal his reactions.

Meanwhile, we were making progress.

The cab laboured up the Rue de Clichy, crossed the outer boulevard and drew up in the Rue Lécluse, a little way from the address that had been tended. It was not possible to go further as the street was obstructed by a large crowd.

In front of No. 39, some two or three hundred people were standing, craning their necks, breathless with excitement. Half a dozen policemen vainly tried to contain them, shouting, 'Move on, please. Move on!'

Alighting from the carriage, we elbowed our way through the bystanders. Just as we reached the doorway of the house, a sergeant pushed us back roughly.

My companion looked him up and down critically, then, drawing himself up to his full height, said:

'Don't you know me? I am Méchinet. And this young man is with me.'

'Please excuse me, sir,' stammered the sergeant, saluting us, 'I didn't recognize you. This way, sir.'

In the hall, a stout, middle-aged woman with a red face, obviously the concierge, was holding forth with much gesticulation amidst a group of tenants.

'Where is he?' asked M. Méchinet abruptly.

'On the third floor, sir,' she replied. 'Third floor, door on the right. Lord God! What a tragedy . . . in a house like ours! And such a decent man!'

I did not hear any more. M. Méchinet was bounding up the stairs, with me on his heels, four at a time, my heart beating as if it would burst.

On the third floor, the door was already open.

We went in, crossed an ante-room, a dining-room, and a parlour, and finally reached the bedroom.

46

If I were to live a thousand years, I would not forget the sight which met my eyes. Even as I write about it now, after a good many years, I can still see it down to the last detail.

Two men were leaning against the mantelpiece in front of the door: the Police Inspector, wearing his sash of office, and the investigating magistrate. On the right hand side, a young man, the latter's clerk, was seated writing at a table.

On the floor, in the middle of the room, lay the corpse of an old man surrounded by a pool of dark, coagulating blood. He was stretched out on his back with his arms extended.

Terrified, I stood rooted to the threshold, so overwhelmed that, in order to avoid falling, I was obliged to support myself against the frame of the door.

My profession had familiarized me with death, I had conquered my repugnance of the operating-theatre a long time ago, but this was the first occasion on which I found myself at the actual scene of a crime.

Because it was obvious that some abominable crime had been committed here.

Less impressed than myself, my companion entered the room with a firm step.

'Ah! It's you, Méchinet,' said the Inspector. 'I'm sorry to have troubled you now.'

'Why is that?'

'Because we no longer have need of your special talents . . . We know the culprit and I have already given the order for his arrest which should have been carried out by now.'

How strange! From the look of M. Méchinet, I would have said that this news failed to please him. He took out his snuff-box, and pretended to take two or three pinches.

'So you know the culprit?'

'Yes, M. Méchinet,' replied the investigating magistrate, 'and our information is quite beyond question. After committing the crime, the murderer fled, believing his victim to be dead. He was mistaken. Providence was watching . . . this poor old man was barely breathing but, summoning up all his strength, he dipped one of his fingers into the blood which was streaming from his wound, and there, on the floor, wrote the name of his assassin in his own blood, thereby handing him over to earthly justice . . . However, look for yourselves.'

47

On the floor, in large, badly formed, though quite legible letters, was written in blood: MONIS . . .

'Well?' asked M. Méchinet.

'They are the first five letters of the name of the deceased's nephew,' replied the Inspector. 'A nephew of whom he was very fond, and whose name is Monistrol.'

'By the devil!' exclaimed M. Méchinet.

'I fancy,' resumed the investigating magistrate, 'that the wretch won't try to deny his guilt. Those five letters are an overwhelming proof against him. And besides, who else could profit from this cowardly crime? He alone, the sole heir of the old man, who leaves him, it is said, a considerable fortune . . . Furthermore, the crime was committed last night, and the only person to visit him last night was this nephew. The concierge saw him arrive at about nine o'clock and leave a little before midnight.'

'It's clear then,' confirmed M. Méchinet, 'quite clear. This fellow Monistrol is a perfect fool.' He shrugged his shoulders. 'Did he steal anything? Did he disturb any of the furniture to put us on the wrong track?'

'Until now nothing has appeared out of order to us,' replied the Inspector. 'As you say, the wretch is not very adept. He will confess as soon as he is arrested.'

On that note, the Inspector and M. Méchinet withdrew into the recess of the window and spoke together in low voices while the investigating magistrate dictated some instructions to his clerk.

## III

As far as M. Méchinet was concerned, I was satisfied.

The profession which my enigmatic neighbour exercised was no longer a mystery to me. His irregular life-style—his absences, his late homecoming, his sudden disappearances, the fears and the complicity of his young wife, the wound which I had dressed for him—was completely accounted for.

What did it matter to me now?

I had gradually recovered my capacity for logical thought, and I examined everything around me with keen interest.

From where I was, propped up against the door jamb, I could

48

take in the whole room at a glance. There was nothing to betray it as the scene of a murder. On the contrary, everything tended to show the easy circumstances and the neat, parsimonious even, habits of the victim.

Everything was as it should be. There was not even a fold out of place in the curtains, and the woodwork of the furniture was bright with polish, indicating the daily attention it received.

It seemed evident, besides, that the theories of the investigating magistrate and the Inspector of Police were correct, and that the unfortunate old man had been assassinated the night before, just as he was about to go to bed.

In fact, the bed was turned down, and night-shirt and night-cap were laid out on the coverlet. On the bedside table, I saw a glass of water, a box of lucifers, and an evening paper.

On the corner of the mantelpiece, a large, heavy copper candlestick shone. But the murderer had fled without blowing it out, for the candle which had lit the crime had burnt away, blackening the alabaster save-all in which it had been fixed.

I noticed these details in a moment, without a conscious act of will. My eyes became the lens of a camera, and the scene of the murder impressed itself on my mind, as if on a photographic plate, so precisely that even today I could draw the apartment of 'the little old man of Batignolles' from memory without forgetting anything, not even the cork with the green wax seal which I still seem to see lying on the floor beneath the chair of the magistrate's clerk.

I was unaware that I possessed this extraordinary faculty, revealed so suddenly in me, for I had previously never had cause to use it, and, too greatly excited, I neglected to analyse my observations.

I had only one desire, obstinate and irresistible: to approach the corpse stretched out two yards away from me.

At first, I fought against this obsessive impulse, but it was stronger than me, and I drew near. My presence had not, I think, been remarked. In any case, no one paid any attention to me now.

M. Méchinet and the Inspector of Police were still talking over by the window, and the clerk was reading back some report to the investigating magistrate in an undertone.

Moreover, I must admit it, I was seized by a sort of fever

49

which rendered me absolutely insensible to what was happening around me, isolating me utterly.

This feeling was so profound that I dared to kneel beside the body, the better to see and examine it. Indeed, I was so far removed from imagining that someone would ask me, 'What are you up to?' that I acted with complete composure.

It seemed to me that this poor old man had seen some seventy or seventy-five winters; he was thin and wiry, but hale all the same, and built, I would have said, to withstand another twenty-five.

He still possessed a good head of yellowish, curly hair. The grey bristles covering his face gave him the appearance of having gone unshaven for five or six days, but they had grown since his death, a phenomenon I had often noted in the hospital mortuary and so was not surprised by.

What did surprise me was the expression on the old man's face. It was calm and, I might say, welcoming. The lips were slightly apart, as if he had been greeting a friend when death had overtaken him so quickly that he still retained his kind demeanour. This was the first thought which came to my mind.

But how could these incongruous circumstances be reconciled? Sudden death and those five letters which I had seen traced on the floor: MONIS. To write them would have required an enormous effort of a dying man. Only the wish to be avenged could have imparted him such energy. And what rage he must have felt to know that death was cheating him of his life before he had completed the name of his murderer . . .

And yet his face seemed to smile.

The poor old man had been struck in the throat, the weapon had slightly severed his neck.

The instrument of the crime could only have been a dagger, or perhaps one of those formidable Catalan knives with blades as large as a man's hand, yet sharp as a razor.

In all my life, I had never been prey to such strange emotions. My temples throbbed with unbelievable violence and my heart swelled as if it would burst.

Was I about to discover something? . . .

Driven on by this same mysterious and irresistible impulse which annihilated my will, I took the rigid, frozen hands of the corpse between my own.

50

The right hand was quite clean . . . it was with one of the fingers of the left, the index finger, that he had written, for it was stained with blood.

What! The old man had written with the left hand! Then . . .

Gripped as if by vertigo, with haggard eyes and bristling scalp, and certainly as pale as the dead man stretched out in front of me, I struggled to my feet and let out a terrible cry.

'God Almighty!'

The others rushed to my side.

'What is it? What is it?' they insisted, with great excitement.

I tried to answer but the words stuck in my throat. I could only point to the hands of the deceased and stammer:

'There! Look, the hands!'

In an instant, M. Méchinet was on one knee beside the body. He saw immediately what I had seen because he was amazed by it as I had been. He rose to his feet in a movement.

'It was not the old man who wrote those letters,' he announced.

And as the investigating magistrate and the Inspector of Police were looking at him with open mouths, he explained to them that the left hand alone was stained with blood.

'And to think I didn't even notice it,' said the Inspector forlornly.

'It is often like that,' said M. Méchinet, energetically helping himself to imaginary pinches of snuff. 'We often don't see the things right in front of our eyes. No matter. The situation is completely changed now, however. Since they were not written by the old man, they must have been written by the murderer . . .'

'Evidently,' concurred the Inspector.

'Well,' continued my neighbour, 'is it possible to imagine a murderer so maladroit as to denounce himself straight off by signing his name beside the corpse of his victim? No, it is not. Hence, we must conclude . . .'

The investigating magistrate had become thoughtful.

'It is clear,' he said. 'We have been misled by appearances . . . Monistrol is not culpable . . . But, then, who is? It is up to you, Méchinet, to uncover him.'

He paused as a policeman entered the room.

'Monistrol has been arrested, sir, and is in custody at the Dépôt,' he said. 'He has confessed everything.'

## IV

The shock was all the greater because it was unexpected. Imagine our amazement in the face of the impossible! What – whilst we had been making every effort to establish Monistrol's innocence, he had formally admitted his guilt!

M. Méchinet was the first to recover himself. He abruptly raised his hand from his snuff-box to his nose five or six times. Then, turning towards the agent, he said:

'Either you've been deceived or you're trying deliberately to mislead us. There is no other alternative.'

'I swear to you, M. Méchinet . . .'

'Hold your tongue, man! Either you have misunderstood what Monistrol has said or else you have been carried away by your desire to surprise us with the announcement that the affair is concluded.'

The policeman, who had been polite and respectful until this point, now protested:

'Excuse me, but I am neither a fool nor a liar. I know what I say.'

It seemed so likely that the discussion would turn into an argument that the magistrate thought it advisable to intervene.

'Calm yourself, M. Méchinet,' he said. 'Listen to all the evidence before pronouncing judgment.'

Then, turning to the agent, he continued:

'Now, my good fellow, tell us everything you know and explain why you are so confident about what you have just said.'

Encouraged by the magistrate, the policeman directed a look of withering irony towards M. Méchinet, and, with an appreciable note of self-importance in his voice, began to speak:

'According to your instructions, sir, and those of the Inspector here, Sergeant Goulard, my colleague Poltin and myself were to proceed to seventy-five Rue Vivienne, the residence of the party Monistrol, a dealer in imitation jewellery, and effect the arrest of the aforementioned Monistrol and charge him with the murder of his uncle.'

'Quite correct,' approved the Inspector gently.

'Acting on these instructions,' continued the man, 'we hailed a cab and proceeded to the same address. Upon arrival, we found M. Monistrol in a small room at the rear of his shop. He was about to sit down to dinner with his wife, a woman of no small beauty, twenty-five to thirty years of age.

'Perceiving the three of us lined up, the accused jumped to his feet and asked us what we wanted, whereupon Sergeant Goulard drew the warrant from his pocket and said. "In the name of the Law, I arrest you."'

'Come to the point, can't you,' interrupted M. Méchinet impatiently.

But the policeman continued in the same level voice as if he had not heard.

'I have arrested a good many people in my time, but I've never seen one take it like him. "You must be joking," he said, "or else you are making a mistake." "No," said Goulard, "there is no mistake." "Well what are you arresting me for?" said Monistrol. "Don't come the child with us. What about your uncle? His body has been found and there is compelling evidence against you." That finished the rogue, eh? He staggered to a chair, crying and stammering I don't know what, half of which was unintelligible anyway.

'On seeing this, Goulard seized him by the collar of his coat and said to him: "If you take my advice, you'll confess. It'll go easier for you if you do."

'He looked at us with bewildered eyes and murmured: "Oh, well, yes. I admit it all."'

'Well done, Goulard,' noted the Inspector with approval.

The policeman enjoyed the moment of triumph and resumed his story:

'We were best getting it over and done with, sir, as we'd been instructed to avoid drawing attention to ourselves. A group of idlers had already begun to gather outside. So Goulard grabbed the accused by the arm and ordered us back to the Préfecture. Monistrol rose to his feet, as best he was able, for both his legs were shaking with fear, and, summoning up his courage like a man, said, "Yes, let's be on our way."

'We thought that the worst was over, but we hadn't reckoned with his wife.

'Until then she had been sitting in her armchair as if she had

fainted, not saying a word, not even looking as if she understood what was going on.

'But when she saw that we really intended to carry off her
husband, she sprang forward like a lioness and blocked the
door. "You shan't pass," she cried. My word, she was good, but
Goulard has had plenty of experience. "Come along now, my
good woman," said he, "don't get in our way. We'll bring back
your husband."

'However, instead of making way for us, she clung even more
resolutely to the doorpost, swearing her husband was innocent,
and declaring that if we took him off to prison, she would follow
him there; one minute threatening and hurling insults at us, the
next imploring us in her most beguiling tones.

'Really, it moved us all, but he was an insensitive devil. He
even had the barbarity to push his poor wife so roughly that she
fell to the ground in the corner of the room . . .

'And that was that, fortunately.

'His wife really had fainted, and we took the opportunity to
pack him off in the cab which had brought us there.

'Pack him off is the right word, too! He had become totally
listless, he couldn't even stand up, and we had to carry him . . .
And not to omit anything, I ought to add that his dog, some kind
of black mongrel, tried to jump into the carriage, and we had
the devil of a job to get rid of it.

'On the way, as is only right, Goulard tried to chat with the
prisoner, take his mind off it . . . But we couldn't get a word out
of him. He seemed to come round only when we reached the
Préfecture. When he had been securely stowed away in one of
the cells put aside for solitary confinement, he threw himself on
the bed, repeating, "What have I done? My God, what have I
done?"

'At this moment, Goulard went up to him and asked for the
second time, "Do you admit it?"

'Monistrol nodded his head and said in a hoarse voice,
"Please, leave me alone."

'Then we arranged for a guard to watch him through the
grille in case he should try to take his own life.

'Goulard and Poltin stayed where they were, and I came here
to report the arrest.'

'Precise,' murmured the Inspector, 'very precise indeed.'

The magistrate was of the same opinion: 'After all that, how can you still have doubts as to his guilt?'

As for me, I was surprised, but my convictions were firm. I was about to say something by way of an objection when M. Méchinet forestalled me.

'That's all very well,' he exclaimed, 'except that if we admit that Monistrol is the murderer, we are also bound to admit that he himself wrote his own name there, on the floor . . . And, well . . . Damn it all! It's a bit thick.'

'Phooey!' interrupted the Inspector. 'Since the accused has admitted it, what's the point of worrying about a circumstance that will certainly be explained at the trial?'

But my neighbour's remark had reawakened all the perplexities of the magistrate, who said, without specifically mentioning them: 'I shall pay a visit to the Préfecture and interrogate Monistrol myself this very night.'

After requesting the Inspector to proceed with the formalities and to attend the pathologists who would conduct the autopsy, he took his leave, followed by his clerk and the policeman who had announced Monistrol's arrest.

'I only hope these doctors won't keep me too long,' grumbled the Inspector, who was thinking of his dinner.

Neither M. Méchinet nor myself answered him. Standing face to face, we were both evidently obsessed by the same idea.

'After all,' murmured my neighbour, 'perhaps it could have been the old man who wrote . . .'

'With his left hand? Is it likely? And how do you account for the fact that his death must have been instantaneous?'

'Are you sure of it?'

'Judging by his injuries, I'd swear to it . . . In any case, the pathologists will be here soon. They will say whether I'm right or wrong.'

M. Méchinet was toying with his nose in a veritable frenzy.

'Perhaps there is a crime to be solved after all. We must wait and see. But let us start the inquiry on a new tack. Shall we have a word or two with the concierge?'

He hurried out to the landing and, leaning over the banister, shouted:

'Down there! The concierge, please. Would you mind stepping up here a moment?'

# V

Waiting for the concierge to appear, M. Méchinet conducted a rapid but thorough examination of the scene of the crime.

The lock on the exterior door of the apartment particularly engaged his attention. The mechanism had not been forced and the key turned easily. This absolutely ruled out any idea of a stranger penetrating the apartment at night by means of some device.

I, for my part, without thinking, or rather, inspired by that amazing instinct which had revealed itself in me so suddenly, returned to the bedroom and picked up the cork with the green wax seal which I had already noticed lying on the floor.

On one side, that of the seal, there was the puncture mark made by the cork-screw; but, on the other side, there was a deep impression obviously caused by a sharp, pointed instrument.

Realizing the importance of my discovery, I showed it immediately to M. Méchinet, who could not prevent an exclamation of delight from escaping him.

'At last,' he chuckled, 'we have a clue! It was the murderer who dropped this cork here . . . He used it to protect the fragile point of the murder weapon. Conclusion: the crime was committed with a fix-blade dagger and not one which closes. With this cork, nothing can prevent me from tracing the murderer.'

The Inspector of Police was in the bedroom completing whatever formalities remained. M. Méchinet and myself were talking alone in the parlour when we were interrupted by the sound of someone on the stairs catching their breath.

A moment later, the portly little gossip arrived whom I had seen lecturing to the tenants in the hall. The concierge was even redder in the face, if that was possible, than when we had arrived.

'What can I do for you, sir?' she asked M. Méchinet.

'Take a seat, please,' he replied.

'But I have such a lot of people downstairs . . .'

'They can wait. Sit down.'

Taken aback by the tone of his voice, she obeyed. M. Méchinet stared at her with his penetrating little grey eyes and said:

'I am making some inquiries, and I would like to ask you some questions. I advise you that it is in your own interest to answer them frankly. First, what is the name of this poor old gentleman?'

'He was called Pigoreau, sir, but he was better known as "Anténor", a name he went by formerly as better suited to his business.'

'How long has he lived here?'

'At least eight years.'

'Where did he live before that?'

'In the Rue Richelieu. He had his shop there, the one which made him his fortune. He was a hairdresser by profession.'

'He was thought to be rich?'

'I have heard his niece say that she wouldn't let his throat be cut for a million francs.'

This could be verified, since an inventory of all the deceased's papers had been carried out.

'Now,' continued M. Méchinet, 'what kind of man was this M. Pigoreau or Anténor?'

'Oh! One of the best, sir,' replied the concierge, 'though you can't imagine a man more obstinate or eccentric than he was. But he wasn't proud. And he could be entertaining when he chose to be. You could spend hours listening to his stories when the mood took him. He knew no end of stories about different people, as you can guess. Being a hairdresser he had had, as he often said, the prettiest women in Paris sitting in his chair.'

'What was his life-style?'

'No different from anyone else. Just like anyone living off their savings, he was not inclined to be extravagant.'

'Can you give me some details?'

'Oh, I should think so, sir, seeing that I did his cleaning for him . . . not that there was much for me to do, him doing most of it himself, sweeping, dusting, polishing. It was one of his fads, you know . . . Anyway, I would bring him up a cup of hot chocolate every day at twelve o'clock. After drinking it, he would swallow a tumbler of water, and that was his breakfast. Then he would get dressed, and that took him until two o'clock for he was very particular about his appearance, he always looked as if he was on his way to a wedding. When he was

57

dressed, he would go out and stroll about Paris until six o'clock when he would eat dinner at a family boarding-house kept by the Mlles Gomet in the Rue de la Paix. After dinner, he would walk to the Café Guerbois, where he took his coffee, and would play cards. He was usually back by eleven o'clock and ready for bed. Really, if he had a fault, it was that he was a bit too fond of women for my liking. Often I used to say to him, "Aren't you ashamed of yourself at your age?" But then, none of us is perfect, and it's understandable coming from an old hair-dresser; after all, he'd had his fair share of luck in his time . . .'

An obsequious smile strayed across the lips of the corpulent concierge, but M. Méchinet remained as grave as ever.

'Did M. Pigoreau receive many visitors?'

'Very few. I saw hardly anyone come here except his nephew, M. Monistrol, whom he used to invite to dinner every Sunday at the restaurant Père Lathuile.'

'And how did they get on together, the uncle and his nephew?'

'They were thick as thieves, sir.'

'They never had any arguments?'

'Never . . . excepting that they were always quarrelling about Madame Clara.'

'Who is Madame Clara?'

'Why, M. Monistrol's wife. A beautiful woman, but old M. Anténor couldn't stand the sight of her and was for ever telling his nephew that he was too much in love with his wife and that, as a result, she was leading him up the garden path. M. Anténor claimed that she didn't care for her husband, that she acted above her station, and that she would end up by doing something foolish. In fact, Madame Clara and the uncle had quite a tiff only last year. She wanted the old man to lend her husband a hundred thousand francs to buy a jeweller's business in the Palais-Royale. But he refused, saying that he didn't mind what they did with his fortune after he was dead, but, until then, having earned it himself, he'd do with it exactly as he pleased.'

I hoped M. Méchinet would pursue this highly suggestive point but, despite the signs I made to him, he continued:

'Who discovered the crime?'

'I did, sir. I discovered the crime,' bewailed the concierge. 'It was frightful! You can't imagine! This morning, as twelve o'clock was striking, I brought up M. Anténor his cup of chocolate as usual. I have my own key to his rooms as I do his cleaning for him. I opened the door and went in . . . And what did I see? Oh my god! . . .'

She started weeping in her shrill voice.

'Your grief shows the goodness of your soul, madame,' observed M. Méchinet earnestly, 'only, as I am very pressed for time, I beg of you to control yourself. What was your first thought when you saw your tenant lying there, murdered?'

'I said to myself that this rogue of a nephew was at the bottom of it, for the inheritance. And I don't mind who hears me say it.'

'Why are you so sure? After all, to accuse a man of such a serious crime is tantamount to sending him to the scaffold.'

'But who else could it be? M. Monistrol came to see his uncle yesterday evening, and left when it was nearly midnight. He always exchanges a greeting with me, but last night he didn't say a word either on arrival or when he departed. And I am sure that no one else went to see M. Anténor before I found him in the morning.'

I must admit that this testimony confounded me.

Uninstructed as I was in the art of interviewing witnesses, I thought it useless to continue. Fortunately, M. Méchinet's experience was more extensive. Moreover, he knew the knack of drawing precise information from those whom he questioned.

'You are quite certain, then,' he insisted, 'that Monistrol came last night?'

'Quite certain.'

'Then you saw him, recognized him? . . .'

'Ah, allow me! I didn't see his face. He passed by very quickly, trying to hide himself, the villain that he is, and the stairs are badly lit . . .'

When I heard this statement of incalculable significance, I jumped up and advanced towards the concierge.

'How dare you state that you recognized Monistrol!' I exclaimed.

She weighed me up, and replied with an ironical smile, 'If I didn't see the face of the master, at least I saw the muzzle of his dog. I'm always kind to the animal, and he came into my room. I

59

was just about to give him a bone of mutton when his master whistled.'

I looked anxiously at M. Méchinet to see what he thought of this reply, but he, impassively, simply asked:

'What breed of dog is M. Monistrol's?'

'A Pomeranian, the sort that used to be trained as guide-dogs. Black all over except for a white patch under one ear. His master calls him Pluto.'

M. Méchinet rose.

'Thank you,' he said. 'That is all. You may go now.'

When she was gone, he said to me:

'His nephew must be guilty – I don't see any other solution.'

However, the police surgeon had arrived during this long conversation, and he told us his conclusions.

'M. Pigoreau's death was definitely instantaneous. Consequently, it could not have been he who wrote the five letters —MONIS—on the floor, by the body.'

I had not been mistaken.

'If it was not him,' pondered M. Méchinet, 'then who was it? Monistrol? What on earth could have put it into his head to do such a thing!'

However, the Inspector, delighted to be able to go to his dinner, mocked the difficulties raised by M. Méchinet. They seemed ridiculous to him since Monistrol had admitted it all.

'Perhaps I am only an old fool,' said M. Méchinet. 'We shall see . . . Meanwhile, my dear M. Godeuil, shall we pay a visit to the Préfecture?'

## VI

We engaged the same hansom to take us to the Préfecture.

M. Méchinet was tremendously preoccupied, his fingers never ceasing to travel from his empty snuff-box to his nose, and I heard him mumble to himself, 'I'll get to the bottom of it yet.'

Then, taking the cork from his pocket, he turned it over and over again, like a monkey inspecting a nut, and muttered, 'A valuable clue. Ah! If only this sealing-wax could speak!'

Ensconced in my corner, I did not say a word. In truth, my situation was rather peculiar, but I did not dwell on it. My mind was completely absorbed in the case. I tried to bring some order to the incongruous elements which I possessed, until the point where I despaired of finding any solution to the problem.

When we arrived it was dark.

The Quai des Orfèvres was silent and deserted: not a sound, not a passer-by. The few shops of the neighbourhood were closed. The only sign of life came from the little restaurant near the corner of the Rue de Jérusalem, and I could see the shadows of the customers against the red curtains of the front window.

'Will they let you see the accused?' I asked M. Méchinet.

'Certainly,' he replied. 'I've been entrusted with the affair, haven't I? Then I must have the right to see the prisoner at any time of the day or night as new evidence comes to light.'

And as he disappeared under the arch with rapid footsteps, he added, 'Come along now, we've no time to lose.'

I had no need of encouragement. As I hurried after him, I was filled with many indefinable emotions and, above all, an uneasy curiosity.

This was the first time in my life that I had crossed the threshold of the Préfecture of Police. And, no doubt, I shared the same prejudices against it as most other Parisians.

'Here,' he whispered, not without a slight shudder, 'here is the secret of Paris.'

I was so lost in my reflections that, forgetting to watch my feet, I almost fell.

This jolt brought my thoughts back to the present.

We walked down a long passage with damp walls and uneven flagstones. Then my companion went into a little room where two men were playing cards while three or four more smoked their pipes stretched out on camp-beds. The words he exchanged with them did not reach me outside. He came out and we set off again.

We crossed a courtyard and hurried down another corridor, and came to a halt in front of an iron gate secured by heavy bolts and a formidable lock.

At a word from M. Méchinet, a guard opened the gate. We passed a vast guardroom, on our right, where there seemed to be a great number of town sergeants and guards, and climbed a steep flight of stairs.

On the landing above, at the entry to a narrow passage lined with little doors, sat a fat, jovial man, who had nothing of the public's conception of the gaoler about him.

'Why, if it isn't M. Méchinet!' he exclaimed when he saw my companion. 'To tell you the truth, I was rather expecting you. I bet you've come to see the man who has been arrested for the murder at Batignolles.'

'Precisely. Is there anything new?'

'No.'

'But the investigating magistrate has been here?'

'Yes, he has only just left.'

'Did he say anything?'

'He only stopped two or three minutes with the accused, but he looked pretty satisfied when he came out. He met the Governor at the bottom of the stairs and I heard him say, "It's in the bag, he made no attempt to deny it . . ."'

M. Méchinet gave a start. The gaoler did not notice it since he continued:

'I can't say I was surprised. As soon as I set eyes on him I said to myself: "Here's a fellow who doesn't know what he's about."'

'What is he doing now?'

'Whining to himself in his cell. I was instructed to watch him in case he tried to kill himself. Well, I do keep an eye on him, but, between ourselves, there's not much point . . . his sort are more worried by how to save their necks.'

'I should like to see him,' interrupted M. Méchinet, 'without him knowing.'

We crept, the three of us, as far as the thick oak door with its tiny observation grille at eye-level.

Through the aperture, you could see everything that happened in the cell, badly lit as it was by a single gas jet.

First of all, the guard peered through the wire mesh, followed by M. Méchinet, then I took my turn.

On a narrow iron bed, covered by a grey blanket with yellow stripes, I could dimly see a man lying on his stomach, his head half-obscured by his arms.

He was weeping: I could hear his sobs. From time to time, a convulsive spasm shook him from head to toe.

'You may open the door now,' said M. Méchinet.

The gaoler did as he was bid, and we went in.

At the sound of the key grating in the lock, the prisoner sat up on his pallet, with drooping arms and legs and his head leaning on his chest, and looked blankly at us.

He was a man of between thirty-five and thirty-eight years of age, of slightly more than average height, broad-chested, with a short apoplectic neck sunk between his powerful shoulders. He was not handsome, his face having been disfigured by small-pox, and his long straight nose and reclining forehead gave him the truly stupid aspect of a sheep. However, his eyes were blue and clear and his teeth exceptionally white.

'Come, come, M. Monistrol,' began M. Méchinet, 'worrying won't do you any good.'

And since the unfortunate man did not reply, he continued, 'I agree, the situation is not very brilliant. But, if I were in your place, I would be keen to show myself as a man. I would use my intelligence and set about proving my innocence.'

'I am not innocent.'

There was no room for ambiguity; this dreadful confession, coming from the very mouth of the accused, was not the garbled report of some dull sergeant.

'What!' exclaimed M. Méchinet. 'It really was you?'

'Yes, it really was me!' shouted the prisoner angrily.

He staggered to his feet. His eyes were blood-shot and his mouth palpitated.

'Me. Alone. How many more times must I repeat it? I signed my confession in front of the judge only five minutes ago. What more do you want? Yes, I know what will happen to me. I'm not afraid. I killed a man and now it's my turn to be killed. Go on, cut off my head! The sooner the better as far as I'm concerned.'

Though at first disconcerted by this, M. Méchinet quickly recovered himself.

'Wait a minute, for God's sake,' he said. 'We don't guillotine people just like that. First, you must be proved guilty. And then the courts will take into consideration your sanity, whether you were provoked, and so on; in fact, all the "extenuating circumstances", as they are called.'

Monistrol gave a groan of anguish.

'You really hated your uncle as much as that?'

'No, not at all.'

'Then, why . . . ?'

63

'For the inheritance. I was ruined. Your inquiries will tell you that. I needed money and my uncle, who was very rich, refused to help me.'

'I see. And you thought that you wouldn't be found out?'

'I hoped so.'

I was surprised at the desultory manner in which M. Méchinet conducted the interrogation. Now I saw the trap he was laying for the prisoner.

'By the way,' he said in an off-hand fashion, 'where did you come by the revolver with which you killed him?'

Monistrol showed no surprise at the question.

'Oh, I've had it for some years,' he replied.

'What did you do with it after the crime?'

'I threw it away outside, in the street.'

'Very good. I will institute a search and we shall find it.'

After a moment of silence, M. Méchinet added:

'What I cannot understand is why you took your dog with you.'

'What! My dog?'

'Yes, your dog, Pluto. The concierge recognized him.'

Monistrol clenched his fists. He opened his mouth as if he was about to say something, but a new thought crossed his mind, and he flung himself on the bed, saying in a tone of unshakeable resolution:

'That's enough torture. You won't wring another word out of me.'

Clearly, no further progress could be made.

We withdrew. When we were outside on the quay, I took M. Méchinet by the arm. 'You heard him as well as I did. He doesn't even know how his uncle died. How can his innocence still be in doubt?'

But this old detective was a great sceptic.

'Perhaps so,' he replied. 'I've seen so many great actors in my time . . . But that's enough for today. I must sleep on it . . . Come home and have a bite to eat with my wife and me.'

## VII

It was nearly ten o'clock when M. Méchinet, still accompanied by myself, rang at the door of his apartment.

64

'I never carry a key,' he told me. 'In this wretched business you never know what is going to befall you next . . . There are plenty of rogues itching to get even with me, and if I am not always so careful about myself, I have to think of my wife.'

It was the pretty Madame Méchinet herself who opened the door.

With a quick, feline grace she slipped her arms around her husband's neck.

'Back at last, then . . . I was beginning to get worried . . .'

But she stopped short when she saw me. Her bright smile faded from her lips and she took a pace backwards.

'What! It's ten o'clock and you've only just left the café? Haven't the pair of you any sense?' she said, directing her remarks to me as much as to her husband.

M. Méchinet had the indulgent smile on his face of the man who is confident of his wife's affection and knows he can make peace with a single word.

'Don't be angry with us, Caroline,' he replied, implicating me in his affairs, 'we left the café hours ago and haven't been wasting our time. I was called out on some business at Batignolles—a murder.'

His wife looked from one to the other of us suspiciously. When she was convinced that she was not being deceived, she said:

'Ah! . . .'

The exclamation was brief enough, yet charged with meaning.

Delivered to her husband, it seemed to say:

'What! Have you confided your profession to this young man? Revealed our secrets to him? How dare you!'

At least, that was how I interpreted the eloquent exclamation, and my neighbour construed it similarly because he replied:

'Well, yes. I didn't see any harm in it. Even if I have to fear the scoundrels I've handed over to the courts, I do not see why I should be afraid of honest folk. I'm not going to lock myself away, and I'm certainly not ashamed of my profession . . .'

'You misunderstand me, my dear,' objected Madame Méchinet.

M. Méchinet did not even hear her.

65

He had mounted his favourite hobby-horse—I was to find that out later—and there is no disputing against hobby-horses.

'Really, my love, you have the most ridiculous ideas. Here I am, one of the sentries at an outpost of civilization. I lose my sleep and risk my life to ensure the safety of society—and you think I should blush for my profession. It's too comical for words . . . I know as well as you do the foolish prejudices which are held against the police. But that's all history now. Do you think it makes any difference to me? Yes, even if those simple-tons look down their noses at us! I would like to see the looks on their faces if we went on strike tomorrow, leaving Paris in the hands of all those rogues we try to keep off the streets!'

No doubt accustomed to displays of this kind, Madame Méchinet wisely did not utter a word, and M. Méchinet, realizing there was no prospect of being contradicted, calmed down as if by magic.

'That's enough for the time being,' he said. 'Just now we have a more important matter: we have not yet eaten. Is there any supper for us?'

Obviously, Madame Méchinet had been taken by surprise in this way too often in the past to be caught out again.

'I'll have something ready in five minutes,' she replied with her pleasant smile.

And, in fact, the next minute there was a succulent joint of cold beef on the table in front of us. Madame Méchinet served us and at the same time kept our glasses filled with an excellent Mâcon wine.

While M. Méchinet plied his knife and fork with determina-tion, I glanced around his peaceful apartment, saw his plump, kindly wife, and I asked myself: 'Is he really one of those violent detectives of the Sûreté that you read about in so many implausible novels?'

However, when we had finished eating, M. Méchinet told his wife of our expedition.

He spoke precisely, entering into the most minute details. She sat beside him, listening intently, clearly no novice to these revelations, interrupting every now and again to clarify some obscure point: a middle-class, French, Delphic oracle, not accustomed merely to be consulted but also prone to expect her advice to be followed.

66

In fact, as soon as M. Méchinet finished his narrative, she said:

'You have made a great error, one you may not be able to remedy . . .'

'What was that?'

'When you left Batignolles, it was not to the Préfecture that you should have gone.'

'But Monistrol . . .'

'Yes, I know. You wanted to interrogate him. But what good has it done you?'

'Well, my dear, it brought to my attention . . .'

'Nothing. You should have gone to the Rue Vivienne and spoken with his wife. You would have caught her while she was still upset about her husband's arrest, and if she is mixed up in this affair, as must be supposed, you might easily have procured her confession.'

I sat up at these words.

'What? Do you really think that Monistrol is guilty, madame?'

She hesitated for a moment.

'Yes,' she said. Then she quickly resumed, 'But I'm certain that it was her idea. Of every twenty crimes committed by men, fifteen are conceived, counselled and procured by their wives. Ask M. Méchinet here. You should have seen the light after what you were told by the concierge. Who is this Madame Monistrol? A great beauty, you were told; flirtatious, ambitious, hankering after wealth, leading her husband by the nose. What is her present situation? Shabby, straitened and precarious. She had had enough of it—and the proof of this is that she asked her husband's uncle to lend him a hundred thousand francs. The old man refused to do so, and all her hopes were destroyed. She must have hated him to death after that. And I bet she used to say to herself, "If only that old miser would die, my husband and I would be rich!" And when she saw him, fit as a fiddle, she said to herself: "He'll live to be a hundred . . . We won't have any teeth in our heads by the time we get our hands on his inheritance . . . Who knows, he might even outlive us." From there, it is not very far to the conception of the crime. Once the idea had taken root, she slowly started to work on her husband: she familiarized him with the idea of being an

67

assassin, virtually put the knife into his hands . . . Until, one day, menaced by bankruptcy and maddened by his wife's complainings, he strikes the fatal blow.'

'All that is logical enough,' concurred M. Méchinet.

Very logical, no doubt, but did it fit the facts?

'Do you think, madame,' I said, 'that Monistrol would have been fool enough to denounce himself by signing his name . . .'

'Fool enough?' she asked with a slight shrug of her shoulders. 'No, I don't think so, since it is the strongest point that you can adduce in favour of his innocence.'

This reasoning was so specious that, for a moment, I was at a loss.

'But he confesses his guilt,' I urged, as soon as I recovered myself.

'An excellent means of inducing the police to establish his innocence.'

'Oh, madame!'

'You, yourself, are the living proof of it, my dear M. Godeuil.'

'But, madame, the poor fellow doesn't even know how his uncle was killed.'

'Excuse me, he *appears* not to know . . . that's not altogether the same thing.'

The discussion was becoming animated, and would have lasted some little while longer if M. Méchinet had not drawn it to a close at that point.

'I think you are rather too romantic tonight, Caroline,' he said.

Then, turning to me, he added:

'Well, I must bid you good night, I'm half-asleep already. Tomorrow morning I will give you a knock and we can go to see Madame Monistrol together . . . Good night.'

He might be able to sleep, but not I. I could not shut my eyes.

A mysterious voice, calling out from the depths of my soul, cried, 'Monistrol is innocent!'

In my imagination, I could picture the sufferings of this unfortunate man, alone in his cell at the Dépôt.

But why had he confessed? . . .

68

# VIII

I lacked experience in those days—I have had occasion to remark it a hundred times since—professional experience; above all, I lacked the exact knowledge of the manner in which the police conduct their investigations.

I vaguely realized that this inquiry had been conducted improperly, negligently even, but I would have been extremely embarrassed if I had been called on to explain where the mistakes had been made or to say what ought to have been done.

All the same, I was as passionately involved as Monistrol.

It seemed to me that his cause was mine. This was not surprising: I had my young vanity at stake! Wasn't it one of my observations which had raised the first doubts as to his guilt?

'For my own sake I must prove him innocent,' I said to myself.

The arguments expressed by Madame Méchinet had so confused me though that I was no longer certain of which fact I should select as the foundation of my defence.

As always happens when the mind is applied too long to the solution of a problem, my ideas at last became a tangled skein and I could see nothing clearly.

At nine o'clock the next morning, when M. Méchinet came to collect me as he had promised, I was as perplexed as before.

'Come along now,' he said, 'we must be off.'

As we hurried down the stairs, I noticed that my worthy neighbour was dressed rather more carefully than usual. He had succeeded in giving himself that prosperous, good-natured appearance which Parisian shopkeepers are so pleased to see in their customers.

He had the high spirits of a man marching off to certain victory.

'Well,' said he, as soon as we were in the street, 'what do you think of my wife? They take me for a wise-blood at the Préfecture, yet, you see, I consult my wife, and she's often right. I believe it was Molière who was in the habit of consulting his servant, wasn't it? Her one failing is that she attributes every miscreant with powers of diabolical cunning; for her, there are no crimes committed as a result of stupidity . . . My failing is just the opposite, I look no further than the facts. Between us, we rarely fall far short of the truth.'

'What!' I exclaimed. 'Have you penetrated the mystery surrounding this Monistrol affair?'

He stopped, took out his snuff-box, and helped himself to three or four imaginary pinches.

'At least I am convinced as to the strategy I must pursue to penetrate it,' he replied in a modest but satisfied voice.

We arrived shortly at the Rue Vivienne, not far from Monistrol's shop.

'Look here,' said M. Méchinet. 'Follow me, but whatever happens don't let on that you are surprised by anything I do.'

He did well to warn me otherwise I would not have been able to hide my astonishment at seeing him abruptly enter a shop selling umbrellas.

As stiff and serious as an Englishman, he examined almost every umbrella in the establishment without, however, finding one which suited him for he finished by asking if it was possible to have an umbrella made to specification.

It seemed there was nothing simpler, and he left promising to call again the next day.

The half-hour he had spent in the shop had not been wasted. Even as he studied the wares which the shopkeeper had displayed to him, he had skilfully learnt from them everything that they knew about Monistrol and his wife.

It was no difficult matter. The murder of 'the little old man of Batignolles' and the arrest of the imitation jeweller had caused a sensation in the district and was the primary topic of conversation.

'There we are!' he sighed when we were on the pavement once again. 'That's the way to gather information which is reliable . . . Why, if they so much as guessed who I was, they would embroider the truth out of all recognition.'

My companion repeated this little comedy in seven or eight other shops in the neighbourhood.

In one of them, where the tradesman was short-tempered and not inclined to talk, he even spent twenty francs.

To my amazement, we spent two hours in this singular fashion, at the end of which time we knew exactly the climate of

70

opinion about M. Monistrol and his wife in the quarter where they had been living since their marriage four years ago.

Opinion was unanimous as to the husband.

He enjoyed a good reputation: he was thought to be good-natured, obliging, honest, intelligent and hard-working. It was through no fault of his that business had not prospered. Fortune does not always smile on those who are most deserving of her favours. He had been unwise enough to take a shop doomed to failure; in fifteen years, four traders had ruined themselves in it.

He was very fond of his wife, everyone was aware of it and talked about it, but he had not displayed his affections ostentatiously, had done nothing to make himself appear ridiculous . . .

No one believed him to be guilty.

'The police must have made some mistake,' they said.

Opinion was divided about Madame Monistrol.

Some found her tastes too elegant for her station; others thought that a jeweller's wife was obliged in the interests of the business to be fashionably dressed.

There was general agreement, however, that she was very attached to her husband.

And everyone wished to praise her modesty, a modesty all the more essential in a woman of remarkable beauty, a woman to whom a man might offer his attentions. But her reputation was uncompromised by even the slightest shadow of a suspicion.

This information clearly troubled M. Méchinet.

'It's unbelievable,' he said. 'No slander, no lies, no back-biting! . . . Caroline has got it wrong this time. According to her, we should find one of those flighty shopkeeper's wives who flaunt themselves more than their husband's merchandise. They rule the household, their husbands being too weak or too blind to raise a hand to them.'

I was as confused as he was and I made no reply.

You would hardly think that these honest traders and the concierge at the Rue Lécluse were describing the same person. In Paris, attitudes vary from quarter to quarter. What is taken as shocking in Batignolles is an exigency in the Bourse.

We had already spent too much time on the inquiry to think of pausing and exchanging impressions and conjectures.

'We had better have a good look at it from the outside before going in,' said M. Méchinet.

Adroit in the art of observing without being observed, even in the bustling streets of Paris, he led me under a covered passageway situated opposite Monistrol's shop.

It was a modest-looking establishment, poor in comparison with those around it. The shop-front was in need of a fresh coat of paint. Above the door, in faded gilt letters, blackened and dingy, was the name, 'MONISTROL'. Across the windows I read, 'Gold and imitation'.

· There was little besides 'imitation' which glittered in the window display. Steel-gilt chains, jet ornaments, tiaras decorated with clusters of rhinestones, imitation coral necklaces, and brooches, rings and cuff-links bright with false stones of every colour.

A glance was all that was necessary to see that there was nothing in this poor cabinet to tempt the poorest window thief.

'Shall we go in?' I said to M. Méchinet.

He had not my impatience, or concealed it better, for, catching me by the arm, he said:

'One moment . . . I should like a glimpse of Madame Monistrol before we go in.'

We waited another twenty minutes at our observation-post, in vain; the shop remained empty and Madame Monistrol did not appear.

'Well, that's enough hanging around,' remarked M. Méchinet at last. 'Come along, M. Godeuil, let us chance it.'

## IX

We had only to cross the street to reach Monistrol's shop.

At the sound of the opening of the door, a little servant girl, fifteen or sixteen years old, came out of the small room at the back of the shop.

'Can I be of assistance, gentlemen?'

'Is Madame Monistrol here?'

'Yes, sir, I'll run and fetch her, she is . . .'

M. Méchinet did not allow the girl to finish. He pushed her roughly aside. 'It's all right, as she's here, I'll speak to her myself,' he said as he strode through into the back room.

I followed hard on his heels, convinced that I would not leave the premises without the solution of the enigma.

The backroom was a cheerless little abode, serving at the same time as parlour, dining-room and bedroom.

It was in a state of considerable confusion and had the incongruous aspect you find in the homes of poor people who pretend to be rich.

The bed, draped with curtains of blue damask, stood at the farthest end, the pillow cases trimmed with lace, whilst on the table in front of the chimney remained the scraps of a most unappetizing meal.

Sitting, or rather, reclining, in an armchair beside the table was a young woman with fair hair. She was holding in her hands some kind of official document.

This was Madame Monistrol. The neighbours had certainly not exaggerated when they spoke of her beauty. I was stunned.

Only the quality of her grief caused me any displeasure: she was dressed in a low-necked, black silk gown, which looked very becoming on her . . .

It showed too much presence of mind in one genuinely afflicted. At that moment, she resembled to me a scheming actress rehearsing the role she intended to play.

She sprang to her feet like a startled doe when she saw us, and asked in a tearful voice:

'What do you want, gentlemen?'

I realized that M. Méchinet had drawn the same conclusions as I had.

'Madame,' he replied, 'I am here by the authority of the court; I am a detective of the Sûreté.'

At this declaration, she fell back into her chair with a dreadful groan.

Then, as if gripped by a fever, with shining eyes and trembling lips, she climbed to her feet again.

'Have you come to arrest me? Bless you, I'm ready, lead me away . . . Lead me to the honest man you arrested last night . . . I will share the same fate as him, whatever it might be . . . He is as innocent as I am. No matter, if he is to be the victim of another of the police's mistakes, I prefer to die alongside him.'

She was interrupted by a protracted growl coming from one of the corners of the room.

I saw a black dog, with bristling fur, bloodshot eyes and bared teeth, ready to attack us.

'Stay, Pluto, stay. Lie down. These gentlemen don't wish me any harm.'

The dog slowly crawled backwards under the bed, still fixing us with his furious eyes.

'You were quite correct in saying that we don't wish you any harm, madame,' said M. Méchinet, 'nor have we come to arrest you.'

She did not appear to be listening.

'I have already received this summons this morning. It requires me to be at the chambers of the investigating magistrate at three o'clock this afternoon. What does he want me for? My God, what does he want?'

'He wants information. Information which I hope will prove your husband's innocence. You mustn't think of me as your enemy. My only interest is in finding out the truth.'

He drew out his snuff-box and hastily helped himself to several pinches.

'That is to say, madame,' he continued in a solemn tone which I had not heard him employ before, 'that the replies you give to the following questions are of the utmost importance. Do you think you can answer me frankly?'

Her blue eyes gazed at my neighbour through her tears. For a long time she made no reply. At last, she said with resignation:

'Ask me what you like, monsieur.'

As I have said before, I was completely without experience in these matters, and yet I was dissatisfied with the manner in which M. Méchinet had commenced the interrogation.

It seemed to me that his own perplexities were too much in evidence and that, rather than pursuing some fixed object, he wandered haphazardly from point to point.

How well I would have conducted it myself—if I had only dared to interrupt!

M. Méchinet sat imperturbably in front of Madame Monistrol.

'You are of course aware of the fact that the night before last, M. Pigoreau, better known as Anténor, your husband's uncle, was mudered at about eleven o'clock.'

'Yes.'

74

'Where was M. Monistrol at this time?'

'It's no good.'

M. Méchinet did not flinch.

'I repeat. Where was your husband the night before last?'

She choked on her sobs, and M. Méchinet allowed her to reply when she was composed.

'The day before yesterday, my husband was away from home all evening.'

'Do you know where he was?'

'Yes, I can tell you that. One of our suppliers who lives in Montrouge was supposed to deliver us a set of false pearls. He hadn't shown up. We were afraid that the person who had ordered them would leave us with them on our hands. We couldn't afford that—business is bad enough as it is. So, while we were having dinner, my husband said to me: "I'd better go and have a word with that fine fellow out in Montrouge." And, sure enough, at nine o'clock, out he went. I walked as far as the corner of the Rue Richelieu with him, where I saw him get on the bus myself.'

I began to breathe again. This could provide the alibi he needed.

M. Méchinet had the same idea.

'If that is so,' he said gently, 'your supplier will certainly confirm that he was with M. Monistrol at eleven o'clock.'

'Unfortunately not.'

'What? Why not?'

'Because he was out. My husband did not see him.'

'This is a catastrophe. Perhaps the concierge will remember M. Monistrol?'

'Our supplier lives in a house which does not have a concierge.'

That might well be true. But as far as the unfortunate prisoner was concerned, it was the end of his last hope.

'And what time did your husband come home?' continued M. Méchinet.

'A little after midnight.'

'Didn't you think that he'd been a long time?'

'Oh, yes. I even reproached him about it. He apologized and said that he had decided to walk back, stopping at a café for a glass of beer on the way.'

'What was he like when he came in?'
'He looked rather annoyed, but that's only natural.'
'What clothes was he wearing?'
'The same as when he was arrested.'
'You didn't notice anything extraordinary about him?'
'No, nothing.'

## X

Standing a little behind M. Méchinet, I was able to study Madame Monistrol's features at my leisure and note each fleeting expression as it crossed her face.

She seemed to be overwhelmed by a boundless grief, large tears streamed down her pale cheeks, and yet, at times, I fancied I could discern a gleam of joy in the depths of her big, blue eyes.

'Is she really guilty?' I wondered.

The idea had occurred to me before, now it returned with greater persistency. I stepped forward.

'But what about you, madame?' I asked gruffly. 'Where were you on that fatal evening, while your husband was wasting his time trotting off to Montrouge to see this supplier?'

She paused and looked at me with a good deal of surprise.

'I was here, monsieur,' she answered softly, 'and I have witnesses who will bear me out.'

'Witnesses!'

'Yes, monsieur. It was very warm that evening and I felt like having an ice-cream. But ice-cream is so tedious when you are on your own that I sent my servant to invite two of my neighbours to join me, Madame Dorstrich, the wife of the shoe-maker who lives next door, and Madame Rivaille, who keeps the glove shop across the road. They both accepted and stayed here until half-past eleven. Go and ask them if you like. With all these other cruel circumstances against us, this accident is a real blessing . . .'

Was it really so accidental? M. Méchinet and I asked ourselves this question as we exchanged quick, doubtful glances.

When chance acts to resolve such an issue so dexterously, it is not easy but to suspect that she has been given some assistance.

Unfortunately, it was hardly a suitable moment to pursue this thought.

'You have never been suspected, madame,' replied M. Méchinet shamelessly. 'The worst that has been supposed was that your husband might have said something to you before committing the crime.'

'Monsieur . . . if you only knew us.'

'Let me finish. We have been told that your business was floundering, that you were hard up . . .'

'Just lately, yes, that's true.'

'Your husband must have been very worried about his precarious situation. He must have suffered, above all, on account of you, the wife he adored, young and beautiful . . . For you far more than for himself, he must have longed for the life of ease and respect which money buys.'

'Monsieur, I can only repeat again, my husband is innocent.'

With a pensive air, M. Méchinet pretended to fill his nose with snuff before unexpectedly asking:

'For God's sake, then, how do you account for his confession? For an innocent man to admit his guilt as soon as the crime of which he is suspected is mentioned is more than unusual, madame. It is prodigious!'

A blush briefly touched the young woman's cheeks.

Her regard, straight and clear until then, vacillated for the first time.

'I suppose,' she replied in a voice muffled with tears and barely audible, 'I suppose that my husband lost his head after finding himself accused of such a dreadful crime.'

M. Méchinet shook his head.

'At the very most we might entertain the idea of a passing delirium . . . but after reflecting all night, M. Monistrol persists this morning in his original confession.'

Was this true? Did my worthy neighbour say that on his own initiative or had he actually been to the Préfecture before calling on me?

However that may be, the young woman nearly fainted and, hiding her head between her hands, murmured:

'God Almighty! My poor husband has taken leave of his senses.'

That was certainly not my opinion. In fact, I was convinced

77

that Madame Monistrol's grief was nothing more than an act and I asked myself whether, for reasons which escaped me, she herself had not chosen the terrible role that her husband should play and, if he was innocent, whether she did not know the identity of the real murderer.

If these opinions were also shared by M. Méchinet, he gave no indication of it.

After addressing the common expressions of consolation to the young woman, without revealing any of his own thoughts, he gave her to understand that she might silence a great many suspicions by allowing him to make a thorough search of her establishment.

She accepted this suggestion with unfeigned enthusiasm.

'Search as much as you like, gentlemen. I shall be most obliged to you. It won't take you very long. We rent only this shop, this room where we are now, a room on the top floor for the servant, and a small cellar. Here are the keys to everything.'

To my great astonishment, M. Méchinet readily accepted the offer and seemed to devote himself to a most meticulous investigation.

What was his objective? Surely he must have some secret purpose because this step would obviously lead nowhere.

When he had the appearance of having finished, he said:

'There just remains the cellar.'

'I'll show you the way, monsieur,' said Madame Monistrol.

On these words, she picked up a lighted candle and conducted us across a courtyard on which the back room had issue and down a flight of slippery steps to a door which she opened herself.

'Here it is . . . go in, gentlemen.'

I began to understand.

M. Méchinet scanned the cellar with a quick, appraising glance. It was ill-kept and untidy. A small barrel of beer was set up in one corner and, just in front, resting on some logs, was a cask of wine. Both were on draught since they were fitted with small wooden taps. On the right, ranged on a metal rack, were four dozen or so bottles of wine.

M. Méchinet took down these bottles one by one, examining them carefully.

He noted, like myself, that not a single bottle was sealed with green wax.

The cork which I had discovered, used by the murderer to protect the point of his dagger, had not come from Monistrol's cellar.

'There's nothing here,' said M. Méchinet, assuming a look of disappointment, 'we may as well go upstairs.'

We did not climb the stairs in the same order as we had descended them. I went first this time, and so it happened that I reached the back room of the shop before the others. As soon as I opened the door that wretched dog sprang from under the bed and set up such a tremendous barking that I took a step backwards.

'That dog of yours has a bad temper,' said M. Méchinet to the young woman.

'Not at all,' she replied, calming the animal with a wave of her hand, 'he's very good. And he's an excellent watch-dog. Jewellers are more vulnerable to burglars than most people so we trained him well.'

When one has been threatened by a dog, the instinctive response is to call it by name, which I proceeded to do.

'Pluto, here boy!'

But instead of coming forward he backed away from me, growling and showing his teeth.

'Oh! It's no use you calling him,' remarked Madame Monistrol carelessly, 'he won't obey you.'

'Really. Why not?'

'This breed of dog is famous for its loyalty. He knows only his master and me.'

This response did not seem to have any particular bearing on the crime we were investigating, but to me it flashed a sudden light on the mystery.

Without thinking—I would hardly do the same today—I asked:

'And where was your dog which is so faithful on the night of the crime?'

This question put point-blank caused her so great a surprise that she almost dropped the candlestick which she still held in her hand.

'I've no idea,' she stammered, 'I can't remember.'

'Perhaps he went with your husband?'

'Yes. I believe he did, come to think of it.'

'Is he trained to follow buses, then? You've already told us that you saw your husband get on the bus.'

She made no reply. I was about to continue when I was interrupted by M. Méchinet. Far from trying to take advantage of Madame Monistrol's confusion, he did everything possible to reassure her and, after strongly advising her not to ignore the magistrate's subpoena, he took his leave.

When we were outside he said to me:

'Have you taken leave of your senses?'

The remark stung me.

'If I have taken leave of my senses, it was because I have found the solution to the problem . . . The dog is the key to the affair, he will lead us to the truth.'

My outburst brought a smile to my neighbour's face.

'You are quite correct,' he said paternally, 'I saw the point you were trying to establish . . . Only, if Madame Monistrol guessed your suspicions as easily as I did, the dog either will be dead or have disappeared before the day is over.'


# XI

I had committed an enormous indiscretion, certainly.

On the other hand, at least I had discovered the weak point in their armour—a chink which could be used to penetrate the strongest defences.

I, a volunteer, had kept my bearings while the old campaigner of the Sûreté had lost his way.

Another man might have been jealous of my success, but not him.

His one thought was how to turn my discovery to best account, which should not prove very difficult now we had a positive point of departure.

Accordingly, we went to a nearby restaurant to hold a counsel of war.

Where was the problem which, an hour ago, had seemed so unlikely of solution?

Even the evidence proclaimed Monistrol's innocence. And although we could only guess as to his reasons for pleading guilty, for the time being the question was a mere detail.

We were equally certain that Madame Monistrol had not left home on the night of the murder, though all the indications pointed to her moral complicity. Even if she had not counselled and procured the crime, she had been fully acquainted with it and consequently knew the murderer well.

But who was the murderer?

Someone whom Monistrol's dog obeyed as he would his master. Had he not followed him all the way to Batignolles?

Consequently, he must be on intimate terms with the Monistrol household.

And he must have a profound hatred of the husband to contrive such an infamous scheme to throw the blame on him.

On the other hand, he must be close to Madame Monistrol's heart; she knew his name but, preferring to sacrifice her husband, refused to denounce him.

There could only be one conclusion. The murderer was some despicable dissembler who had abused the confidences of the husband to seduce his wife.

In short, notwithstanding her reputation, Madame Monistrol had, without doubt, a lover; and this lover, inevitably, was the murderer.

Convinced of this, I racked my brains to devise some infallible scheme to lead us to the wretch.

'It seems to me,' I said to M. Méchinet, 'that the way we should proceed is this. Madame Monistrol and the murderer must have agreed not to see each other for the time being, just after the crime. It would be a most elementary precaution. She will be becoming impatient to see her accomplice again though. If you order one of your men to follow her night and day, we will have him before half a week is out.'

M. Méchinet played implacably with his empty snuff-box, muttering unintelligibly to himself between his teeth, without replying. He turned towards me suddenly:

'That won't do. You have a genius for the profession, I am sure of it, but you are deficient in the practical aspects. Fortunately, I am here. A chance remark put you on the right track and now you don't want to follow it any further . . .'

'How do you mean?'

'We must make use of the dog.'

'I still don't understand you.'

'Well, wait and see. Madame Monistrol will have to leave the shop at two o'clock to be at the Palais-de-Justice for three. The little servant girl will be on her own in the shop. And now not a word more . . .'

Of course, I implored him to explain himself, but he would not be drawn, taking a mischievous pleasure in paying me back for his own failures.

I had no choice but to accompany him to the nearest café where he forced me to play dominoes.

My mind was not on the game, and he took advantage of my distraction to beat me unmercifully until, at last, two o'clock sounded.

'Once more into the breach,' said he, abandoning the hand.

We paid and left the café, and a moment later we were once more standing in the covered passageway from where we had surveyed Monistrol's shop previously.

Ten minutes later Madame Monistrol appeared in the doorway opposite. She had added a black crêpe veil to complete the same black silk dress she had been wearing earlier. She looked like a widow.

'Dressed to kill, I see! I hope the magistrate likes it,' grumbled M. Méchinet.

She gave some last instructions to the servant and hurried off.

My companion waited five long minutes before he was satisfied that she was not coming back.

'It is time,' he said. And for the second time that day we entered the jeweller's shop.

The girl was sitting alone behind the counter, absent-mindedly sucking lumps of sugar stolen from the bowl of her employer.

She recognized us immediately and stood up, flushed and a little frightened.

'Where is Madame Monistrol?' asked M. Méchinet before she had had chance to utter a word.

'She has gone out, monsieur.'

'Gone out? Impossible! She's there, in the back room.'

'Gentlemen, I swear to you ... but, please, see for yourselves.'

M. Méchinet tapped his forehead as if greatly inconvenienced.

'How annoying! Poor Madame Monistrol will be most upset about it.'

The girl stared at him with wide eyes and open mouth.

'But perhaps you can help me out,' he continued. 'I've only come back because I've lost the address of the gentleman whom madame asked me to visit on her behalf.'

'Which gentleman would that be?'

'You know, Monsieur ... Confound it! I've even forgotten his name now! Monsieur ... Monsieur ... You know, the gentleman that dog of yours obeys so readily.'

'Ah! Monsieur Victor.'

'That's the name! Do you know what he does?'

'He's a jewellery worker, a great friend of Monsieur Monistrol. They used to work together before Monsieur set up his own business. That's why he can do what he likes with Pluto.'

'Then you must know where M. Victor lives?'

'Of course, he lives at twenty-three Rue du Roi-Doré.'

The poor girl was so pleased to be so helpful that I could not help regretting the unsuspecting manner in which she betrayed her mistress.

Such scruples did not appear to trouble M. Méchinet's more hardened nature.

As I opened the door, our business concluded, he even launched a grim jest over his shoulder:

'Thank you. You have been most helpful. You have just rendered your mistress a great service. She will be most satisfied with you.'

## XII

I had only one thought in my head when we were outside on the pavement.

M. Méchinet and I should unite our forces on the spot and hasten to the Rue du Roi-Doré to arrest this Monsieur Victor who was clearly the real murderer.

But M. Méchinet immediately threw cold water on my enthusiasm.

'There are formalities, you know,' he said. 'I can do nothing without a warrant of arrest. It is to the Palais-de-Justice that we must go.'

'And if Madame Monistrol sees us there? She will warn her accomplice and . . .'

'Perhaps so,' replied M. Méchinet with undisguised bitterness, 'perhaps we shall observe the formalities only to see our quarry disappear . . . Well, I might be able to do something about that. But we must make haste.'

Hurrying, we arrived at the Palais-de-Justice and mounted four at a time the steep flight of steps leading to the chambers of the investigating magistrate, stopping only to ask the chief usher if the magistrate charged with the affair of 'the little old man of Batignolles' was in his office.

'Yes, he is,' replied the attendant, 'but he has a witness with him at the moment—a young woman in black.'

'That must be Madame Monistrol,' whispered my companion to me; then he turned to the man again, 'You know who I am, don't you? Quickly, give me something on which to write him a brief note. You can take it in for me.'

The usher departed, dragging his feet along the dusty flagstones of the gallery, returning shortly to say that the magistrate would see us in an adjoining room, No. 9.

The magistrate, leaving Madame Monistrol under the watchful eye of his clerk, received us in the room of a colleague.

'What is it?' he asked in a tone which did nothing to disguise the distance which separates a judge from a humble detective.

M. Méchinet gave a brief but clear account of our achievements, hopes and disappointments.

Needless to say, the magistrate hardly seemed inclined to share our views.

'But he admits it!' he repeated, with a persistency which exasperated me.

However, after a series of protracted explanations, he consented:

'Oh, very well. I'll sign this warrant for you.'

As soon as he was in possession of this indispensable

document, M. Méchinet rushed from the building so precipi-
tously that I almost fell down the stairs following him. Outside,
there was not a cab to be seen; nonetheless we covered the
distance to the Rue du Roi-Doré in less than a quarter of an
hour.

'Take care now,' he said to me. And he himself was completely composed as we turned into the narrow alley of the
house bearing the number 23.

'Where will I find M. Victor, please?' he asked the concierge.

'Fourth floor, door on the right.'

'Is he in?'

'Yes.'

M. Méchinet took a step in the direction of the staircase,
then seemed to change his mind.

'I 'must treat my old friend to a good bottle of wine,' he
observed to the concierge. 'Which is the nearest wine shop that
he patronizes?'

'The one over the way.'

To reach it we had only to cross the street.

'A bottle of wine, please, a good one . . . The one with the
green seal,' he said, as if he were an habitué.

I must admit that this simple idea had not occurred to me.

As soon as the bottle was brought, my companion produced
the cork which I had found in the bedroom at Batignolles. The
seals were undoubtedly identical.

It was not with moral certitude alone that M. Méchinet
knocked firmly at M. Victor's door—now we had material
proof.

'Come in, it's open,' replied a voice with a pleasant ring to it.

The door was on the latch and we went in. The room
was clean and tidy, and a pale, slightly-built man of thirty
was bent over a workbench. Our visit did not seem to trouble
him.

'What can I do for you?' he asked politely.

M. Méchinet strode forward and caught him by the arm.

'In the name of the Law, I arrest you.'

The man blanched but did not lower his eyes.

'You've a damned cheek!' he said insolently. 'What am I
supposed to have done?'

M. Méchinet shrugged his shoulders.

85

'Don't come the child with me,' he replied. 'Your account is settled. You were seen leaving the house at Batignolles and in my pocket I have the cork which you used to protect the point of your dagger.'

These words were a crushing blow for the wretch. He collapsed into a chair.

'I didn't do it,' he stammered.

'You can tell that to the judge,' said M. Méchinet without emotion, 'but I fear he won't believe you. Your accomplice, Monistrol's wife, has confessed everything.'

Victor sprang resiliently to his feet.

'Impossible! She knew nothing about it.'

'So you delivered the blow on your own? Very well . . . That will do for a confession.'

M. Méchinet turned to me and continued confidently:

'My dear M. Godeuil, if you would be good enough to look in the drawers I think you will probably find the dagger belonging to this fine fellow; in any case, you'll come across his mistress's portrait and her love letters.'

The murderer clenched his teeth and I could read the rage in his eyes, but the relentless iron grip of M. Méchinet extinguished all hope of resistance in him.

In a chest of drawers I found the items my companion had mentioned.

And twenty minutes later, M. Victor was securely stowed away between M. Méchinet and myself in a cab rolling towards the Préfecture of Police.

I was amazed by how simple it had been. Was there no more than this to arresting a man destined for the scaffold?

Later I learnt to my cost that there are more dangerous criminals.

This one, however, gave himself up for lost as soon as he saw his cell at the Dépôt. In despair, he recounted the details of his crime to us.

He had known old M. Pigoreau a good many years, he explained. His single objective for murdering him, though, had been to compromise Monistrol in the crime—for whom he had reserved the full penalty of the Law. That was the reason he had dressed as Monistrol and taken Pluto with him. And once he had killed the old man, he dipped one of the fingers of the cadaver into the pool of blood and wrote those five letters which so nearly cost an innocent man his life.

'Oh, it was a clever scheme all right,' he added with cynical effrontery. 'If it had only succeeded, I would have killed two birds with one stone: I would have got rid of that fool whom I hated, and profited by winning the woman I love.'

'Unfortunately,' interposed M. Méchinet, 'you lost your head at the last minute. It always happens like that. Your mistake was to pick on the left hand of the body . . .'

Victor sprang to his feet.

'What!' he exclaimed. 'That's what gave me away?'

'Exactly.'

With the typical gesture of the misunderstood genius, he shook his fists at the heavens.

'God! What it is like to be an artist!' he shouted.

And looking at us with pity, he added:

'Didn't you know? M. Pigoreau was left-handed!'

And so an error in the investigation led to the discovery of the murderer.

The lesson was not lost on me, as I will prove at a later date by narrating some circumstances happily rather less dramatic than these.

Monistrol was released the next day.

The judge severely rebuked him at the same time for placing the outcome of justice in jeopardy with his persistent lies. He simply replied: 'I love my wife. I thought she was guilty. I chose to sacrifice myself for her . . .'

Was she guilty? I would swear to it.

She was arrested; but was acquitted by the same judge who condemned Victor to life imprisonment with hard labour.

Today, the Monistrols keep a wine shop of ill repute on the Cours de Vincennes. Their uncle's inheritance is long spent and they live in fearful poverty.

## 2

# MAURICE LEBLANC
## The Mysterious Railway-Passenger

I had sent my motor-car to Rouen, by road, on the previous day.
I was to meet it by train and go on to some friends who have a
house on the Seine.

A few minutes before we left Paris, my compartment was
invaded by seven gentlemen, five of whom were smoking. Short
though the journey by the fast train is, I did not relish the
prospect of taking it in such company, the more so as the
old-fashioned carriage had no corridor. I therefore collected
my overcoat, my newspapers and my railway-guide and sought
refuge in one of the neighbouring compartments.

It was occupied by a lady. At the sight of me, she made a
movement of vexation which did not escape my notice and leant
towards a gentleman standing on the footboard: her husband,
no doubt, who had come to see her off. The gentleman took
stock of me and the examination seemed to conclude to my
advantage, for he whispered to his wife and smiled, giving her
the look with which we reassure a frightened child. She smiled,
in her turn, and cast a friendly glance in my direction, as though
she suddenly realised that I was one of those decent men with
whom a woman can remain locked up for an hour or two, in a
little box six feet square, without having anything to fear.

Her husband said to her:

'You mustn't mind, darling, but I have an important appointment and I can't wait.'

He kissed her affectionately and went away. His wife blew
him some discreet little kisses through the window and waved
her handkerchief.

Then the guard's whistle sounded and the train started.

At that moment and in spite of the warning shouts of the
railway-officials, the door opened and a man burst into our

carriage. My travelling-companion, who was standing up and arranging her things in the rack, uttered a cry of terror and dropped down upon the seat.

I am no coward, far from it, but I confess that these sudden incursions at the last minute are always annoying. They seem so ambiguous, so unnatural. There must be something behind them, else . . .

The appearance and bearing of the newcomer, however, were such as to correct the bad impression produced by the manner of his entrance. He was neatly, almost smartly dressed; his tie was in good taste, his gloves clean; he had a powerful face . . . But, speaking of his face, where on earth had I seen it before? For I had seen it: of that there was no doubt. Or, at least to be accurate, I found within myself that sort of recollection which is left by the sight of an oft-seen portrait of which one has never beheld the original. And at the same time, I felt the uselessness of any effort of memory that I might exert, so inconsistent and vague was that recollection.

But, when my eyes reverted to the lady, I sat astounded at the pallor and disorder of her features. She was staring at her neighbour – he was seated on the same side of the carriage – with an expression of genuine affright; and I saw one of her hands steal trembling towards a little wrist-bag that lay on the cushion a few inches from her lap. She ended by taking hold of it and nervously drawing it to her.

Our eyes met and I read in hers so great an amount of uneasiness and anxiety that I could not help saying:

'I hope you are not unwell, madame? . . . Shall I open the window?'

She made no reply, but, with a timid gesture, called my attention to the man. I smiled as her husband had done, shrugged my shoulders, and explained to her by signs that she had no cause for alarm, that I was there and that, besides, the gentleman seemed quite harmless.

Just then, he turned towards us, and after contemplating us, one after the other, from head to foot, huddled himself into his corner and made no further movement.

A silence ensued; but the lady, as though summoning all her energies to perform an act of despair, said to me, in a hardly intelligible tone:

'You know he is in our train?'

'Who?'

'Why, he . . . he himself . . . I assure you.'

'Whom do you mean?'

'Arsène Lupin!'

She had not removed her eyes from the passenger; and it was at him rather than at me that she flung the syllables of that dread name.

He pulled his hat down upon his nose. Was this to conceal his agitation, or was he merely preparing to go to sleep?

I objected:

'Arsène Lupin was sentenced yesterday, in his absence, to twenty years' penal servitude. It is not likely that he would commit the imprudence of showing himself in public today. Besides, the newspapers have discovered that he has been spending the winter in Turkey, ever since his famous escape from the Santé.'

'He is in this train,' repeated the lady, with the more and more marked intention of being overheard by our companion. 'My husband is a deputy prison governor, and the station inspector himself told us that they were looking for Arsène Lupin.'

'That is no reason why . . .'

'He was seen at the booking-office. He took a ticket for Rouen.'

'It would have been easy to lay hands upon him.'

'He disappeared. The ticket collector at the door of the waiting-room did not see him; but they thought that he must have gone round by the suburban platforms and stepped into the express that leaves ten minutes after us.'

'In that case, they will have caught him there.'

'And supposing that, at the last moment, he jumped out of the express and entered this, our own train . . . as he probably . . . as he most certainly did?'

'In that case, they will catch him here. For the porters and the police cannot have failed to see him going from one train to the other and, when we reach Rouen, they will nab him finely.'

'Him? Never! He will find some means of escaping again.'

'In that case, I wish him a good journey.'

'But think of all that he may do in the meantime!'

90

'What?'

'How can I tell? One must be prepared for anything.'

She was greatly agitated; and, in point of fact, the situation, to a certain degree, warranted her nervous state of excitement. Almost in spite of myself, I said:

'There are such things as curious coincidences, it is true . . . But calm yourself. Admitting that Arsène Lupin is in one of these carriages, he is sure to keep quiet and, rather than bring fresh trouble upon himself, he will have no other idea than to avoid the danger that threatens him.'

My words failed to reassure her. However, she said no more, fearing, no doubt, lest I should think her troublesome.

As for myself, I opened my newspapers and read the reports of Arsène Lupin's trial. They contained nothing that was not already known and they interested me but slightly. Moreover, I was tired, I had had a poor night, I felt my eyelids growing heavy and my head began to nod.

'But, surely, sir, you are not going to sleep!'

The lady snatched my paper from my hands and looked at me with indignation.

'Certainly not,' I replied. 'I have no wish to.'

'It would be most imprudent,' she said.

'Most,' I repeated.

And I struggled hard, fixing my eyes on the landscape, on the clouds that streaked the sky, and soon all this became confused in space, the picture of the excited lady and the drowsy man was obliterated from my mind and I was filled with a great, deep silence of sleep.

It was soon made agreeable by light and incoherent dreams, in which a being who played the part and bore the name of Arsène Lupin occupied a certain place. He turned and shifted on the horizon, his back laden with valuables, clambering over walls and stripping country houses of their contents.

But the outline of this being, who had ceased to be Arsène Lupin, grew more distinct. He came towards me, grew bigger and bigger, leapt into the carriage with incredible agility and fell full upon my chest.

A sharp pain . . . a piercing scream . . . I awoke. The man, my fellow-traveller, with one knee on my chest, was clutching my throat.

I saw this very dimly, for my eyes were shot with blood. I also saw the lady, in a corner, writhing in a violent fit of hysterics. I did not even attempt to resist. I should not have had the strength for it, had I wished to: my temples were throbbing, I choked . . . my throat rattled . . . Another minute . . . and I should have been suffocated.

The man must have felt this. He loosened his grip. Without leaving hold of me, with his right hand he stretched a rope, in which he had prepared a slip-knot, and, with a quick turn, tied my wrists together. In a moment, I was bound, gagged, rendered motionless and helpless.

And he performed this task in the most natural manner in the world, with an ease that revealed the knowledge of a master, of an expert in theft and crime. Not a word, not a fevered movement. Sheer coolness and audacity. And there was I on the seat, tied up like a mummy, I, Arsène Lupin!

It was really ridiculous. And, notwithstanding the seriousness of the circumstances, I could not but appreciate and almost enjoy the irony of the situation. Arsène Lupin 'done' like a novice! Stripped like a first-comer—for of course the scoundrel relieved me of my pocket-book and purse! Arsène Lupin victimized in his turn, duped, defeated! What an adventure!

There remained the lady. He took no notice of her at all. He contented himself with picking up the wrist-bag that lay on the floor and extracting the jewels, the purse, the gold and silver knick-knacks which it contained. The lady opened her eyes, shuddered with fright, took off her rings and handed them to the man, as though she wished to spare him any superfluous exertion. He took the rings and looked at her: she fainted away.

Then, calm and silent as before, without troubling about us further, he resumed his seat, lit a cigarette, and abandoned himself to a careful scrutiny of the treasures which he had captured, the inspection of which seemed to satisfy him completely.

I was much less satisfied. I am not speaking of the twelve thousand francs of which I had been unduly plundered: this was a loss which I accepted only for the time; I had no doubt that those twelve thousand francs would return to my possession after a short interval, together with the exceedingly important papers which my pocket-book contained: plans, estimates, specifications, addresses, lists of correspondents, letters of a compromising character. But, for the moment, a more immediate and serious care was worrying me: what was to happen next?

As may be readily imagined, the excitement caused by my passing through the Gare Saint-Lazare had not escaped me. As I was going to stay with friends who knew me by the name of Guillaume Berlat and to whom my resemblance to Arsène Lupin was the occasion of many a friendly jest, I had not been able to disguise myself after my wont and my presence had been discovered. Moreover, a man, doubtless Arsène Lupin, had been seen to rush from the express into the other train. Hence it was inevitable and fated that the commissary of police at Rouen, warned by telegram, would await the arrival of the train, assisted by a respectable number of constables, question any suspicious passengers and proceed to make a minute inspection of the carriages.

All this I had foreseen and had not felt greatly excited about it; for I was certain that the Rouen police would display no greater perspicacity than the Paris police and that I should have been able to pass unperceived: was it not sufficient for me, at the wicket, carelessly to show my deputy's card, thanks to which I had already inspired the ticket-collector at Saint-Lazare with every confidence? But how things had changed since then! I was no longer free. It was impossible to attempt one of my usual moves. In one of the carriages the commissary would discover the Sieur Arsène Lupin, whom a propitious fate was sending to him bound hand and foot, gentle as a lamb, packed up complete. He had only to accept delivery, just as you receive a parcel addressed to you at a railway station, a hamper of game or a basket of vegetables and fruit.

And to avoid this annoying catastrophe what could I do, entangled as I was in my bonds?

The train was speeding towards Rouen, the next and only stopping place; it rushed through Vernon, through Saint-Pierre . . .

I was puzzled also by another problem, in which I was not so directly interested, but the solution of which aroused my professional curiosity. What were my fellow-traveller's intentions?

If I had been alone, he would have had ample time to alight quite calmly at Rouen. But the lady? As soon as the carriage door was opened, the lady, meek and quiet as she sat at present, would scream and throw herself about and cry for assistance!

Hence my astonishment. Why did he not reduce her to the same state of helplessness as myself, which would have given him time to disappear before his two-fold misdemeanour was discovered?

He was still smoking, his eyes fixed on the view outside, which a hesitating rain was beginning to streak with long, slanting lines. Once, however, he turned round, took up my railway guide and consulted it.

As for the lady, she made every effort to continue fainting, so as to quiet her enemy. But a fit of coughing, produced by the smoke, gave the lie to her pretended swoon.

Myself, I was very uncomfortable and had pains all over my body. And I thought . . . I planned . . .

Pont-de-l'Arche . . . Oissell . . . The train was hurrying on, glad drunk with speed . . . Saint-Etienne . . .

At that moment, the man rose and took two steps towards us, to which the lady hastened to reply with a new scream and a genuine fainting fit.

But what could his object be? He lowered the window on our side. The rain was now falling in torrents and he made a movement of annoyance at having neither umbrella nor overcoat. He looked up at the rack: the lady's *en-tout-cas* was there; he took it. He also took my overcoat and put it on.

We were crossing the Seine. He turned up his trousers and then, leaning out of the window, raised the outer latch.

Did he mean to fling himself on the permanent way? At the rate at which we were going, it would have been certain death. We plunged into the tunnel through the Côte Sainte-Catherine. The man opened the door and, with one foot, felt for the step. What madness! The darkness, the smoke, the din all combined to lend a fantastic appearance to any such attempt. But, suddenly, the train slowed up, the Westinghouse brakes counteracted the movement of the wheels. In a minute, the pace from fast became normal and decreased still more.

94

Without a doubt, there was a gang at work repairing this part of the tunnel; this would necessitate a slower passage of the trains, for some days perhaps; and the man knew it.

He had only, therefore, to put his other foot on the step, climb down to the footboard and walk quietly away, not without first closing the door and throwing back the latch.

He had scarcely disappeared when the smoke showed whiter in the daylight. We emerged into a valley. One more tunnel and we should be at Rouen.

The lady at once recovered her wits and her first care was to bewail the loss of her jewels. I gave her a beseeching glance. She understood and relieved me of the gag which was stifling me. She wanted also to unfasten my bonds, but I stopped her:

'No, no: the police must see everything as it was. I want them to be fully informed as regards that blackguard's actions.'

'Shall I pull the alarm signal?'

'Too late: you should have thought of that while he was attacking me.'

'But he would have killed me! Ah, sir, didn't I tell you that he was travelling by this train? I knew him at once, by his portrait. And now he's taken my jewels.'

'They'll catch him, have no fear.'

'Catch Arsène Lupin! Never.'

'It all depends on you, madame. Listen. When we arrive, be at the window, call out, make a noise. The police and porters will come up. Tell them what you have seen, in a few words: the assault of which I was the victim and the flight of Arsène Lupin. Give his description: a soft hat, an umbrella—yours—a grey frock overcoat . . .'

'Yours,' she said.

'Mine? No, his own. I didn't have one.'

'I thought that he had none either when he got in.'

'He must have had . . . unless it was a coat which some one had left behind in the rack. In any case, he had it when he got out and that is the essential thing . . . A grey frock overcoat, remember . . . Oh, I was forgetting . . . tell them your name to start with. Your husband's position will stimulate their zeal.'

We were arriving. She was already leaning out of the window. I resumed, in a louder, almost imperious voice, so that my words should sink into her brain:

'Give my name also, Guillaume Berlat. If necessary, say you know me . . . That will save time . . . we must hurry on the preliminary inquiries . . . the important thing is to catch Arsène Lupin . . . with your jewels . . . You quite understand, don't you? Guillaume Berlat, a friend of your husband's.'

'Quite . . . Guillaume Berlat.'

She was already calling out and gesticulating. Before the train had come to a standstill, a gentleman climbed in, followed by a number of other men. The critical hour was at hand.

Breathlessly, the lady exclaimed:

'Arsène Lupin . . . he attacked us . . . he has stolen my jewels . . . I am Madame Renaud . . . my husband is a deputy prison governor . . . Ah, here is my brother Georges Andelle, manager of the Crédit Rouennais . . . What I want to say is . . .'

She kissed a young man who had just come up and who exchanged greetings with the commissary of police. She continued, weeping:

'Yes, Arsène Lupin. . . . He flew at this gentleman's throat in his sleep . . . Monsieur Berlat, a friend of my husband's.'

'But where is Arsène Lupin?'

'He jumped out of the train in the tunnel, after we had crossed the Seine.'

'Are you sure it was he?'

'Certain; I recognised him at once. Besides, he was seen at the Gare Saint-Lazare. He was wearing a soft hat . . .'

'No, a hard felt hat, like this,' said the commissary, pointing to my hat.

'A soft hat, I assure you,' repeated Madame Renaud, 'and a grey frock overcoat.'

'Yes,' muttered the commissary, 'the telegram mentions a grey frock overcoat with a black velvet collar.'

'A black velvet collar, that's it!' exclaimed Madame Renaud, triumphantly.

I breathed again. What a good, excellent friend I had found in her!

Meanwhile, the policeman had released me from my bonds. I bit my lips violently till the blood flowed. Bent in two, with my handkerchief to my mouth, as seems proper to a man who has long been sitting in a constrained position and who bears on his face the blood-stained marks of the gag, I said to the commissary, in a feeble voice:

'Sir, it was Arsène Lupin, there is no doubt of it . . . You can catch him, if you hurry . . . I think I may be of some use to you . . .'

The coach, which was needed for the inspection by the police, was slipped. The remainder of the train went on to Le Havre. We were taken to the station master's office through a crowd of onlookers who filled the platform.

Just then, I felt a hesitation. I must make some excuse to absent myself, find my motor-car and be off. It was dangerous to wait. If anything happened, if a telegram came from Paris, I was lost.

Yes, but what about my robber? Left to my own resources, in a district with which I was not very familiar, I could never hope to come up with him.

'Bah!' I said to myself. 'Let us risk it and stay. It's a difficult hand to win, but a very amusing one to play. And the stakes are worth the trouble.'

And, as we were being asked provisionally to repeat our depositions, I exclaimed:

'Mr Commissary, Arsène Lupin is at this moment getting a start on us. My motor is waiting for me in the station yard. If you will do me the pleasure to accept a seat in it, we will try . . .'

The commissary gave a knowing smile:

'It's not a bad idea . . . such a good idea, in fact, that it's already being carried out.'

'Oh?'

'Yes, two of my officers started on bicycles . . . some time ago.'

'But where to?'

'To the entrance of the tunnel. There they will pick up the clues and the evidence and follow the track of Arsène Lupin.'

I could not help shrugging my shoulders:

'Your two officers will pick up no clues and no evidence.'

'Really!'

'Arsène Lupin will have arranged that no one should see him leave the tunnel. He will have taken the nearest road and, from there . . .'

'From there made for Rouen, where we shall catch him.'

97

'He will not go to Rouen.'

'In that case, he will remain in the neighbourhood, where we shall be even more certain . . .'

'He will not remain in the neighbourhood.'

'Oh? Then where will he hide himself?'

I took out my watch:

'At the present moment Arsène Lupin is hanging about the station at Darnétal. At ten-fifty, that is to say, in twenty-two minutes from now, he will take the train which leaves Rouen, from the Gare du Nord, for Amiens.'

'Do you think so? And how do you know?'

'Oh, it's very simple. In the carriage, Arsène Lupin consulted my railway guide. What for? To see if there was another line near the place where he disappeared, a station on that line and a train which stopped at that station. I have just looked at the guide myself and learnt what I wanted to know.'

'Upon my word, sir,' said the commissary, 'you possess marvellous powers of deduction. What an expert you must be!'

Dragged on by my conviction, I had blundered into displaying too much cleverness. He looked at me in astonishment and I saw that a suspicion flickered through his mind. Only just, it is true, for the photographs dispatched in every direction were so unlike, represented an Arsène Lupin so different from the one that stood before him, that he could not possibly recognise the original in me. Nevertheless, he was troubled, restless, perplexed.

There was a moment of silence. A certain ambiguity and doubt seemed to interrupt our words. A shudder of anxiety passed through me. Was luck about to turn against me? Mastering myself, I began to laugh:

'Ah, well, there's nothing to sharpen one's wits like the loss of a pocket-book and the desire to find it again. And it seems to me, that, if you will give me two of your men, the three of us might, perhaps . . .'

'Oh, please, Mr Commissary,' exclaimed Madame Renaud, 'do what Monsieur Berlat suggests.'

My kind friend's intervention turned the scale. Uttered by her, the wife of an influential person, the name of Berlat became mine in reality and conferred upon me an identity which no suspicion could touch. The commissary rose:

'Believe me, Monsieur Berlat, I shall be only too pleased to see you succeed. I am as anxious as yourself to have Arsène Lupin arrested.'

He escorted me to my car. He introduced two of his men to me: Honoré Massol and Gaston Delivet. They took their seats. I placed myself at the wheel. My chauffeur started the engine. A few seconds later we had left the station. I was saved.

I confess that, as we dashed in my powerful 35-hp Moreau-Lepton along the boulevards that skirt the old Norman city, I was not without a certain sense of pride. The engine hummed harmoniously. The trees sped behind us to right and left. And now, free and out of danger, I had nothing to do but to settle my little private affairs, with the co-operation of those two worthy representatives of the law. Arsène Lupin was going in search of Arsène Lupin.

Ye humble mainstays of the social order of things, Gaston Delivet and Honoré Massol, how precious was your assistance to me! Where should I have been without you? But for you, at how many cross-roads should I have taken the wrong turning! But for you, Arsène Lupin would have gone astray and the other escaped!

But all was not over yet. Far from it. I had first to capture the fellow and next to take possession, myself, of the papers of which he had robbed me. At no cost must my two satellites be allowed to catch a sight of those documents, much less lay hands upon them. To make use of them and yet act independently of them was what I wanted to do; and it was no easy matter.

We reached Darnétal three minutes after the train had left. I had the consolation of learning that a man in a grey frock overcoat with a black velvet collar had got into a second-class carriage, with a ticket for Amiens. There was no doubt about it: my first appearance as a detective was a promising one.

Delivet said:

'The train is an express and does not stop before Monté-rolier-Buchy, in nineteen minutes from now. If we are not there before Arsène Lupin, he can go on towards Amiens, branch off to Clères, and, from there, make for Dieppe or Paris.'

'How far is Montérolier?'

'Fourteen and a half miles.'

'Fourteen and a half miles in nineteen minutes . . . We shall be there before him.'

It was a stirring race. Never had my trusty Moreau-Lepton responded to my impatience with greater ardour and regularity. It seemed to me as though I communicated my wishes to her directly, without the intermediary of levers or handles. She shared my desires. She approved of my determination. She understood my animosity against that blackguard Arsène Lupin. The scoundrel! The sneak! Should I get the better of him? Or would he once more baffle authority, that authority of which I was the embodiment?

'Right!' cried Delivet . . . 'Left! . . . Straight ahead! . . .'

We skimmed the ground. The milestones looked like little timid animals that fled at our approach.

And suddenly, at the turn of a road, a cloud of smoke, the north express!

For half a mile, it was a struggle, side by side, an unequal struggle, of which the issue was certain. We beat the train by twenty lengths.

In three seconds we were on the platform, in front of the second class. The doors were flung open. A few people stepped out. My thief was not among them. We examined the carriages. No Arsène Lupin.

'By jove!' I exclaimed. 'He must have recognized me in the motor, while we were going alongside, and jumped out!'

The guard of the train confirmed my supposition. He had seen a man scrambling down the embankment, at two hundred yards from the station.

'There he is! . . . Look! . . . At the level crossing!'

I darted in pursuit, followed by my two satellites, or rather by one of them, for the other, Massol, turned out to be an uncommonly fast sprinter, gifted with both speed and staying power. In a few seconds, the distance between him and the fugitive was greatly diminished. The man saw him, jumped a hedge and scampered off towards a slope, which he climbed. We saw him further still, entering a little wood.

When we reached the wood, we found Massol waiting for us. He had thought it wiser not to go on, lest he should lose us.

'You were quite right, my dear fellow,' I said. 'After a run like this, our friend must be exhausted. We've got him.'

I examined the skirts of the wood, while thinking how I could best proceed alone to arrest the fugitive, in order myself to effect certain recoveries which the law, no doubt, would only have allowed after a number of disagreeable inquiries. Then I returned to my companions.

'Look here, it's quite easy. You, Massol, take up your position on the left: you, Delivet, on the right. From there, you can watch the whole rear of the wood and he can't leave it, unseen by you, except by this hollow way, where I shall stand. If he does not come out, I'll go in and force him back towards one or the other. You have nothing to do, therefore, but wait. Oh, I was forgetting: in case of alarm, I'll fire a shot.'

Massol and Delivet moved off, each to his own side. As soon as they were out of sight, I made my way into the wood, with infinite precautions, so as to be neither seen nor heard. It consisted of close thickets, contrived for the shooting, and intersected by very narrow paths, in which it was only possible to walk by stooping, as though in a leafy tunnel.

One of these ended in a glade where the damp grass showed the marks of footsteps. I followed them, taking care to steal through the undergrowth. They led me to the bottom of a little mound, crowned by a rickety lath-and-plaster hovel.

'He must be there,' I thought. 'He has chosen a good post of observation.'

I crawled close up to the building. A slight sound warned me of his presence and, in fact, I caught sight of him through an opening, with his back turned towards me.

Two bounds brought me upon him. He tried to point the revolver which he held in his hand. I did not give him time, but pulled him to the ground, in such a way that his two arms were twisted and caught under him, while I held him pinned down with my knee upon his chest.

'Listen to me, old chap,' I whispered in his ear. 'I am Arsène Lupin. You've got to give me back my pocket-book and the lady's wrist-bag, this minute and without fuss . . . in return for which I'll save you from the clutches of the police and enrol you among my pals. Which is it to be: yes or no?'

'Yes,' he muttered.

'That's right. Your plan of this morning was cleverly thought out. We shall be good friends.'

I got up. He fumbled in his pocket, fetched out a great knife, and tried to strike me with it.

'You ass!' I cried.

With one hand I parried the attack. With the other, I caught him a violent blow on the carotid artery, the blow which is known as the 'carotid hook'. He fell back stunned.

In my pocket-book, I found my papers and bank notes. I took his own out of curiosity. On an envelope addressed to him I read his name: Pierre Onfrey.

I gave a start. Pierre Onfrey, the perpetrator of the murder in the Rue Lafontaine at Auteuil! Pierre Onfrey, the man who had cut the throats of Madame Delbois and her two daughters! I bent over him. Yes, that was the face which, in the railway carriage, had aroused in me the memory of features which I had seen before.

But time was passing. I placed two hundred-franc notes in an envelope, with a visiting-card bearing these words:

'Arsène Lupin to his worthy assistants, Honoré Massol and Gaston Delivet, with his best thanks.'

I laid this where it could be seen, in the middle of the room. Beside it I placed Madame Renaud's wrist-bag. Why should it not be restored to the kind friend who had rescued me? I confess, however that I took from it everything that seemed in any way interesting, leaving only a tortoise-shell comb, a stick of lip salve, and an empty purse. Business is business, when all is said and done! And, besides, her husband followed such a disreputable occupation! . . .

There remained the man. He was beginning to move. What was I to do? I was not qualified either to save or to condemn him.

I took away his weapons and fired my revolver in the air:

'That will bring the two others,' I thought. 'He must find a way out of his difficulties. Let fate take its course.'

And I went down the hollow way at a run.

Twenty minutes later, a cross-road, which I had noticed during our pursuit, brought me back to my car.

At four o'clock I telegraphed to my friends from Rouen that

an unexpected incident compelled me to put off my visit. Between ourselves, I greatly fear that, in view of what they must now have learnt, I shall be obliged to postpone it indefinitely. It will be a cruel disappointment for them!

At six o'clock, I returned to Paris by L'Isle-Adam, Enghien and the Porte Bineau.

I gathered from the evening papers that the police had at last succeeded in capturing Pierre Onfrey.

The next morning—why should we despise the advantages of intelligent advertisement?—the *Echo de France* contained the following sensational paragraph:

Yesterday, near Buchy, after a number of incidents, Arsène Lupin effected the arrest of Pierre Onfrey. The Auteuil murderer had robbed a lady of the name of Renaud, the wife of the deputy prison governor, in the train between Paris and Le Havre. Arsène Lupin has restored to Madame Renaud the wrist-bag which contained her jewels and has generously rewarded the two detectives who assisted him in the matter of this dramatic arrest.

# 3
# MAURICE LEBLANC
## Drops That Trickle Away

The courtyard bell, on the ground floor of the Baronne
Assermann's imposing residence in the Faubourg St Germain,
rang loudly, and a moment later the maid brought in an
envelope.

'The gentleman says he has an appointment with madame
for four o'clock.'

Madame Assermann slit the envelope. Taking out a card,
she held it gingerly between her finger-tips, and read:

THE BARNETT AGENCY
*Information Free*

'Show the gentleman into my boudoir,' she drawled.

Valérie Assermann—the beautiful Valérie she had been
called for some thirty years—still retained a measure of good
looks, although she was now thick-set, past middle-age and
elaborately made-up. Her haughty and at times harsh expression had yet a certain candour which was not without charm.

As the wife of Assermann, the banker, she took pride in her
vast house with its luxurious appointments, in her large circle of
acquaintances and in all the pomp and circumstance of her
social position. Behind her back society gossips whispered that
Valérie had been guilty of various rather more than trifling
indiscretions. Even hardened Parisian scandalmongers pro-
fessed themselves shocked at her behaviour. There were
those who suggested that the baron, an ailing old man, had con-
templated getting a divorce.

Baron Assermann had been confined to his bed for several
weeks with heart trouble, and Valérie rearranged the pillows
under his thin shoulders and asked him, rather absent-mindedly, how he was feeling, before proceeding to her boudoir.

Awaiting her there she found a curious person—a sturdily built, square-shouldered man, well set up, but shockingly dressed in a funereal frock-coat, moth-eaten and shiny, which hung in depressed creases over worn, baggy trousers. His face was young, but the rugged energy of his features was spoiled by a coarse, blotchy skin, almost brick-red in tone. Behind the monocle, which he used for either eye indifferently, his cold and rather mocking glance sparkled with a boyish gaiety.

'Mr Barnett?' Valérie asked, on a rising inflection, making no effort to keep the scorn out of her voice.

He bowed, and, before she could withdraw it, he had kissed her hand with a flourish, following this gallantry by a not quite inaudible click of the tongue—suggesting his appreciation of the perfumed flavour.

'Jim Barnett—at your service, madame la baronne. When I got your letter I stopped just long enough to give my coat a brush . . . that was all . . .'

The baronne wondered for a moment whether she should show her visitor the door, but he faced her with all the composure of a man of rank, and, a little taken aback, she merely said:

'I've been told that you are quite clever at disentangling rather delicate and complicated matters . . .'

He gave a self-satisfied smirk.

'Yes—I've rather a gift for seeing clearly; seeing *through* and *into* things—and people.'

While his voice was soft, his tone was masterful and his whole demeanour conveyed a suggestion of veiled irony. He seemed so sure of himself and his powers that it was impossible not to share his confidence, and Valérie felt herself coming under the influence of this unknown common detective, this head of a private inquiry bureau. Resenting the feeling, she interrupted him:

'Perhaps we had better—er—discuss terms . . .'

'Quite unnecessary,' replied Barnett.

'But surely'—it was she who was smiling now—'you do not work merely for glory?'

'The services of the Barnett Agency, madame la baronne, are entirely free.'

She looked disappointed, and insisted: 'I should prefer to arrange some remuneration—your out-of-pocket expenses, at least.'

'A tip?' he sneered.

She flushed angrily. Her satin-shod foot tapped the carpet. 'I cannot possibly . . .' she began.

'Be under an obligation to me? Don't worry, madame la baronne, I shall see to it that we end up quits for whatever slight service I may be able to render you.'

Was there a note of menace in the suave voice?

Valérie shuddered a trifle uneasily. What was the meaning of this obscure remark? How did this man propose to recoup himself? Really, this Jim Barnett aroused in her almost the same sort of dread, the same queer kind of nightmare emotion that one might feel if suddenly confronted with a burglar! He might even be . . . yes, he was quite possibly some undesirable, unknown admirer. She wondered what she had better do. Ring for her maid? But he had so far dominated her that, regardless of the consequences, she found herself submitting passively to his questioning as to what had caused her to apply to his agency. Her account was brief, as Barnett seemed to be in a hurry, and she spoke frankly and to the point.

'It all happened the Sunday before last,' she began. 'After a game of bridge with some friends, I went to bed rather early and fell asleep as usual. About four o'clock—at ten minutes past, to be exact—a noise woke me and then I heard a bang which sounded to me like a door closing. It came from my boudoir—this room we are in, which communicates with my bedroom and also with a corridor leading to the servants' staircase. I'm not nervous, so after a moment's hesitation I got up, came in here and turned on the light. The room was empty, but this small show-case'—she indicated it—'had fallen down, and several of the curios and statuettes in it were broken. I then went to my husband's room and found him reading in bed; he said he had heard nothing. He was very much upset and rang for the butler, who at once made a thorough search of the house. In the morning we called in the police.'

'And the result?' asked Barnett.

'They could find no trace of the arrival or departure of any intruder. How he entered and got away is a mystery. But under a footstool among the debris of the curios someone found half a candle, and an awl set in a very dirty wooden handle. Now on the previous afternoon a plumber had been to repair the taps of the wash-basin in my husband's dressing-room. The man's employer, when questioned, identified the tool and, moreover, the other half of the candle was found in his shop.'

'On that point, then,' interrupted Jim Barnett, 'you have definite evidence.'

'Yes, but against that is the indisputable and disconcerting fact that the investigation also proved that the workman in question took the six o'clock express to Brussels, arriving there at midnight—four hours before the disturbance which awakened me.'

'*Really?* Has the man returned?'

'No. They lost track of him at Antwerp, where he was spending money lavishly.'

'Is that all you can tell me?'

'Absolutely all.'

'Who's been in charge of this investigation?'

'Inspector Béchoux.'

'What! The worthy Béchoux! He's a very good friend of mine. We've often worked together.'

'It was he who mentioned your Agency.'

'Yes, because he'd come up against a blank wall, I suppose.'

Barnett crossed to the window and leaning his head against the pane thought hard for a few minutes, frowning ponderously and whistling under his breath. Then he returned to Madame Assermann and continued:

'You and Béchoux, madame, conclude that this was an attempted burglary. Am I right?'

'Yes. An unsuccessful attempt, since nothing has been taken.'

'That's so. But all the same there must have been a definite motive behind this attempt. What was it?'

Valérie hesitated. 'I really don't know,' she said after a moment. But again her foot tapped restlessly.

The detective shrugged his shoulders; then, pointing to one of the silk-draped panels which lined the boudoir above the wainscoting he asked:

'What's under that panel?'

'I beg your pardon,' she said in some bewilderment; 'what do you mean?'

'I mean that the most superficial observation reveals the fact that the edges of that silk oblong are slightly frayed, and here and there they are separated from the woodwork by a slit: there is every reason to suppose that a safe is concealed there.'

Valérie gave a start. How on earth could the man have guessed from such imperceptible indications . . . Then with a jerk she slid the panel open, disclosing a small steel door. As she feverishly worked the three knobs of the safe an unreasoning fear came over her. Impossible as the hypothesis seemed, she wondered whether this queer stranger might somehow have robbed her during the few minutes he had been left alone in the room!

At length, taking a key from her pocket, she opened the safe, and gave a sigh of relief. There it was—the only object the safe contained—a magnificent pearl necklace. Seizing it quickly, she twined its triple strands round her wrist.

Barnett laughed.

'Easier in your mind now, madame la baronne? Yes, it's quite a pretty piece of jewellery, and I can understand its having been stolen from you.'

'But it's not been stolen,' she protested. 'Even if the thief was after this, he failed to steal it.'

'Do you really think so?'

'Of course. Here is the necklace in my hands. When anything's stolen it disappears. Well—here it is . . .'

'Here's *a* necklace,' he corrected her quietly; 'but are you sure that it is *your* necklace and that it has any value?'

'What *do* you mean?' she asked in unconcealed annoyance. 'Only a fortnight ago my jeweller valued it at half a million francs.'

'A fortnight ago—that is to say, five days before that night . . . And now? Please remember I know nothing; I have not valued the necklace; it is merely a supposition. But are you yourself entirely without suspicion?'

Valérie stood quite still. What suspicion was he hinting at? In what connection? A vague anxiety crept over her as his suggestion persisted. As she weighed the mass of heaped-up pearls in her outstretched hand it seemed to get lighter and lighter. As she looked she discovered variations in colouring, unaccustomed reflections, a disturbing unevenness, a changed graduation—each detail more disturbing than the last, until in the back of her mind the terrible truth began to dawn, distinct and threatening.

Jim Barnett gave vent to a short chuckle.

'Just so. You're getting there, are you? On the right track at last—one more mental effort and all is clear as day! It's all quite logical. Your enemy doesn't just steal—he substitutes. Nothing disappears, and except for the noise of the falling show-case everything would have been carried out in perfect secrecy and have gone undiscovered. Until some fresh development, you would have been quite unaware that the real necklace had vanished and that you were displaying on your snowy shoulders a string of imitation pearls.'

Valérie was so absorbed in her own thoughts that she hardly noticed the familiarity of the man's words and manner.

Barnett leaned towards her.

'Well—that settles the first point. And now we know what he stole, let's look for the thief. That's the procedure in all well-conducted cases. And once we've found the thief we shan't be far from recovering the object of the theft.'

He gave Valérie's hand a friendly pat of reassurance.

'Cheer up, madame. We're on the right scent now. Let's begin by a little guess-work—it's an excellent method. We'll suppose that your husband, in spite of his illness, had sufficient strength to drag himself from his own room to this one, armed with the candle, and, anyway, with the tool the plumber left behind; we'll go on to suppose that he opened the safe, clumsily overturned the show-case and then fled in case you had heard the noise. Doesn't that throw a little light on it all? How naturally it accounts for the absence of any trace of arrival or departure, and also for the safe being opened without being forced, since Baron Assermann must many a time in all these years have come in here with you in the evening, seen you work the lock, noted the clicks and intervals and counted the number of notches displaced—and so, gradually, have discovered the three letters of the cipher.'

This 'little guess-work', as Jim Barnett termed it, seemed to appal the beautiful Valérie as he went on 'supposing' step by step. It was as if she saw it all happening before her eyes. At last she stammered out distractedly:

'What you suggest is madness. You don't suppose my husband . . . If someone came here that night, it couldn't have been the baron. Don't be absurd!'

'Had you a copy of your necklace?' he interjected.

She paused. When she spoke it was slowly, with forced calm.

'Yes . . . my husband ordered one, for safety, when we bought it—four years ago.'

'And where is the copy?'

'My husband kept it,' she replied, her voice a mere whisper.

'Well,' said Barnett cheerfully, 'that's the copy you've got in your hands; he has substituted it for the real pearls which he has taken. As for his motive—well, since his fortune places Baron Assermann above any suspicion of theft, we must look for something more intimate . . . more subtle . . . Revenge? A desire to torture—to injure—perhaps to punish? What do you think yourself? After all, a young and pretty woman's rather reckless behaviour may be very understandable, but her husband is bound to judge it fairly severely . . . Forgive me, madame. I have no right to pry into the secrets of your private life. I am merely here to locate, with your help, the present whereabouts of your necklace.'

'No,' cried Valérie, starting back. 'No!'

Suddenly she felt she could no longer endure this ally who, in the course of a brief, friendly, almost frivolous conversation, had fathomed with diabolical ease all the secret circumstances of her life by a method quite unlike the ordinary methods employed by the police. And this man was now pointing out with an air of good-natured banter the precipice to whose edge fate seemed to be forcing her. The sound of his sarcastic voice became all at once intolerable. She hated the mere thought of his searching for her necklace.

'No,' she repeated obstinately.

He bowed, insolently servile.

'As you wish, madame. I have not the slightest desire to seem importunate. I am simply here to serve you in so far as you want my help. Besides, as things are now, you can safely dispense, with my aid, since your husband is quite unfit to go out and will scarcely have been so imprudent as to entrust the pearls to anyone else. If you make a careful search, you will probably discover them hidden somewhere in his room. I need say no more—except that if you should need me, telephone me at my office between nine and ten any night. And now I respectfully withdraw, madame la baronne.'

Again he kissed her hand and she dared not resist him. Then he took his leave jauntily, swinging along with an irritating air of utter complacency. The courtyard gate clanged behind him. To Valérie it brought a curious premonition of doom—as if a prison gate had now closed upon her.

That evening Valérie summoned Inspector Béchoux, whose continued attendance seemed only natural, and the search began.

Béchoux, a conscientious detective and a pupil of the famous Ganimard, adhered to the approved methods of his profession —and proceeded to examine the baron's bathroom and private study in sections. After all, a necklace with three strands of pearls is too large an object to remain hidden from an expert searcher for very long. Nevertheless, after a week's persistent search, including several night visits when, owing to the baron's habit of taking sleeping draughts, he was able to examine even the bed and the bedclothes, Béchoux admitted himself discouraged. The necklace could not possibly be in the house.

In spite of her instinctive aversion, Valérie was tempted to get in touch once more with the impossible man at the Barnett Agency. Despite the repugnance with which he inspired her, she felt positive he would know how to perform the miracle of finding the necklace.

Then matters were brought to a head by a crisis which came suddenly, though not unexpectedly. One evening the servants summoned their mistress hastily—the baron lay choking and prostrate on a divan near the bathroom door. His distorted features and the anguish in his eyes were indicative of acute suffering.

Almost paralysed with fright, Valérie was about to telephone for the doctor, but the baron stammered out the words, 'Too late . . . it's . . . too . . . late . . .'

Then, trying to rise, he gasped out: 'A drink . . .' and would have staggered to the wash-stand.

Quickly Valérie thrust him back on to the divan.

'There's water here in the carafe,' she urged.

'No . . . I want it . . . from the tap . . .' He fell back, exhausted.

She turned on the tap quickly, fetched a glass and filled it, but when she took it to him, he would not drink.

There was a long silence except for the sound of the water running in the basin. The dying man's face became drawn and sunken. He motioned to his wife and she leaned forward—but, doubtless to prevent the servants hearing, he repeated the word 'Closer', and again 'Closer'.

Valérie hesitated, as though afraid of what he might want to say, but his imperious glance cowed her and she knelt down with her ear almost touching his lips. Then he whispered, incoherently, and she could scarcely so much as guess what the words meant.

'The pearls . . . the necklace . . . you shall know before I'm gone . . . you never loved me . . . you married me . . . for . . . my money . . .'

She began to protest indignantly at his making such a cruel accusation at this solemn moment, but he seized her wrist and repeated in a kind of confused delirium: '. . . for my money, and your conduct has proved it. You have never been a good wife to me—that's why I wanted to punish you—why I'm punishing you now—it's an exquisite joy—the only pleasure possible to me—and I can die happily now because the pearls are vanishing away . . . Can't you hear them, falling, dropping away into the swirling water. Ah, Valérie, my wife . . . what a punishment! . . . the drops that trickle away! . . .'

His strength failed him again, and the servants lifted him on to his bed. The doctor came very soon after, and two elderly spinster cousins who had been summoned settled themselves in the room and refused to budge. The final paroxysm was prolonged and painful. At dawn Baron Assermann died, without uttering another word.

At the formal request of the cousins, a seal was placed on every drawer and cupboard in the room. Then the long death vigil began . . .

Two days later, after the funeral, the dead man's lawyer called and asked to speak to Valérie in private. He looked grave and troubled and said at once:

'Madame, I have a most painful duty to perform, and I prefer to get it over as quickly as possible, while assuring you beforehand that the injustice done to you was subject to my profound disapproval and contrary to my advice and entreaty. But it was useless to oppose an unshakable determination . . .'

'I beg you, monsieur,' stammered Valérie, 'to make your meaning clear.'

'I am coming to it, madame la baronne—it is this. I hold a will drawn up by Baron Assermann twenty years ago, appointing you his sole heiress and residuary legatee. But I have to tell you that last month the baron confided to me that he had made a fresh will . . . by which he left his entire fortune to his two cousins . . .'

'He made a new will?' cried Valérie.

'Yes.'

'And you have it?'

'After reading it to me he locked it in that desk. He did not wish it to be read until a week after his death. It may not be unsealed before that date.'

Now Valérie realised why, a few years before, after a series of violent quarrels, her husband had advised her to sell all her own jewellery and purchase a pearl necklace with the money. Disinherited, with no fortune of her own, and with an imitation pearl necklace in place of the real one, she was left penniless.

The day before the seals were to be broken, a car drew up in the Rue Laborde in front of rather dingy premises bearing the sign:

THE BARNETT AGENCY
OPEN FROM TWO TO THREE
*Information Free*

A veiled woman in deep mourning got out of the car and knocked on the glass panel of the inner door.

'Come in,' called a voice from within.

She entered.

'Who's that?' went on the voice in the back room, which was separated from the office by a curtain. She recognized the tones.

'Baronne Assermann,' she replied.

'Excuse me, madame. Please take a seat. I won't keep you a moment.'

While she waited, Valérie looked round the office. It was comparatively empty; the furniture consisted of a table and two old armchairs. The walls were quite bare and the place was innocent of files or papers. A telephone was the only indication of activity. An ashtray, however, held the stubs of several expensive cigarettes, and a subtle fragrance hung in the air.

The curtain swung back and Jim Barnett appeared suddenly, alert and smiling. He wore the same shabby frock-coat, the same impossible, made-up tie, the same monocle at the end of a black ribbon.

He seized and kissed his visitor's gloved hand.

'How do you do, madame. This is indeed a pleasure. But what's the matter? I see you are in mourning—nothing serious, I hope—oh, but how absent-minded I am—of course—Baron Assermann, was it not? So sad! A charming man, and such a devoted husband. I should so much like to have met him. Well, well. Let's see—how did matters stand?'

As he spoke, he took from his pocket a slender notebook which he fingered pensively.

'Baroness Assermann—there we are—I remember. Imitation pearls—husband the thief—pretty woman. . . . A very pretty woman . . . She is to telephone me. . . . Well, dear lady,' he concluded, with increasing familiarity, 'I am still awaiting that telephone call.'

Once more, Valérie felt disconcerted by this man. Without wishing to pretend overwhelming sorrow at the death of her husband, she yet felt sad, and mingled with her sadness was a haunting dread of future poverty. She had had a bad time during the last days—and her wan face showed the ravages of terror and futile remorse resulting from her nightmare visions of ruin and distress . . . And here was this impertinent upstart detective, not seeming to grasp the position at all.

With great dignity she recounted all that had happened, and although she avoided idle recriminations, she repeated what her husband's lawyer had said.

'Ah, yes; quite so,' interposed the detective, smiling approval. 'Good . . . that all fits in admirably. It's quite a pleasure to see how logically this enthralling and well-constructed drama is working itself out.'

'A pleasure?' asked Valérie tonelessly.

'Certainly—a pleasure which my friend Inspector Béchoux must have enjoyed—for I suppose he's explained to you . . .'

'What?'

'What? Why, the key to the mystery, of course. Isn't it priceless? Old Béchoux must have rocked with mirth!'

Jim Barnett, at any rate, was laughing heartily.

'That wash-basin trick now—there's a novelty! It's certainly farcical rather than dramatic—but so adroitly worked in—of course I spotted the dodge at once when you told me about the plumber, and saw the connection between the repairing of the wash-basin and the baron's little plans. That was the crux of the whole thing. When he planned the substitution of the false necklace, your husband arranged a good hiding-place for the real pearls; it was essential for his purpose. Merely to deprive you of them and throw them or cause them to be thrown into the Seine like worthless rubbish, would only have been half a revenge. For it to be complete and on the grand scale he had to keep them close at hand, hidden in a spot at once near and inaccessible. And that's what he did.'

Jim Barnett was thoroughly enjoying himself and went on jocularly: 'Can't you imagine your husband explaining it all to the plumber? "See here, my man, just examine that waste-pipe under my wash-basin. It goes down to the wainscotting and leaves the bathroom at an almost imperceptible gradient, doesn't it? Well, reduce that gradient still more—take up the pipe in this dark corner, so as to form a sort of pocket—a blind alley, where something could be lodged if necessary. When the tap is turned on the water will fill the pocket and carry away the object lodged there. You understand? Then drill a hole about half an inch in diameter in the wall side of the pipe, where it won't be noticed. Yes—there! Done it? Now plug it up with this rubber stopper. Does it fit? That's all right then. Now, you understand, don't you—not a word to anyone! Keep your mouth shut. Take this and catch the Brussels express tonight. These three cheques you can cash there—one every month. In three months' time you may come back to Paris. Good-bye. That's all, thanks." . . . And that very night you heard a noise in your boudoir, the imitation pearls were substituted for the real ones, and the latter secreted in the hiding-place prepared for them in the pocket of the pipe. Now do you see? Believing that the end has come, the baron calls out to you: "A glass of water—not from the carafe—from the tap there." You obey. And the terrible punishment is brought about by your own hand as it turns on the tap—the water runs, carries away the pearls, and the baron stammers out: "Do you hear? They're trickling away—away!"'

The baronne listened in distracted silence. What impressed her most in Barnett's terrible story was not the full revelation of her husband's rancour and hatred, but the one fact which it hammered home.

'Then you knew the truth?' she murmured at last.

'Of course,' he replied, 'it's my job. The Barnett Agency, you see . . .'

'And you said nothing of this to me?' Her tone was an accusation.

'But, my dear baronne, it was you yourself who stopped me from telling you what I knew, or was just about to discover. You dismissed me—somewhat peremptorily, I fear—and not wishing to be thought officious, I did not press the matter. Besides, I had still to verify my deductions.'

'And have you done so?' she faltered.

'Yes. Just out of curiosity, that's all.'

'When?'

'The same night.'

'What! You got into the house that night—into our rooms? I heard nothing . . .'

'Oh, I've a little way of working on the quiet. Even Baron Assermann didn't hear me. And yet . . .'

'What?'

'Well, just to make sure, I enlarged that hole, you see . . . the one through which he had pushed the pearls into the pipe.'

She started.

'Then you saw them?'

'I did.'

'My pearls were actually there?'

He nodded.

Valérie choked, as she repeated under her breath: 'My pearls were there in the pipe and you could have taken them? . . .'

'Yes,' he admitted nonchalantly, 'and I really believe that but for me, Jim Barnett, at your service, they would have dropped away as the baron intended they should on the day of his death, which he knew was not far off. What were his words: "They're vanishing . . . can't you hear them? . . . drops that trickle away . . . !' And his plan of revenge would have come off— too bad—such a beautiful necklace—quite a collector's piece!'

Valérie was not given to violent explosions of wrath, likely to upset her complexion. But at this point she was worked up to such a pitch that she rushed up to Barnett and convulsively seized the collar of his coat.

'It's theft! You're a common adventurer! I suspected it all along—a crook!'

At the word 'crook' the young man hooted with joy.

'I—a crook? How frightfully amusing!'

She took no notice. Shaking with passion, she rushed up and down the room shrieking: 'I won't have it, I tell you. Give me back my pearls at once or I'll call the police!'

'Oh—how ugly that sounds,' he exclaimed, 'and how tact-less for a pretty woman like yourself to behave like this to a man who has shown himself assiduous in serving you and only wants to co-operate peaceably with you for your good!'

She shrugged her shoulders and demanded again: 'Will you give me my necklace!'

'Of course! It's absolutely at your disposal. Good heavens, do you suppose that Jim Barnett robs the people who pay him the compliment of seeking his help! What do you think would become of the Barnett Agency, which owes its popularity to its reputation for absolute integrity and disinterested service? I don't ask my clients for a single penny. If I kept your pearls I should be a thief—a crook, as you would say—whereas I am an honest man. Here, dear lady, is your necklace.'

He produced a small cloth bag containing the rescued pearls and laid it on the table.

Thunderstruck, Valérie seized the precious necklace with shaking hands. She could hardly believe her eyes; it seemed incredible that this man should restore her property in this way, and with a sudden fear lest he was merely acting on a momentary impulse, she made abruptly for the door without a word of thanks.

'You're in rather a hurry all at once,' laughed Jim Barnett. 'Aren't you going to count them? Three hundred and forty-five. They're all there . . . and they're the real ones, this time.'

'Yes,' said Valérie, 'I know that . . .'

'You're quite sure? Those really are the pearls your jeweller valued at five hundred thousand francs?'

'Yes; they are the ones.'

'You'd swear to that?'

'Certainly,' she said positively.

'In that case, I'll buy them from you.'

'You'll buy them! What do you mean?

'Well, being penniless, you've got to sell them. Why not to me, then, since I can offer you more than anyone else will—I'll give you twenty times their value. Instead of five hundred thousand francs, I'll give ten million. Does that startle you? Ten millions's a pretty figure.'

'Ten million!'

'Exactly the reputed gross amount of the baron's estate.'

Valérie lingered at the door, her fingers twisting the handle.

'My husband's estate,' she repeated. 'I don't see any connection. Please explain.'

With gentle emphasis Jim Barnett continued: 'It's very simple. You have your choice—the pearl necklace or the estate!'

'The pearl necklace . . . the estate?' she repeated, puzzled.

'Certainly. As you yourself told me, the inheritance turns on two wills: the earlier one in your favour and the second in favour of those two old cousins, who are as rich as Crœsus and apparently correspondingly mean. But suppose Will Number Two can't be found, Will Number One is valid.'

'But tomorrow,' she said in faltering accents, 'they intend to

**break** the seals and open the desk—and the second will is there.'

'The will may be there—or it may not,' suggested Barnett, rather contemptuously. 'I'll go so far as to say that in my humble opinion it is not.'

'Is that possible,' she asked, staring at him in amazement.

'Quite possible—even probable—in fact, I seem to remember now that when I came to investigate the waste-pipe on the evening after our talk, I took the opportunity of looking round your husband's rooms as he was sleeping so soundly.'

'And you took that will,' she asked haltingly.

'This rather looks like it, doesn't it?'

He unfolded a sheet of stamped paper and she recognised her husband's writing as she caught sight of the words: *'I, the undersigned, Léon Joseph Assermann, banker, in view of certain facts well known to her, do hereby declare that my wife Valérie Assermann shall not have the slightest claim upon my fortune and that . . .'*

She read no further. Her voice caught in her throat and falling limply into an armchair she gasped:

'You stole that paper—and expect me to be your accomplice . . . I won't. My poor husband's wishes must be obeyed . . .'

Jim Barnett threw up his hands enthusiastically.

'How splendid of you, dear lady. Duty points to self-sacrifice, and I commend you the more when your lot is so especially hard—when for two old cousins who are quite undeserving of pity, you are prepared to sacrifice yourself with your own hands to gratify Baron Assermann's petty spite. You bow to this injustice to expiate those youthful peccadilloes. The beautiful Valérie is to forgo the luxury to which she is entitled and be reduced to abject poverty. But, before you finally make this choice, madame, I beg you to weigh your decision carefully and realize all it means. Let me be quite plain: *if that necklace leaves this room*, the lawyer receives Will Number Two tomorrow morning and you are disinherited.'

'And if it stays?'

'Well, there's no will in that desk and you inherit the whole estate—ten million francs in your pocket, thanks to Jim Barnett.'

His sarcasm was obvious, and Valérie felt like a helpless animal trapped in his ruthless grasp. There was no way out. If she refused him the necklace, the will would be read out next day. He was relentless, and would turn a deaf ear to any entreaties.

He stepped into the back room for a moment and then returned from behind the curtain, calmly wiping off his face the grease paint with which he had covered it, like an actor removing his make-up. His appearance was now completely changed—his face was fresh and young-looking, with a smooth, healthy skin. A fashionable tie had replaced the made-up atrocity. He had changed the old frock-coat and baggy trousers for a well-cut lounge suit. And his attitude of smiling confidence made it clear he did not fear denunciation or betrayal. In return, Valérie knew he would never say a word to anyone, even to Inspector Béchoux—the secret would be kept inviolate.

He leaned towards her and, laughing, said: 'Well—I believe you're looking at it more reasonably now. That's good! Besides, who'll know that the wealthy Baronne Assermann is wearing imitation pearls? Not one of your friends will ever suspect it. You'll keep your fortune and possess a necklace which everyone will think is genuine. Isn't that lovely? Can't you just see yourself leading a full and happy life, with plenty of opportunity for fun and flirtation? Aha!' He waggled a jovial forefinger in her angry face.

At that moment Valérie had not the slightest desire for fun or flirtation. She glared at Jim Barnett with suppressed fury, and, drawing herself up, made her exit like a society queen withdrawing from a hostile drawing-room.

The little bag of pearls remained on the table.

'And they call that an honest woman!' said Jim Barnett to himself, his arms folded in virtuous indignation. 'Her husband disinherits her to punish her for her naughty ways, and she disregards his wishes! There's a fresh will—and she filches it! She deceives his lawyer and despoils his old cousins. Tut, tut! And how noble is the part of the lover of justice who chastises the culprit and sets everything to rights again!'

He slipped the necklace deftly back into its place in the

depths of his pocket, finished dressing, and then, his monocle carefully adjusted, and a fat cigar between his teeth, he left the office, and went forth in search of fresh amusement.

# 4
# GASTON LEROUX
## The Mystery of the Four Husbands

The old sea-dogs who spent their evenings seated on the
terrace of the inn which overlooked the sea had never seen
Zinzin arrive in such a condition before. His eyes were popping
from his head, and he was as pale as death. As soon as he had
had time to drop into a chair, they pressed anxiously around
him.

'What is the matter, Zinzin? What is the matter, old fellow?'
Captain Michel asked.

Zinzin made a sign that he was still unable to speak, but at
last he wiped his forehead.

'I have just come from the police commissioner,' he began,
'and he gave me a most horrible bit of news.'

'Tell us about it before it becomes old stuff,' Gobert exclaimed. 'The story is sure to change with time.'

'Oh, this doesn't date from yesterday,' Zinzin murmured
with a sinister laugh.

'Then why so much excitement today?'

'I'll tell you why shortly,' the other replied dismally. 'I was
mixed up in it when I was very young. It narrowly missed
making me a landlubber for ever with a little garden plot over
me! On my word! It's not the fault of the damned wedding story
if I'm not fertilizing a crop of dandelions today. It caused a lot of
stir in its time. They even took the case up to the court of
assizes!'

'Stories of marriages exist by the legion,' grouchy old
Chaulieu remarked. 'I know ten myself.'

'I only know one,' Zinzin replied with a groan, 'but I warn
you that it is more horrible than all ten of Chaulieu's put
together!'

He sighed heavily again and lighted his pipe. 'I never told

you anything about it before,' he spat out, 'because it seemed such an utterly fantastic affair, but today I must talk! Good God! Good God!'

'Well, what is it? What is it, Zinzin?'

'It is a horrible story,' Zinzin choked.

'Perhaps,' Chaulieu added quietly and sceptically.

Zinzin cast him a murderous look. 'In all my life I have only been in love once,' he went on, 'and it was that time. It never happened again because I never met another such girl. Her name was Olympe, and there were a dozen of us who wanted to marry her.'

'And here the impossible begins,' sneered Chaulieu.

'Twelve, I tell you! I'll give you their names in a moment, and that doesn't include those who did not openly propose. There wasn't a man in the whole country who would not have wanted to. She wasn't rich, but she came of good family—and beautiful! At the time of which I speak she was just seventeen years old. Her section of the country was noted for its beautiful women—a big pleasant suburb worth visiting if only to watch the girls come home from church on Sundays.

'Well! In all the town there was not one girl fit to tie her shoes, and that meant a lot . . . Listen, if you have ever gone to Cagnes, perhaps you have seen Renoir's portraits of young girls . . . Those pictures are pure fantasy—pictures of flowers and sunlight, not humans. Well, Olympe was like that: a ray of sun and the petals of a rose. A dream! But a dream with eyes and a mouth! . . . enormous childish eyes with supernatural purity in their gaze, and the mouth of a woman! The mouth alone was of flesh and blood! Olympe was like an angel come down to earth to kiss!

'We were all crazy about her. She lived alone with her grandmother, who had taken her from school at the death of her parents and entrusted her to the safe care of the servant Palmire, who was the girl's willing slave. Olympe was still much of a child, often playing with the country urchins, returning home with armfuls of wild flowers, baskets filled with wild strawberries. She would run behind the flocks with the sheepdogs when she crossed them on the road, and often scandalized the old women by returning home at night astride a goat!

'In nice weather the old people would sit outside their doors on little wooden benches and wait for her to come. She had a wonderful imagination and told them stories which she made up as she went along.

'The grandmother, who in her day had been the beautiful Madame Gratien, lived in a big old house on the Place de l'Abbaye. The gardens were closed in by walls and at the back looked out on the open country. She knew all the élite of the neighbourhood and had maintained connections in the city.

'The behaviour of her granddaugher had amused her in the beginning but at last it began to preoccupy her. Olympe seemed very thoughtless for her age . . . What would happen when she was alone in the world? Madame Gratien suddenly decided to marry her off as soon as possible.

'She had already received several offers for the hand of her granddaughter, and when it was known that she no longer discouraged suitors, they besieged her on all sides. This flood of admirers was a new game for Olympe. Finally one Sunday we were all gathered in the living-room, when the grandmother gave Olympe a little talking-to. She told her that she was beginning to be very tired and weary with life and that she would like to see Olympe settle down before she died. Olympe greeted this announcement with tears. We thought that the prospect of the old lady's death saddened her, but Olympe explained it differently. "As though it were gay to marry!" she said when we tried to cheer her up.

'We burst out laughing at that and all swore that her husband would be perfectly willing to be her slave.

'"First of all, I do not want to leave Grandmother," she said, "nor Palmire . . . And secondly I want to live in our old house."

'"Agreed, agreed," we answered in chorus.

'"And now," said good Madame Gratien, "which one are you going to choose?"

'"Oh, we'll talk of that later," said Olympe. "This is no way to marry people off. You're not really serious about it, Grandmother!"

'"For six months you've said the same thing: that you'd talk it over later. Now, it's become a joke. You know that I have

124

always done everything you wanted before . . . Come; if you were obliged to choose one of these gentlemen, which would you take?"

'Olympe suddenly became serious, and we watched her anxiously . . . In spite of our apparent acceptance of the whole thing as a joke, we were deadly serious . . .

'She stood up, walked around us, and sized us up from head to foot with such funny expressions that we were more than a little embarrassed. If I live to be a thousand, I'll never forget that scene! What an examination! To be truthful, we hardly dared breathe.

'She made us stand, lined us up, placing us, changing us—advancing a man to the head of the line and then, after looking him straight in the eyes, sending him back to third or fourth position. The grandmother encouraged us from time to time with a "Hold yourselves well, gentlemen! . . . Hold yourselves well! . . . Be serious."

'It was funny when one thinks that we were not all young men either! I well remember the arrival of the town registrar, respectable M. Pacifire, who for two years had openly bid for Olympe's hand. He came late and naturally did not know what it was all about.

'She met him at the door and placed him, dumbfounded, at the end of the line. He had the last number! You can imagine how we laughed. But you can bet that when he knew what it was all about, he did not laugh at all!

'"At last! It is done!" she announced. "If I marry I'll take Monsieur Delphin *first*, then Monsieur Hubert, then Monsieur Sabin, then my little Zinzin (as you see, I was number four), then Monsieur Jacobini . . ." and she went on down the whole twelve of us . . . I'll enumerate them: first, Monsieur Delphin, a nice fellow with a great future ahead of him, son of the town pharmacist; he had taken his degree in science, was working for a fellowship in chemistry and was very well spoken of at the university. Second, Monsieur Hubert, still young, about twenty-five, head forest warden. Third, Dr Felix Sabin, just out of college, and as merry as a lark . . . I think he had settled himself in the country with the idea of getting into politics. Fourth, yours truly, who had already taken to the sea but who would have given it all up to stay with Olympe. Fifth,

Lieutenant Jacobini, son of a colonel in the Guards, a distinguished, smart fellow who had just come back from a mission in South Africa where he had made something of a name for himself. Sixth, the son of a big landowner with lots of money. Seventh, a young lawyer. Eighth, the son of a solicitor. Ninth, an old notary. Tenth, a travelling salesman. Eleventh, the assistant of the district attorney. Twelfth, M. Pacifire, the registrar . . . yes, that makes twelve. We were only twelve that day!

'Six months later, Olympe married number one, young Delphin. Well all went to the wedding—but not to have a good time. I tried to reason against it, but I would have given anything to be in Delphin's shoes. The following year, however, I no longer envied him. He was dead!

'No one knows exactly what he died of. They say that he was poisoned by some laboratory work, but nothing was certain. The physician who attended him, Dr Sabin, shook his head when he was questioned. I think that in reality he thought of only one thing, in short, that he had now become number two and that if anything were to happen to the forest warden who preceded him, he might yet hope for a chance!

'It seemed impossible, but Olympe had become even lovelier since her marriage. Now, when she passed in her widow's weeds, she was something to kneel before and worship. But she did not mourn her dead husband for long. In fact, if one can believe old Palmire, Monsieur Delphin was not excessively gay and for a young husband spent too much time in his laboratories, leaving his young wife for entire days while he searched for heaven knows what in the bottoms of his test-tubes.

'Monsieur Hubert's turn was bound to arrive, and he did not lose time in pressing his suit and in promising her all the gaieties that she had missed since her first marriage. He was a jolly fellow, that Hubert, fond of good food, an excellent drinker and hunter as was fitting in a man of his position and name.

'Big celebrations and big parties now took place at Olympe's. She began to ride horseback and there was not another like her for fifty miles around. It was a sight to see her hunt the deer and wild boar. Nothing frightened her. We had trouble to keep up

126

with her, and afterwards she presided over the banquet with a sparkle and an ardour that gave us all fever.

'She was more courted than ever, but she made fun of us, and kept her loveliest and gayest smiles for Dr Sabin. "He is number three," she exclaimed, laughing. "Everyone in turn!"

'"Hey!" Hubert interrupted. "I never felt better in my life!"

'"And I take care of him," replied the doctor. "He is the one man whom I'm not permitted to kill. Thank the fortune, Hubert, which prohibits me from choosing my victims!"

'This was all very nice, but it seemed to me that Dr Sabin made too much use of his position as family doctor in order to be familiar with Olympe. They were often seen alone in the park behind the house, or even going for a little outing in the forest when Hubert, called away on business or to some bachelor party in the neighbouring town, left Olympe for a few hours. She had become the general topic of conversation in the village. She scandalized the habitués of the five o'clock teas at Mme Tabureau's, the mayor's wife, or at Mme Blancmougin's, the wife of the solicitor whose son had received number eight in the general classing. Mme Blancmougin never ceased congratulating herself on her son's lucky escape.

'In fact, after the death of old Mme Gratien, which had occurred in the meantime, Olympe no longer kept her desires within any limits and she frightened many people by the liberty of those desires. Hubert made no attempt to restrain her. He was amused and flattered by the number of victims won by those innocent blue eyes and that bright mouth which seemed to be always asking for a kiss.

'He was a good liver, that Hubert, but not a real lover. "My!" Palmire would whisper to those who liked to be informed of all that went on in the house, "he certainly loves his food more than his bed. If madame were not so honest, that fact might give him a bad jolt!"

'And so saying, she shook her head on seeing Olympe and Dr Sabin come in from one of the driving lessons. Those lessons had started a lot of gossip which was cut short by a new misfortune in Place de l'Abbaye.

'Delphin had installed a laboratory in an isolated building in a far corner of the grounds and this Hubert had made into a sort of hunting-pavilion. He had furnished it with his guns, his knives, his rifles, his pistols, and had also stored his ammunition there. It was like a little armoury, with the exception of the walls, which were decorated with the usual trophies. It was a pleasant little spot, covered with climbing vines and flowers, and there was a fine view of the fields and country beyond. He often had lunch served there in order to be alone with his wife or friends, away from the ears of the servants.

'It was there that Hubert was found one afternoon in August with a pistol in his hands and a bullet through his heart.

'Suicide or accident? Several even murmured the word "crime"! . . . but it was said so low that no one heard them.

'You can imagine what a stir it caused. An inquest was held. The assistant district attorney, who was number eleven, managed the affair. It was Dr Sabin, number three, who was called to give his opinion on the nature of the death. He pronounced it accident. The inquest hesitated a long time between accident and suicide, but they finally concluded with the theory of an accident.

'"My goodness!" Palmire sighed when she was besieged by many people wanting to know what madame had to say about the death of her husband. "What should she say? She knew nothing about it, of course. She had lunched in the little pavilion with monsieur . . . They both had seemed very gay. She left him at about two-thirty in order to dress, for she was going to town with Dr Sabin. About three o'clock the gardener heard a shot and ran to the pavilion. He found monsieur stretched out dead. And now you know as much as we do. Why should he have committed suicide? Life was beautiful and so was Olympe. He had everything to make him happy. And now Olympe is crying her eyes out, which is a stupid thing to do. No one is responsible for an accident, and it was his fault for not being more careful!"

'So spoke Palmire. The next year Olympe married Dr Sabin.'

'I expected it,' interrupted Chaulieu; 'if your blue-eyed angel with the passionate mouth had to give herself to all twelve of those gentlemen we haven't finished and it's not going to be a funny tale.'

'I didn't promise you a funny story. I told you that it was

horrible. Olympe did not give herself to all twelve, since I was number four and I'm still alive. Nevertheless, I excuse Chaulieu for his remark because in the village they began to say: "They'll all go. She's capable of it."

'"And why not? If it pleases Olympe?" Palmire replied whenever she heard something of that kind. And she added, scratching her long chin, "She would be wrong in hesitating over it as far as the worth of those men is concerned!"

'It was a terrible thing that she said, in the ignorance of a servant ready to perjure her soul for her mistress.

'Dr Sabin was certainly a courageous fellow to marry into a household which seemed destined to misfortune. Some good old woman of the kind particularly skilful in slipping in a malicious remark between a frown and a smile, remarked, however, "Oh, nothing will happen to *him*. He knows what he is doing!"

'The town was a-buzz with horrible remarks. Poor doctor! He did not deserve what was said, since he, too, died, exactly three months to the day after his wedding. He lasted an even shorter time than the others.'

'Good Lord!' Gaubert whistled.

'And so came your turn,' said Captain Michel.

'It's beginning to be very amusing,' remarked Chaulieu.

But they all stopped joking. Zinzin had become terribly pale and his hand trembled as he put down his glass. He looked with wild eyes at a man who was approaching the table.

'Hello,' exclaimed the captain, 'here's the police commissioner's orderly.'

It was he in fact, and he bent over and whispered in Zinzin's ear:

'We've just had a telephone message. She has been dead ten years. You don't need to worry any longer.' And with that he departed.

As for Zinzin, he staggered into the captain's arms and had to be taken home.

'Let's hope he doesn't kick it before the end of his story,' said Gaubert gently.

Chaulieu shrugged his shoulders. 'Bah,' he said, 'he is working for a climactic effect.'

Nevertheless we did not discover the end of the story until

eight days later. Zinzin certainly had been very ill. This time we listened without interrupting him.

'It was my turn then, number four's turn. But I was still ignorant of the fact. I was sailing in the Baltic Sea when the thing happened, and I did not learn it until my return ashore. I threw myself on a train for home and on the way met Lieutenant Jacobini, number five, who had himself returned only a short while ago.

'Our trip was not a merry one. I confess that in spite of the certainty I now had of being able to marry Olympe and in spite of the hope Lieutenant Jacobini had of soon being able to cheer up my widow, this double prospect did not fill us with merriment. The house on Place de l'Abbaye seemed less like a place of joy to us now and more like a tomb!

'Naturally the first thing I asked Jacobini, after he had told me the sinister news, was if he could give me a few details on the doctor's death. How had he died? He answered gloomily that he hadn't the faintest idea and that no one else had either; but that he more than anyone wanted to get to the bottom of it. That was the reason for his return.

'"And you?" he asked me.

'"Oh," I answered, "as for me, you can understand that I am interested in the matter at least as much as you are."

'"Yes," he replied without the slightest sarcasm, "I understand that . . . It is an even more urgent matter for you."

'"But," I went on, "they must have called his death by some name!"

'"Not any more of a name than they gave the death of Olympe's first husband. They claimed that Delphin was poisoned by some laboratory experiment, but the thing was never proved. And as far as Dr Sabin is concerned it can't be that."

'"All these deaths are certainly very strange! Tell me, Jacobini, aren't the police interested in this?"

'"Yes. Our assistant district attorney, number eleven, has ordered an investigation. I ought to add that Olympe was the first to ask it . . . They did an autopsy on the body . . ."

'"And?"

'"And found nothing . . . But that doesn't prove a thing," he added in a tone which struck me.

'"What do you mean? Have you a suspicion?"

'"In such matters," replied Jacobini, "it is not permissible to have suspicions. One must be certain or keep still." And he kept still.

'But all this did not tend to quiet my anxiety.

'"Then he died in his bed? Was he ill?"

'"No! Olympe found him at about five o'clock in the afternoon in his room, stretched out on the floor with a table and chair overturned, his mouth still foaming and his face distorted with horror . . . It was proved that he had been in the room alone from three o'clock on and that the house was completely deserted, as the servants had gone to a nearby fair."

'"And—Madame Sabin?"

'"She had lunched with him in the little pavilion at the end of the garden and had remained there to embroider with Palmire."

'"Then what was the conclusion of the inquest?"

'"That Dr Sabin died from an attack of epilepsy."

'"Was he subject to it?"

'"No, but it seems that that does not always follow."

'We were silent a long time. Then I sighed.

'"We ought to be sincerely sorry for Olympe," I said, "because otherwise it would be too horrible."

'"Yes," he replied after thinking a moment, "you are right! It would be too horrible . . . She must be pitied. Besides, Palmire says that she is completely crushed. No one ever sees her now. She never goes out. According to gossip she wants to enter a convent . . . It is natural enough that after three unfortunate marriages like these she should be sick of matrimony—and —and I congratulate you," he added with a strange laugh. Then he went on quickly, because he was an extremely polite fellow: "I hope I haven't pained you in saying that?"

'"I don't know," I answered.

'We arrived an hour later. We hadn't forewarned anyone and it was already late at night. We had decided to go directly to the Hôtel de Bourgogne, and I was surprised to find the solicitor's son, number eight, waiting for us on the platform. I remember his name now; he was called Juste. There is nothing to say about him except that he was an honest fellow, and that Dr Sabin had often treated him for rheumatism.

'"I knew that you had landed," he said to me, "and that you were taking this train. What hotel are you going to?"

'"To the Bourgogne with Lieutenant Jacobini."

'Juste had been so preoccupied with me that he hadn't noticed my companion. He shook him warmly by the hand and said that he would go with us.

'I was growing more puzzled every moment. At the hotel he followed me to my room and gave me a packet for which he asked a receipt.

'"This was entrusted to my honour," he said, "with the mission of giving it into your own hands."

'I examined the sealed envelope quickly and recognized the writing immediately. My name was written on the outside with the addition: "To be delivered after my death".

'"Yes," the other replied, "I have accomplished my mission and I am only accountable to him; but since I haven't the faintest idea of what is contained in that letter, I want a receipt, to be on the safe side."

'I gave him his receipt.

'"In giving you this letter," I asked, "Dr Sabin said nothing special?"

'"Not a thing," he replied. "He told me nothing, absolutely nothing."

'Upon which he shook my hand and took leave of me a bit hurriedly. He seemed free of a great weight. I opened the letter feverishly.

'Ten minutes later someone knocked at Jacobini's door. He was just about to get into bed and called out, asking who was there. As no one answered him, he went to the door and opened it impatiently. A ghost with a letter in its hands entered his room. This ghost was I and I hadn't strength enough even to speak. He sat me down, took the letter from my hands, locked the door and read.

'I will never forget him as he stood there, bent over the lamp. The letter which had plunged me into a sort of prostration had an entirely different effect on him. Everything about him seemed to tighten up while with me there had been a complete loosening of my willpower. He frowned heavily, his eyebrows

132

were knitted, his chin grew more prominent, and a dangerous flame like the cold steel flash of a sword lit the eyes intent on reading the document, a document which had been written by the trembling hand of a man who knew himself condemned to death.

'This is what Dr Sabin had written. The original has long been in the police files but this is a copy:'

Dear Zinzin:

Before marrying Olympe I want you to read this: it is a man who is about to die who is writing to you. I have been horribly poisoned. No one knows it except the guilty one or guilty ones and me. I have not complained, for I have got only what I deserved. Thanks to strong drugs I have been able at times to overcome the pain which is destroying me and still to appear human. Thus I have been able to see Juste without giving anything away to him, nor will you tell him anything unless he, too, should want to marry Olympe—in which case you will show him this letter. But I hope that this will be the end of the matter and that after my death no one will wish to take my place, our place, the place of the three men who have entered this house full of health and life and who have disappeared from it, carrying with them the enigma of their triple misfortune.

As far as possible keep scandal from Olympe. I have loved her too much. I still love her, perhaps. No scandal, therefore, unless it be absolutely necessary. And besides, I am certain of nothing. In such a case, proof of the guilt is necessary, and I have none. I might be able to accuse her with a chance of not making a mistake, but I haven't the right; and I will tell you why. You know that after Hubert's death I returned a verdict of suicide. But Hubert did not commit suicide. Hubert was murdered!

And I knew the truth at my first sight of the body by the position of the pistol in his hand. The weapon had been placed in his hand, after his death! I won't go into details, but I could have proved it very easily. I had been called immediately after the discovery of the body in the hope that perhaps life still stirred within him, but it was all over. Next to the corpse stood Olympe in tears. Before looking at the woman I had seen the pistol and had already reached a conclusion. Then I looked at the woman. You may have suspected the affectionate ties that bound us already. Besides, Olympe made no effort to hide the truth, and I had spoken to her about it more than once. Looking at her, it seemed to me that her eyes wavered after catching mine and they left me the impression of an ardent and silent plea. Even today I am sure that I was not mistaken and I feel a chill of horror. That woman killed Hubert in order to be mine! It was horrible, but I adored her, and not only did I not denounce her, but without her noticing and for pity of her I slipped the pistol into the correct position. I made the matter easy for the board of experts. You see, Zinzin, old man, I'm not hiding anything from you. You understand now why I haven't the right to accuse this woman. My cowardice has made me her accomplice.

I think we loved each other like the damned, trying to forget in the embrace of love a lost paradise. Between us there never came a thought of Hubert or of Delphin. One would have said that Olympe had never known those two men. But I, I was curious to know how Delphin had died and I began a cunning investigation which one day they must have noticed. From that day on, I am sure, my death was decided.

Certain contradictory remarks made by Palmire concerning Delphin's experiments and the rather mysterious circumstances of his death led me to certain clues in which I found almost certainty of Olympe's guilt in the poisoning of Delphin with Palmire as an accomplice. I had not said anything yet to Olympe, who did not seem to suspect my thoughts. I attempted to keep as hidden as possible the hideous suspicions. But one day I felt that I had been struck! A high fever, a strange uneasiness and dull pains warned me that I had been poisoned. I still said nothing because I wanted to know—to know. And I believed that I had done the necessary things to save me in time from a drug which was already attacking the sources of life—and which I could not rid myself of.

How did they go about it? . . . To make sure that it was she,

I ate nothing except what she gave me, and we drank from the same glass. Yes, but we did not eat from the same plate! Ah, what horror! . . . And this is where the matter rests today as I write you this letter . . . I have just had an attack which I have concealed from her. Is she really ignorant of it? Or does she find pleasure in it? Lord God! And yet my face has changed in these last weeks and several times I have pushed her from my arms. Still she seems to have noticed nothing. Oh, the monster! The two monsters! Yes, two, because I have discovered Palmire spying on me and the two of them are always together. Nevertheless, Olympe said to me yesterday: 'It's funny how men change after a few weeks of marriage! After a short while they are unrecognisable. They are no longer interesting!'

Zinzin, you will have this letter and I am going to talk to her. But I won't be telling her anything she doesn't already know. She must believe by now that I know by whose hands her first two husbands were killed; but I must tell her that I know that she is killing the third and that she must stop there!

Ah, Olympe, our Olympe! . . . If you knew, Zinzin, you would understand—and you would pardon me . . . Perhaps, after all, she is not guilty—perhaps Palmire is responsible, perhaps Palmire did it all alone. Ah, my God, if that could be true! . . . This is an idea which has come to me a little late—too late! . . . Think it over, Zinzin. I am past thinking now. I suffer too much . . . And yet I do not like to die without knowing. If she could only prove to me that it is Palmire who did it alone! I love her still, Zinzin!

'After this last line the writing was so disordered and jumbled that it was difficult to read, and the signature which followed seemed to express the supreme effort of a man from whom life is escaping. And yet Dr Sabin could not have died that day. Probably by the feverish use of some medicine he was able to suspend his destiny. We know that the unfortunate man did not die until after lunch the next day . . .

'I made the copy which you have just read,' Zinzin continued, 'that same night, because Lieutenant Jacobini demanded the original. He had the right to it, *since he was going to take my place*! I said all the things that you or anyone would say in such horrible circumstances; but I realized that his mind was made up and that there was nothing more to do. Of course, it was no longer a question of love for Olympe.

'He had made a vow, a vow to punish her for her crimes. He would force her to confess, make her give herself up, and then we would see! . . .

'He did not tell me what we would see, but it was easy enough to understand on catching sight of his fierce, terrible look when he spoke.

'"Dr Sabin got his just deserts," he said to me, "and I do not pity him; but that poor Hubert was my friend, and Delphin I loved as a younger brother and *I may be responsible for his death*. Therefore, I, Jacobini, am going to avenge them."

'To accomplish that he decided to marry Olympe.

'"And if she doesn't want to marry?" I asked him.

'He laughed a horrible laugh. "A woman like her will not refuse a man like me!"

'He was right. Olympe married number five and I was best man for Jacobini. He insisted upon it. During the ceremony he stood with his arms crossed at the foot of the chancel beside his kneeling bride and looked already like a statue of vengeance. Olympe was no longer the girl we had all known and loved. There was something strangely funereal in her beauty and it seemed already to be bending under the hand of death. She looked like the figures in marble one sees on tombstones. I never expected to see her again, for the next day I set out to sea.

'At every port I threw myself on the newspapers; I opened my mail with trembling, feverish hands. No news reached me of the hideous tragedy that I felt must have been happening at home during my absence. When, three months later, I returned, my first question was . . . yes, you have guessed it . . .

'"Is nothing changed around here?"

'"Goodness, no."

'"And how are the Jacobinis?"

'"The Jacobinis are fine," I was told.

'The next day Jacobini came to call on me. He knew that I had just returned. He looked exceedingly well and had prolonged his furlough, since Olympe refused to leave the house even though he hated it. "At heart I can't blame her," he explained. "She believes that if she leaves the house and this town where she spent such a happy youth it will look as though the evil tongues which claim she had a hand in the death of her three husbands have some cause for their suspicions."

'I looked at Jacobini, but he met my gaze clearly.

'"I understand your astonishment," he said, "but Olympe is not to be suspected."

'"So much the better, so much the better. Let's drop the subject, then."

'"Zinzin!"

'"Yes, Jacobini!"

'"I have come to talk to you and you must listen to me. The first thing I did on returning to the house after the wedding was to show her Dr Sabin's letter. Olympe cried, but did not seem in the least astonished.

'"'I had a suspicion of that,' she confessed to me. 'Everybody thinks I am a monster. I wonder that you wanted to marry me.'

'"'I will tell you why in due time,' I replied, 'but for the moment we are concerned with Dr Sabin's letter.'

'"'What can I say?' she continued bitterly. 'I am no more guilty of Hubert's death, of which they suspect me, than I am of my first husband's. Sabin loved me madly, and there were moments when his love was strangely like hatred. He let drop words from time to time that made me understand his horrible thought . . . and he started an abominable investigation. He questioned Palmire, who repeated everything to me. I tried to quiet him. Above all I wanted to avoid any scandal. I told myself his state of mind would pass with time and that as I had nothing to hide, he would end by understanding that we were all the victims of a horrible fate. Then suddenly he believed himself poisoned. He did not tell me in the beginning. I myself did not mention the word "poison", so that nothing definite should happen between us. I did not want to be forced to call in the police or to send him from the house, but as he continued to suffer I suggested that he consult a doctor. He did nothing. The day of his death he was under the influence of a strong drug that made him delirious. He insisted on coming to the table, and as I knew what he suspected I made a point of drinking only what he drank and of eating from the same plate.

137

At the dessert he threw himself at my feet and begged my pardon for having suspected me. He said he knew now that he was being poisoned by "that horrible Palmire". And he begged me to aid him in fastening the guilt on her. As I tried naturally to defend her, he left me abruptly and locked himself in his room. You know the rest. It was I who asked for an autopsy.'"

'Lieutenant Jacobini stopped.

'"And that convinced you of her innocence?" I asked.

'"No," he answered. "If Olympe expected something of the nature of Sabin's letter, I was ready for an explanation such as she gave me with a few tears thrown into the bargain. My next remark to my bride of an hour was very abrupt. 'And what about the tali-tali, Olympe? What have you done with it?' I asked.

'"She started and turned a deathly white. 'Oh,' she moaned, 'so you think that I poisoned him with tali-tali?'*

'"I took her by the wrist and it was like holding a hand of marble. 'Listen, Olympe: Hubert died of an accident. I'll grant that and it doesn't matter to me; but Delphin was my friend and he and Dr Sabin died the same death. They were both poisoned by the tali-tali which leaves no trace. It was I who gave the poison to Delphin that he might analyse it and find an antidote if possible. I brought it back with me on my last return from Africa and I want to know what has become of it. It is a

* The tali-tali of which Lieutenant Jacobini speaks here is certainly a close relative of the poison described in André Demaison's work. In the *Diato* is written: 'A man was hovering over the cauldron in which boiled the roots and bark of the sacred tree. At its name the children were terrified and the adults lost their mind: but the sorcerer, who was now pouring rice into the horrible soup, had declared that the poison could only harm those who sucked the marrow from the bones of their own kind . . .' And this is the picture of those put to the test: 'The unfortunates fell to the ground, letting out hoarse and horrible cries of pain. The bodies curled into a ball like partridges wounded by the hunter's bullet, or ducks with their necks cut before life is lost with the flow of blood.' The tali-tali of which Lieutenant Jacobini speaks produces fulminating effects if taken in a large dose. In other cases the poisoning may be slow. Sometimes it takes twenty-four hours for it to manifest itself in all its force. The victim, as happened to Dr Sabin, seems to have fallen from an epileptic fit.

138

terrible poison which the wizards down there give to the unfortunates who are suspected of having brought the anger of bad spirits on the village. Its victims are legion ... I am responsible for what it has done in France ... What have you done with the tali-tali, Olympe?'

'"Olympe looked up at me with frozen eyes. She was no longer crying. 'There is no more tali-tali,' she answered.

'"'Since when?' I asked brutally, trying to gain control over her obstinate mind, which was clearly fighting against me now.

'"'Since I asked Delphin to destroy it. That was a gift, sir, which you should never have made, not that I believe that he died of it, but because it would have been your fault if he had killed me with it. Was it the poison that was closed in the belly of a mahogany fetish covered with bizarre signs and curious designs burned into the wood?'

'"'That was it, Olympe. There is no possible error. You know the tali-tali well.'

'"'Yes, Delphin used this poison and the barks of the tree which you brought him to make some experiments which interested me, much more than the rest of his work, as a matter of fact. His test-tubes and apparatus amused me in the beginning, but one tires of everything. I soon noticed, however, that Delphin was not well, and I blamed his languor on the bad air of the laboratory. I asked him to give up his work for a little while. He would not, so I asked him at least to do me the favour of destroying the tali-tali. He answered that there was nothing to fear because the tali-tali was only fatal to those who drank it and that he was certainly not crazy enough to drink the liquid, which he had already tried out on chickens and rabbits. He was amused at my childishness, but I gave him no peace until he had destroyed the tali-tali in front of me and Palmire. Tired of fighting with me about it he threw the fetish and the poison into the fire and it was burned up in a moment.'

'"'How did the poison act in the fire?'

'"'First there was a long green flame like a sky rocket and that was followed by a suffocating vapour which we ran from. As for the fetish itself, it was nothing more than an ember which flashed a last grimace before falling into ashes. That is all, sir, and I have nothing else to tell you, but if it was to hear this that you married me you might as well have dispensed with the

139

ceremony. I would have given you the information just the same, and perhaps I would have loved you afterwards. But now please leave this house and never let me see you again.'"

'When Jacobini reached this point he stopped and rolled himself a cigarette.

'"And then?" I asked.

'"Then I left her to question Palmire. I forced her to tell of the tali-tali also. I attacked her from all sides. She's an ignorant peasant and she could not have invented the chemical effects which she had seen in the fire. All she said agreed to the letter with what Olympe had told me. I asked her all kinds of questions which Olympe could not have foreseen. I went on into other matters and at the end of my investigation I went back to Olympe and threw myself on my knees before her. She pardoned me, Zinzin, because besides being honest she is also very good."

'"Possibly," I said, "but she is not proud!"

'As you can well imagine, I did not go to call on them, but I saw Jacobini eight days later. An awful anguish was visible on his pale, restless face.

'"Zinzin," he said to me in a hoarse voice, "I think I'm infected with it, too. But perhaps it is only an idea. Yes, an idea! Even the thought of that tali-tali is enough to drive one mad."

'I didn't have time to say a word. He had already gone and I was never to see him alive again.

'And this is the frightful tragedy which occurred the next day according to the police, who with help from the dying Jacobini and Palmire's statements reconstructed the scene.

'At noon, Jacobini, who had not seen his wife since morning, went to the pavilion. He was filled with the darkest presentiments in spite of the fact that he tried to free himself of the idea of poison by trying to believe that his illness was due to swamp fevers which he had suffered from in the tropics.

'Luncheon was served there, and, as Jacobini entered, a door closed hurriedly at the end of the room. At the same time he heard furtive steps and the sound of a box being closed. He ran to the door, half opened it and saw Olympe engaged in low conversation with Palmire. She seemed very much troubled.

'At that moment a terrible cramp seized him in the intestines and he let the door close, having only strength enough to drop on the sofa. With one hand he had unconsciously taken hold of Olympe's work-box, which was badly closed and showed bits of fine linen. Jacobini's fingers, clutching at the lid feverishly from pain, opened it and fumbled in the lace. Suddenly they struck a hard object and he stood up, haggard and mad . . .

'In his hand he held the fetish of death, the horrible phial, the hideous tali-tali which Olympe and Palmire had sworn was destroyed, burned before them. Olympe had lied. Olympe had poisoned him as she had poisoned the other two. He was to suffer the atrocious death which had tortured his predecessors.

'Overcoming the agony for a few minutes, Jacobini poured what was left of the poison into a bottle of wine on the table; there was enough left for a terrible dose. And then he waited for his wife.

'She was not long in coming. She kissed him and asked him how he felt this morning. He replied that he felt much better, but that the fever had not completely left him and that he was thirsty.

'"Then you must drink something, darling," she said.

'He did not wait for her to pour the wine out and filled two glasses himself.

'"But you know that the doctors have forbidden me wine," she said, "and that I only drink water."

'He insisted that she drink with him in the same glass, as they had often done. She turned her head away. He seized her brutally, threw her head back and savagely pinched her nostrils, thus forcing her to drink. As she cried with fear, she spoke. "Perhaps you would have preferred another glass," he said, and showed her the tali-tali.

'She cried for help, but suddenly put her hand to her abdomen and was taken with a horrible cramp. At the same time the pain clutched at him, and they fell together on the sofa. They shrieked together, agonized together, clutched and scratched and bit each other. They pulled at each other like wild beasts. They twisted and writhed, contorting themselves in the same hell.

'Jacobini had still strength enough to insult her, naming the first victims. "You won't kill any more. You are going to die. You are going to die with me."

'But the pain was too great. It seemed as though there was hell within him. He pulled weapons down from the walls, and he tried to stab himself with a knife and so end the horror at one blow; but he only succeeded in making a terrible wound. Then he turned the steel towards Olympe and slit her open from top to bottom like an animal. The room echoed with her last howl.

'Possessed by a thousand demons he smashed her skull, pierced her like a pin-cushion, pulled out her eyes and cut her into pieces. She was nothing more than a bleeding, nameless horror when the servants rushed into the room.

'But Jacobini did not die until the next morning and in his few moments of lucidity narrated the hideous details of their abominable martyrdom. The assistant district attorney who at one time had hoped to marry her was present, and he returned home and went to bed ill. During the night he was so delirious that they thought he would lose his mind and so add one more victim to the list.'

Zinzin stopped. Perspiration beaded his temples. He let out a sort of groan.

'The most horrible part,' he went on, 'is the fact that she had done nothing.'

'Oh!' the others exclaimed.

'Yes, she was innocent. I learned that the other day, only the other day.'

'Palmire had done it all!' Gaubert exclaimed.

'As to her,' said Zinzin with a terrible laugh, 'the police took her and kept her. You can well understand that I did everything in my power to have her given full punishment. All she did was to say no, and to cry about Olympe. Concerning her mistress, however, she gave us explanations which dumbfounded us. They were so utterly stupid or naive. For example, when she was asked, "If your mistress was innocent, she would not have told her husband that the tali-tali had been destroyed before the two of you," Palmire answered, "Bah, that is simple. We agreed between us to say that it had been because there were already rumours about and we did not want to be suspected; besides we did not know what had become of the tali-tali because we really believed that Monsieur Delphin had burned it all the day that he threw a few drops in to please Madame."

142

'Yes, she said just that,' Zinzin went on, 'and she was hissed and hooted. I cried louder than the rest.'

'And what was she sentenced to?' asked Chaulieu.

'Death,' replied Zinzin in a whisper.

'But they don't execute women?'

'No . . . Her sentence was changed to life imprisonment. She died in her cell about ten years ago. I learned that the other day also.'

'And did she repent? Did she confess?' Michel asked.

'No,' Zinzin answered, looking at us like a madman, 'and she had nothing to confess . . . *She, too, was innocent!*'

'Good God!' Chaulieu exclaimed.

'But then, who was guilty?' Gaubert asked.

'A man who has just died and confessed on his deathbed. After the tragedy he left the town and settled not far from here. Yes, he died the other day at Mourillon. That man had owned some property which touched the edge of Olympe's estate in the far corner where the pavilion was.'

'But who was the man?—one of the twelve?'

'Yes, one of the twelve—the twelfth, to be exact! He naturally could not ever hope to marry Olympe, because of course she would never go through with eleven husbands after such deaths, but he eliminated those who had been happier than he . . . and at the end he had fixed it so that the evidence all pointed to Olympe.

'Do you remember, when the twelfth suitor arrived that day when we were all lined up in the drawing-room – the arrival of Monsieur Pacifire, the registrar—what fun Olympe made of him and how we had all laughed when she placed him at the foot of the line? Yes, we made fun of Monsieur Pacifire when he came into the room! Well, he avenged himself, that man!'

# 5

# GEORGES SIMENON
## Storm Over the Channel

### I

It was as if some malign influence had taken advantage of Maigret's recent retirement to bring home to him ironically the most flagrant proof of the fragility of human testimony. And, this time, the famous Superintendent, or rather he who had still carried that rank three months ago, was on the other side of the counter, the client side, if one can call it that, since it was to him that the question, accompanied by an insistent gaze, was directed:

'You're sure that it was half-past six, a bit before if anything, and that you were sitting by the chimney?'

Maigret now realized, with a dreadful clarity, how a small group of people, half a dozen in this case, could be suddenly paralysed by the simple question:

'What precisely were you doing between the hours of six and seven o'clock?'

If only it had been a matter of tumultuous or dramatic or stirring events! But no! It concerned all in all half a dozen people who, because of the bad weather, had been dragging their heels, waiting for dinner, in the two or three rooms open to them in a family boarding-house. And Maigret the client, Maigret the witness, hesitated like a naughty schoolboy or like a witness who was lying.

Bad weather, that was putting it mildly. At the Gare Saint-Lazare, a placard had warned: 'Storm over the Channel. Dieppe–Newhaven crossing cancelled.'

The numerous English were seen turning round and going back to their hotel.

At Dieppe, along the main street, it looked as if the wind

would tear down the shop-signs. You had to brace yourself to open some of the doors. The rain came down in torrents, sounding like the waves breaking on the stony beach. Occasionally, a silhouette slipped by, someone who was forced to go out and ran along the wall with his overcoat over his head.

It was in November. The street-lamps had been on since four o'clock. At the harbour station, the ferry which should have departed at two o'clock was still on the quay near some fishing boats whose masts were knocking against each other.

Mme Maigret, resigned, had gone up to fetch from her bedroom the knitting which she had started in the train, and sat by the stove where the guest-house's unfamiliar ginger cat had come to find her and curl up in her lap.

From time to time, she raised her head and threw a sorry glance at Maigret, who didn't know what to do with himself.

'We'd be better off at the hotel,' she sighed. 'You'd be sure to find somebody to play cards with you . . .'

Of course. Only the thrifty Mme Maigret had obtained, from God knows which friend, the address of this family boarding-house lost at the end of the quay, in a quarter which was dark and deserted during the summer and where the shutters were closed and the doors barricaded throughout the winter.

They were, however, on holiday. The only one, in fact, that the couple had treated themselves to since their honeymoon twenty-five years ago.

Maigret was off duty, at last! He was free of the Quai-des-Orfèvres and was able to go to sleep in the evening certain that he would spend the night in his bed and that a telephone call would not suddenly send him out to examine some still-warm corpse.

Since Mme Maigret had dreamed of visiting England for a long time, he had made up his mind:

'We will have a fortnight in London. I shall take the opportunity to go and shake hands with some colleagues at Scotland Yard with whom I worked during the war . . .'

So much for that! Storm over the Channel! The boat which wouldn't leave! This gloomy guest-house which had suddenly occurred to Mme Maigret where the walls sweated meanness and boredom!

The proprietress, Mlle Otard, was in her sour fifties, a fact

145

which she tried to hide under her sugary smiles. Her nostrils twitched every time she encountered the trace of pipe smoke which Maigret left in the wake of his comings and goings. Several times, she had been on the point of remarking that she didn't allow pipes to be smoked, especially not without respite, in the overheated little rooms when ladies were present. At these times, Maigret, who felt the approach of the storm, looked her in the eyes with such tranquillity that she preferred to turn away.

She was no more enamoured of him when she saw the ex-Superintendent, who had never been able to give up the habit, hover round the stoves, grasp the poker and rake over the unconsumed coal so vigorously that the chimneys roared like engines.

The house wasn't large. It was a two-storey villa that had been converted into flats. You came in along a corridor but, for reasons of economy, this corridor hadn't a light, nor had the stairs leading to the first and second floors, so that now and then you could hear someone trip up on the steps or a hand which groped before finding a door handle.

The main room, at the front, was the sitting-room, with its peculiar little green-velvet armchairs and a table of very old and tattered magazines.

Then, there was the dining-room where you could remain in between meals as well.

Mme Maigret was in the sitting-room. Maigret went from one room to the other, from one stove to the other, from one poker to the other.

At the back, there was the office where Irma, the little fifteen-year-old maid, was busy that afternoon cleaning the cutlery with chalk.

After that, the kitchen, the domain of Mlle Otard and Jeanne, the elder maid, a girl of between twenty-five and thirty years old, always in slippers, always badly groomed, of dubious morality, always bad-tempered as well, who threw out distrustful, aggressive stares.

The guest-house didn't employ any other staff. A bewildered kid of four, whom Maigret learned from the younger maid was Jeanne's son, was ceaselessly being shaken, scolded and slapped.

146

Perhaps, with the weather, it wasn't a very pleasant time anywhere. At Mlle Otard's, it was dismal. There seemed to be more seconds in a minute there than anywhere else, because the hands on the face of the black marble clock standing under a glass jar on the mantelpiece didn't advance.

'Make use of a lull to go to the café . . . I'm sure you'll find someone who'll play cards with you . . .'

You were never left the opportunity to talk, because you were never left alone. Mlle Otard went from the kitchen to the sitting-room, opened a drawer or cupboard, sat down, went out again, like someone who felt the need constantly to watch over everyone lest some catastrophe should occur. You would have thought that, if she absented herself for a quarter of an hour, someone would have taken the opportunity to pinch one of the old back numbers of *Mode du Jour* or set fire to the sideboard.

From time to time Irma would come in as well, specifically to return the cutlery to the drawer of the sideboard and to take out some more.

As for the sad lady—Maigret called her that because he didn't know her name—she was sitting up straight in a chair by the stove in the dining-room. She was reading a book of which it was impossible to see the title, because it no longer had a cover.

As far as one could tell, she had been there for a couple of weeks. She must have been thirty, and in poor health; perhaps she had come to convalesce after undergoing an operation? In any case, she moved carefully, as if she was afraid of breaking something. She ate little, and when she was eating sighed, as if she resented the minutes wasted on this vulgar function.

As for the other one, the young bride, as Maigret called her with a grim smile, it was exactly the contrary. She created a palpable draught as she moved from one chair to another.

The young bride was between forty and forty-five. She was small and stout, but not what you could call homely; the proof of it was that her husband was at her beck and call but had an obedient yet ashamed look about him.

Her husband was in his thirties, but it wasn't necessary to study him long to realize that he hadn't married for love but had sacrificed his freedom for a meal ticket in his old age.

Their name was Mosselet: Jules and Emilie Mosselet.

147

If the hand didn't advance quickly, it advanced all the same. Maigret remembered, with a shock, noting the time just as Jeanne served the sad lady with a mint tea. It had been a few minutes past five, and Jeanne had seemed to him even slyer than ever.

A little later, the young Englishman, Mr John, had come in from outside and let the cold and the rain enter the house, leaving patches of water from his soaked raincoat on the sitting-room floor.

He had a fresh complexion caused by the freezing wind and the news he carried. He announced in a thick accent:

'The boat's going to sail. Could you see to my bags, *s'il vous plaît, Mademoiselle la patronne . . .*'

He had been rushing around since morning, because he was in a hurry to return to England, and just now he had come back from the harbour station where he had learnt that the ferry was going to attempt the crossing.

'Have you my bill?'

Maigret hesitated for a moment. He was on the verge of following his wife's advice, even if it meant a soaking, and running along by the houses as far as the Brasserie des Suisses where, at least, there was life and movement.

He even went as far as the coat-stand in the corridor, noticed Mr John's three large suitcases half-concealed in the darkness, shrugged his shoulders and returned to the sitting-room.

'Why didn't you go out? You're making yourself bad-tempered for no reason . . .'

Just because of this remark, he sank heavily into an armchair and picked up the first magazine which came to hand and started to leaf through the pages.

What was remarkable was that he had absolutely nothing to do and nothing was able to interest him either. Logically, he should have been in a perfectly receptive state.

The house wasn't large. Wherever you were, you could hear the slightest noise, to such an extent that in the evening, when the Mosselet couple locked themselves in their bedroom, it was embarrassing.

Maigret saw nothing, heard nothing, hadn't the shadow of a presentiment.

He realized vaguely that Mr John paid his bill and slipped

148

into the office to give Irma a tip. He vaguely acknowledged the Englishman's vague farewell and noted that Jeanne, who was stronger than the young man, was charged with carrying two of the suitcases to the boat.

But he didn't see her leave. That didn't concern him. He happened to be reading. And because the magazine which he had picked up at random was an agricultural weekly, it was a long article, in small print, on the habits of field-mice, and he ended up, stupidly, engrossed in it.

From then on, the hands were able to advance silently around the dull green face of the clock without anyone noticing. Mme Maigret, counting the stitches of her knitting, moved her lips soundlessly. Occasionally, a lump of coal crackled in one of the stoves, or a gust of wind made a roar in the chimney.

The rattle of crockery announced that Irma was laying the table. There was the subdued odour of frying which advertised the customary evening meal of whiting.

And suddenly, there were voices surging out of the night, animated voices which seemed to be born out of the storm and which came closer, buffeting against the shutters and stopping only on the doorstep where they drew to a crescendo with the most violent knocking that the house had ever known.

Even at this moment, Maigret didn't jump. For hours, he had dreamed of a diversion from the monotony of the day and, at the moment when it presented itself, so much more impressively than could have been hoped for, he remained engrossed in his study of field-mice.

'Yes, this is the house,' Mlle Otard could be heard saying.

A gust of air came in, and water, and damp clothes, and red, excited faces, and it was impossible to avoid looking up and catching sight of the uniform of a Town Sergeant and the dark overcoat of a small man whose cigar was out.

'You have, haven't you, a certain Jeanne Fénard in your service?'

Maigret noticed that the kid came out just at that moment, God knows where from, probably the back of the kitchen.

'This person was killed by a bullet fired from a revolver as she crossed the Rue de la Digue . . .'

Mlle Otard's first reaction was incredulity and suspicion.

149

One felt that she wasn't the sort of woman who allowed herself to be influenced by anything anyone told her. Her pinched lips pronounced the magnificent word:

'Really!'

But what followed didn't leave any room for doubt, because the man with the extinct cigar continued:

'I am the Superintendent of Police. I must ask you to come with me to identify the body. I must also ask that no one else leaves the house . . .'

Maigret's eyes shone with malice. His wife looked at him as if to say, 'Why don't you tell him who you are?'

But he had retired too recently, and savoured the pleasures of anonymity. He sank lower in his armchair with a real delight. He studied the Superintendent with a critical eye.

'Will you put on your coat and follow me?'

'Where to?' protested Mlle Otard again.

'To the morgue . . .'

This provoked a shriek and groan from the sad lady, whom Maigret had forgotten about. Either a genuine fit of hysterics or one acted well enough to be real.

Irma rushed out from the office, holding a dish in her hand. 'Jeanne is dead?'

'That's none of your business,' ordered Mlle Otard. 'You can serve the dinner while you're waiting for me to come back . . .'

She looked at the kid who hadn't understood anything and was wandering between the legs of the grown-ups.

'Lock him in his room . . . He'll go to sleep . . .'

Where was Mme Mosselet at this moment? The question seemed easy but Maigret couldn't have answered it. On the other hand, Mosselet, who wore ridiculous red felt slippers about the house, was there, by the side of the corridor. He had probably heard the noise from his bedroom and come down.

'What is it?' he asked.

But the Superintendent was in a hurry. He said something in a low voice to the uniformed policeman who took off his cap and cape, lit a cigarette and deposited himself in front of the fire, a man who was making himself comfortable for a long wait.

As Mlle Otard, who had put on Wellington boots and a

yellow waterproof, was being led out, she looked over her shoulder one last time and flung out at Irma:

'Serve the dinner quickly! . . . The fish will be burnt! . . .'

Irma cried automatically, as if out of politeness, because someone was dead. She cried as she served the table, turning her head so that her tears wouldn't fall on to the dishes.

Maigret noticed that Mme Mosselet was there, hardly affected, but curious.

'What I should like to know is how is it possible . . . That it happened in the street? . . . Are there gangsters in Dieppe, then? . . .'

Mosselet ate heartily. Mme Maigret still didn't understand why this case seemed to leave her husband indifferent after he had spent a lifetime concerned only with crimes.

The sad lady looked at her whiting with very nearly the same expression as her whiting looked at her. From time to time, she opened her mouth, not to eat, but to let out some air by way of a sigh.

As for the policeman, he had taken a chair, installed himself astride it and watched the others eat, impatient to play a part.

'It was me who found her!' he said self-importantly to Mme Mosselet, who seemed the most interested.

'How?'

'It was really out of luck . . . I live in the Rue de la Digue, a little street which goes from the quay right to the end of the harbour, over yonder, past the cigarette factory. It's as much to say that no one ever goes down there. I was walking along with my head down when I saw something dark . . .'

'How dreadful!' said Mme Mosselet without conviction.

'I thought it was a drunk at first, because you find them on the pavement every day . . .'

'Even in winter?'

'Above all in winter, because one starts drinking to warm oneself up . . .'

'While in summer one drinks to cool oneself down!' joked Jules Mosselet, looking pointedly at his wife.

'If you like . . . I felt it . . . I guessed that it was a woman . . . I gave a shout and when we had carried her to the chemist's on

151

the corner of the Rue de Paris, we found out that she was dead
. . . I recognized her then, as well, because I know everyone in
the district by sight. I said to the Superintendent, "That
there lass, she's the maid at Otard's guest-house . . ."'

Then Maigret, like someone who is reluctant to get involved
with something which doesn't concern him, asked timidly:

'Weren't there any suitcases near her?'

'Why should there have been any suitcases?'

'I don't know . . . I was also wondering if she was pointing
towards the harbour or coming this way . . .'

The policeman scratched his head.

'Wait a second . . . I think, from her position, that she was
coming here when it happened . . .'

He hesitated for a moment, decided to pick up the bottle of
red wine and pour himself a glass, murmuring:

'You don't mind?'

The movement had brought him to the table. There remained two stiff fish in the dish. He hesitated again, took one of
them, ate it without either a knife or a fork and went to throw
the bones in the coal-scuttle.

Then he studied each of the faces, assured himself that there
were no competitors for the second whiting and ate it like the
first, took another drink, and sighed:

'It must be a crime of passion . . . She wasn't half a trollop . . .
One of the wildest at the dance-hall on the end of the harbour
. . .'

'It's different in that case,' murmured Mme Mosselet who,
because it was a crime of passion, seemed to find the thing quite
natural.

'What surprises me,' continued the policeman, whom Maigret couldn't take his eyes off, 'was that it was done with a revolver . . . The sailors, you know, would rather use a knife . . .'

At this moment, Mlle Otard came in. The wind which was
reddening the cheeks of the others had turned hers pale.
Besides, the incident had made her aware of her own importance and her attitude seemed to say:

'I know something, but don't count on me to tell it . . .'

She looked round the table, at the diners and the plates, and
noticed the fish bones. Harshly she asked Irma, who was
snivelling, pressed against the door jamb:

'Why are you waiting to serve the veal?'

Then finally, to the policeman:

'I hope you were given something to drink? . . . Your superior will be here soon . . . He's busy telephoning Newhaven at the moment . . .'

Maigret gave a start and she noticed it. His surprise didn't seem genuine to her and it was clearly possible to see a suspicion flicker across her face.

The proof of this was that she felt it necessary to add:

'. . . At least, I suppose . . .'

She didn't suppose: she knew. Then the Superintendent of Police had heard tell of Mr John and his abrupt departure.

For the time being, as a result, the official line of inquiry would be that of the young Englishman.

'All this will make me ill again!' the sad lady, who hardly opened her mouth three times all day except to sigh, murmured plaintively.

'And me?' complained Mlle Otard, who couldn't tolerate that anyone should be more upset than her by the incident. 'Do you think this does my business any good? A girl I've been training these last couple of months . . . Irma! When are you going to think of bringing the gravy?'

The most obvious result of all these comings and goings was to allow the house to be flooded with cold air: instead of evaporating in the surrounding warmth, it created little draughts which circulated and caught you in the back of the neck, provoking a shiver between the shoulders.

Maigret got up to poke the fire, indifferent to the empty coal-scuttle. Then he filled a pipe and put a scrap of paper to it which he had lit from the fire and unconsciously took up his favourite stance, the one for which he was known at the Quai-des-Orfèvres, pipe between teeth, back to the fire, hands crossed in the small of his back, with that indefinable look, obstinate or absent, which he had when the disparate elements started to come together in his mind to form a germ still far removed from the truth.

The arrival of the Superintendent didn't succeed in making him budge. He heard:

'The ferry hasn't arrived. I will be informed . . .'

It was not difficult to imagine the steamer struggling across the blackness of the Channel where one could see only the white crests of the waves. And the sick passengers, the deserted restaurant, the worried shadows in the shadow of the deck with, for their only guide, the intermittent flicker of the lighthouse at Newhaven.

'I see that I am obliged to interrogate these ladies and gentlemen one at a time . . .'

Mlle Otard understood. She declared:

'The communication door can be closed. You can install yourself in the sitting-room.'

The Superintendent of Police hadn't eaten yet, but there were no more fish on the table and he didn't dare to plunge his fingers in the dish where the pieces of veal were congealed.


## II

It was by accident. The policeman had looked around to see whom he could send in first. His glance had met with that of Mme Maigret who had seemed docile enough to make an example of.

'Go on . . .' he had said to her, opening, then closing behind her the sitting-room door, while a slight smile crept across the lips of the ex-Superintendent.

Though the door was closed, one could hear nearly everything which was said on the other side and Maigret's smile became more pronounced when his colleague in the next room asked:

'With an "ai" or an "é"?'

'An "ai" . . .'

'Like the famous detective?'

The good woman contented herself by replying, 'Yes!'

'Are you related to him?'

'I'm his wife.'

'But then . . . it's . . . your husband who is with you?'

And, the next moment, Maigret was in the sitting-room in front of a gentleman who was beaming but, at the same time, a little bit uneasy.

'Confess that you were trying to have me on! . . . When I think that I was going to interrogate you like the others . . . Mind you, I'm only here as a matter of form and to kill some

154

time, waiting for news from Newhaven . . . But you, who were on the spot, who saw the tragedy unfold, as it were, you should have a clearer idea and I would be grateful for . . .'

'I swear to you that I haven't the slightest idea.'

'In fact, who knew that this girl was about to go out?'

'The people in the house, of course. But at this stage I realize how difficult is the duty of the witness: I am incapable of determining with exactitude who was in the house at that moment.'

'You were preoccupied?'

'I was reading . . .'

He didn't dare add that he was reading an article on the life of moles and field-mice.

'I vaguely heard some commotion . . . Afterwards . . . Mme Mosselet, for example! Was she or wasn't she downstairs? And, if she was downstairs, where abouts? What was she doing?'

The Superintendent of Police wasn't satisfied. He wasn't far from thinking that his illustrious colleague was happy to let him sort everything out all on his own and he promised himself that he would show him how he, a small provincial detective, knew how to lead an inquiry.

The sad lady was called. Her name was Germaine Moulineau and she was a primary teacher on sick leave.

'I was in the dining-room,' she stammered out. 'I remember that I thought it was unfair to make that poor girl carry the Englishman's cases when there were strong men about who didn't know what to do with themselves.'

She had said that for Maigret, and to prove it she threw a glance at his broad shoulders as she made her allusion to strong men.

'From that moment, you never left the dining-room again?'

'Excuse me! I went up to my room.'

'Did you stay there long?'

'Nearly a quarter of an hour . . . I took a pill and waited for it to take effect . . .'

'You must excuse the question I'm about to ask you, but I shall ask it to all the guests in the house and I consider it merely as a formality. I suppose that you haven't been out today and that all your clothes, consequently, are dry?'

155

'No . . . I went out for a minute some time in the middle of the afternoon . . .'

A new proof of the relativity of witnesses! Maigret hadn't noticed either that she had gone out nor that she had been absent from the dining-room for a quarter of an hour!

'You probably went to fetch those pills from the chemist's?'

'No . . . I wanted to view the harbour in the wind and rain . . .'

'Thank you . . . Next, please!'

The next person to come in was Irma, who sniffed continually and clutched the corner of her apron between her fingers.

'Do you know if your companion Jeanne had any enemies?'

'No, monsieur . . .'

'Have you noticed any change in her mood which might indicate that she felt threatened?'

'She said to me only this morning that she wouldn't be staying in this dump much longer, those were her very words . . .'

'You're not well looked after?'

'I didn't say that,' she hurriedly avowed with a look at the door.

'At least, you know if Jeanne had any boyfriends?'

'Of course she did.'

'Why do you say, "Of course she did"?'

'Because she was always afraid of getting pregnant.'

'You don't know their names?'

'There was a fisherman called Gustave who used to come now and then and whistle from the street.'

'Which street do you mean?'

'The street at the back . . . You can go straight through to it, across the kitchen yard . . .'

'Did you go out this afternoon?'

She hesitated, on the verge of saying no, hesitated once more, and ended up admitting:

'Only for a second . . . I went to the baker's to buy a croissant . . .'

'At what time?'

'I don't remember . . . Probably about five o'clock . . .'

'What did you want a croissant for?'

156

'We're not given a lot to eat,' she mumbled in a voice hardly audible.

'Thank you.'

'You won't repeat it?'

'You needn't worry about that . . . Next, please!'

This time, Jules Mosselet came in, looking as casual as possible.

'Yours to command, Superintendent.'

'Did you go out this afternoon?'

'Yes, Superintendent . . . I went out to get some cigarettes . . .'

'At what time?'

'It must have been five to five or ten to five . . . I came back nearly straight away. The weather was very bad . . .'

'Did you know the victim?'

'Not at all, Superintendent . . .'

He was dismissed like the others and his wife took his place, and was posed the question which had become a ritual:

'Did you go out this afternoon?'

'I'm obliged to reply, of course?'

'It would be better for you . . .'

'In that case, I must ask you not to speak to Jules about it. You will understand. He's a lad who has had a lot of success with women. Since he's got a weak character, I am suspicious. When I heard him go out, I followed him to find out where he was going.'

'And where was he going?' asked the Superintendent, winking at Maigret.

The least you could say was that the answer was unexpected.

'I don't know . . .'

What do you mean, you don't know? You just admitted that you were following him . . .'

'Precisely! I thought I was following him. Believe me! But by the time I'd put on my coat and opened my umbrella, he was already at the corner of the first street. When I got there in my turn, I caught sight of a silhouette in a brown raincoat and I followed hard on his heels. It wasn't until five minutes later, when the silhouette stepped in front of a lighted shop-window, that I realized that it wasn't Jules . . . Then, I came back here and pretended not to have done anything . . .'

'How much longer after you was he coming back?'

'I don't know . . . I was upstairs . . . He could have been downstairs for some time . . .'

Just at that moment, the bell rang violently and a uniformed policeman delivered a note to the Superintendent. He opened it and, a second later, handed it over to Maigret:

*Neither John Miller nor anyone answering to his description disembarked from the Dieppe–Newhaven ferry.*

Though it did not particularly please him to do so, given the attitude of his colleague who seemed disposed to give him as little help as possible, the Superintendent of Police had politely offered to let Maigret stand in on the inquiry if he was interested.

Nevertheless, while they were walking together past the houses from which there was a danger of receiving a tile on the head—here and there the fragments could be seen on the pavement—he explained:

'As you can see, I don't want to leave anything to chance. I will be very surprised if there isn't more to this John Miller than meets the eye. The proprietress of the guest-house told me that he had been there for a couple of days but had replied evasively to her questions. He paid in French currency; but, and here was a curious detail, he gave her an unheard of amount of small change. He went out very little, and only in the morning. Mlle Otard met him two days running at the market where he seemed to be interested in butter, eggs and vegetables . . .'

'Unless it was in the shoppers' purses!' broke in Maigret.

'You think he is a pickpocket?'

'That would certainly explain why he should have entered England under another name and wearing different clothes to the ones you described . . .'

'That won't stop me looking for him. We're going to Victor's now, the café near the fish market. I will be happy to meet that fellow Gustave there, whom the little maid spoke about, to find out if he is the same Gustave, called Chipped-Tooth, whom I've had to deal with a couple of times . . .'

'According to your policeman, the blokes around here prefer playing about with knives rather than guns,' objected Maigret

158

once more, while jumping over a deep puddle and still splashing himself.

A few minutes later, they went into Victor's. The floor was greasy and a dozen tables were occupied by fishermen in jerseys and wooden sabots. The lights in the café were too bright and a phonograph poured out shrill music while the owner and two slovenly waitresses bustled around.

It was obvious from the looks of the men that they had recognized the Superintendent of Police who, accompanied by Maigret, had gone to sit in a corner and ordered a beer. When one of the girls brought it, he held her by her apron and spoke to her in a low voice:

'What time did Jeanne come in this afternoon?'

'What Jeanne?'

'Gustave's girlfriend . . .'

The girl hesitated, looked at one of the groups of men and thought it over:

'I don't think I've seen her!' she said at last.

'She often turns up here though, doesn't she?'

'Sometimes . . . But she doesn't come in . . . She looks round the door to see if he's here and, if he is, he goes to join her outside.'

'Gustave has been here all night?'

'You'd better ask my friend Berthe . . . Me, I went out . . .'

Maigret wore a beatific smile. He appeared to be ravished to see that he was not the only one unable to provide a reliable eye-witness.

Berthe was the other waitress. She squinted. Perhaps it was this which gave her such a disagreeable air.

'If you're interested,' she replied to the Superintendent, 'why don't you ask him yourself. I'm not paid to keep law and order.'

But, by this time, the first waitress had already spoken to a red-haired man in Wellington boots who got up, hitching up his thick duck trousers which were tied with string, spat on the ground, and came over to the Superintendent. When he opened his mouth, he exhibited, right in the middle, a broken tooth.

'It's me you're after?'

'I would like to know if you've seen Jeanne this evening . . .'

'What business is that of yours?'

'Jeanne is dead.'

'It's not true . . .'

'I'm telling you she's dead, in the street, killed by a bullet from a revolver.'

The man was genuinely surprised. He looked at them and shouted:

'Look here! What's all this about? Jeanne is dead?'

'Answer my question. Have you seen her?'

'All right, I'd better tell the truth. She came here . . .'

'At what time?'

'I can't remember . . . I was gambling for the aperitifs with fat Hipolyte . . .'

'It would be after five o'clock?'

'Surely.'

'Did she come in?'

'I don't let her come in the cafés I frequent. I saw her head in the door. I went to tell her to leave me in peace . . .'

'Why?'

'Because!'

The owner had stopped the record-player and silence reigned in the bar as the customers tried to catch scraps of the conversation.

'Did you have an argument?'

Chipped-Tooth shrugged his shoulders like a man who knew he would have all the trouble in the world to make himself understood.

'Yes and no . . .'

'Explain yourself!'

'Let us say that I had designs on somebody else and she was jealous . . .'

'Who else?'

'Somebody who came to the dance-hall with Jeanne once . . .'

'Her name?'

'Even I don't know it . . . Never mind, since you want to know it! . . . And I haven't even laid a finger on her, so you won't be able to make any trouble for me on that account, in spite of her age . . . It's the kid who works with Jeanne at the guest-house . . . That's all! When Jeanne came, I just went out to the pavement, and I told her that if she didn't leave me in peace, she'd get a pasting.'

'And after that? You came straight back into the café?'

'Not straight away . . . I went to see the ferry for Newhaven leave . . . I thought it would botch up the manoeuvre because of the current . . . Are you going to arrest me?'

'Not yet . . .'

'Don't put yourselves out, eh? We're beginning to get used to always getting it in the neck for others . . . To think that she's dead! . . . She didn't suffer, at least?'

It was a strange feeling for Maigret, to be there and have nothing to do. He still was not used to being a citizen like any other. He heard a voice other than his own posing some questions and he had to make an effort not to interfere, to approve or to disapprove.

Occasionally, he burned to ask a question, and it was a real torture to keep it to himself.

'Are you coming with me?' the Superintendent of Police asked Maigret, as he got up and threw some coins on the table.

'Where are you going?'

'To the police station. I must draft my report; then I can go to bed, there is nothing more we can do today . . .'

Once they were on the pavement, he murmured as he turned up the collar of his overcoat:

'Of course, I shall put a man on Chipped-Tooth . . . That's my method and I believe it's yours too . . . It's a mistake to try and obtain immediate results at any price because you only end up tiring yourself out and losing your temper . . . I'll have enough to do tomorrow with the people from the DPP.'

Maigret preferred to leave him under the red lantern of the police station; he had nothing to do in the office where his colleague would be conscientiously applying himself to drafting a detailed report.

The wind had died down, but the rain was still falling, more finely, it seemed, than earlier on, because it fell vertically now. Very few people passed in front of the shop windows which were still illuminated.

As used to happen to him in the old days, when an affair started badly, Maigret began by wasting his time, meaning by this that he went into the Brasserie des Suisses and, for a good

161

quarter of an hour, unthinkingly watched his two neighbours playing backgammon.

His feet were damp in his shoes and he felt that he had caught a cold. It was this which decided him, after he had finished his beer, to order a grog of rum which brought the blood to his head.

'Well, well! . . .' he sighed, as he got up.

It was none of his business! Of course, that made him a bit sick at heart, but he had been looking forward long enough to reaching his retirement age not to grumble now that that time had come.

Outside, at the far end of the quay, a good way after the deserted harbour station where only a solitary arc-lamp shone, he glimpsed a purple stain on the wet pavement and he remembered a certain dance-hall which had been mentioned.

Without having decided to go there, and still not admitting to himself that he had taken up the case, he found himself in front of a peculiar façade tastelessly painted and illuminated by coloured light bulbs. When he opened the door, he received a blast of Java music in the face, but was disappointed to find that the establishment was nearly empty.

Two women were dancing, factory girls probably, who wanted to have their money's worth, and the three musicians were playing for them alone.

'By the way, which day of the week is it today?' he asked the boss as he planted himself down at the bar.

'Monday . . . Not many people will come today . . . Here, it's mainly Saturdays and Sundays, and a bit on Thursdays . . . A few couples later on, after the cinema, but in this weather . . . What are you having?'

'A grog.'

He regretted it as he watched the man concoct his grog with fancy rum and water boiled in a dubious saucepan.

'It's your first time here? Just passing through Dieppe, are you?'

'Yes, I'm just passing through . . .'

And the man, misjudging him, explained:

'You know, in my establishment, you won't find any professionals. You can dance, offer the young girls a drink, but, for anything else, it's more difficult . . . Especially today!'

'Because there's nobody here?'

'Not just that . . . Look! Those kids who are dancing . . . Do you know why they're dancing?'

'No . . .'

'To chase away the gloom . . . Earlier on, one of them was crying while the other stared straight in front of her . . . I offered them a drink to help them get over it . . . It's no joke to learn that one of your friends has been killed . . .'

'Ah! There's been an accident?'

'A crime, yes! In a little street less than a hundred yards from here . . . A young maid was found with a bullet in her head . . .'

And Maigret said to himself, 'To think that it never occurred to me to ask if she had been shot in the head or the stomach!'

Then, aloud:

'The shot was fired from close by, then . . .'

'As close as possible because in the darkness, and with a storm like this, it would have been difficult to see three feet in front of you . . . Mind you, I would swear it wasn't anyone from round here . . . If it had been done with the fists, I don't say . . . Every Saturday, I have to throw a couple of them out before there is a free-for-all . . . Look! I've felt pretty bad myself since I was told about it . . .'

It was so true that he poured himself a small glass and smacked his lips.

'Would you like me to introduce you to them?'

Maigret didn't have time to object before the boss had already beckoned over the two girls with a familiar gesture.

'Here's a gentleman who is feeling bored and would like to offer you a drink . . . Come over here . . . You will be better off in this corner . . .'

He indicated to Maigret with a leer that he could even take liberties here without being seen.

'What would you like? Grogs?'

'Make it grogs . . .'

It was embarrassing. He hadn't the manner. The two young girls studied him furtively and tried to get a conversation going.

'Don't you dance?'

'I don't know how to dance . . .'

'Wouldn't you like us to teach you?'

No! Certainly not that! He could not imagine himself

163

revolving round the dance-floor under the amused glances of the three musicians!

'Are you a travelling salesman?'

'Yes . . . I'm passing through . . . The boss just told me that your friend . . . well, that something unpleasant has happened . . .'

'She wasn't our friend!' riposted one of the girls.

'Oh! I thought . . .'

'If it had been one of our friends, we wouldn't be here! But we knew her, like we know all the regulars. Now that she's dead, you can't reproach her for anything. It's sad enough as it is . . .'

'Naturally . . .'

He had to agree. It was above all a matter of knowing how to wait without frightening his companions.

'Was she a bit wild?' he ventured, however.

'That's not the half of it . . .'

'Be quiet, Marie! She's dead . . .'

Some customers came in. One of the young girls danced a couple of times with some strangers. After some time, Maigret caught sight of Gustave Chipped-Tooth, dead drunk, leaning on the bar.

The drunk man looked at him as if he was going to recognize him and Maigret feared an unpleasant scene. But nothing came of it. The man was too drunk to see anything clearly and the boss was only waiting for an opportunity to throw him out.

In exchange for the favour which he had rendered Maigret by introducing him to the two local beauties, he forced a round of grogs on him every quarter of an hour or so.

So that at one o'clock in the morning, when he left, the ex-Superintendent of the Police Judiciaire brushed against the frame of the door, had some trouble doing up the buttons of his overcoat, and splashed through all the puddles on his way back to the boarding-house.

He had forgotten that guests who came back after eleven o'clock had to ring a special bell which sounded in Mlle Otard's bedroom. He shook the bell violently, woke everybody up, and was let in with as much bad grace as possible by the proprietress, who had slipped a coat over her nightdress.

'On a day like today! . . .' he heard her grumbling.

Mme Maigret had gone to bed but she turned on the light when she heard footsteps on the staircase, and looked in amazement at her husband whose bearing seemed exaggeratedly heavy and who tore off his false collar with an unaccustomed gesture.

'I wonder where you've been? . . .' she murmured, turning over towards the wall.

And he repeated:

'Where I've been? . . .'

Then, once again, with a peculiar smile:

'Where I've been? . . . Suppose I'd been to Villecomtois . . .'

She frowned, racked her memory, and was certain that she had never heard this name before.

'Is it near here?'

'It's in the Cher . . . Villecomtois! . . .'

It was better to leave the trouble of questioning him until the next day.

## III

Whether she was on holiday or not, whether she had gone to bed early or late—the latter almost never occurred—Mme Maigret had a mania for getting up at unearthly hours. Only the other day, the ex-Superintendent had made a fuss about this, on finding her, at seven o'clock in the morning, already dressed and not knowing what to do with herself.

'I can't get used to staying in bed,' she had replied. 'I always feel as if there is some housework to be done . . .'

And it was the same this morning. He opened one eye, from time to time, because this eye was in the yellow glare of the electric light bulb. It was not daylight yet and already his wife was filling the room with unobtrusive watery noises.

'What is that word again?' wondered Maigret, half-asleep, as he acknowledged irritably that he would have a headache.

The famous word of last night, the name of a small town or village, which he had trumpeted to his wife as he came in, had so hypnotized him that, as often happens, he had forgotten it by dint of thinking about it.

He thought he was only half-asleep, because he was aware of some small things going on around him; in this way, he realized

165

the light had been turned off and that a pitiful daylight had replaced the rays of the light bulb. Then he heard an alarm-clock somewhere in the house, the footsteps of someone on the staircase, and the front door-bell ring twice.

He would have liked to know if it was still raining and if the storm had dropped, but he had not the courage to open his mouth and ask, and suddenly he sat up in bed because his wife was shaking his shoulder; he saw that day had completely broken; his watch, on the bedside table, showed half-past nine.

'What's up?'

'The Superintendent is downstairs . . .'

'What has that got to do with me?'

'He wants to see you . . .'

Because yesterday night he might have had one grog too many—without intending to, of course—Mme Maigret felt it necessary to take on a maternal and protective air.

'Drink your coffee while it is hot . . .'

On such mornings getting washed is always unpleasant, and Maigret was tempted to put off the trouble of shaving until the next day.

'What was the word I said to you, last night?' he asked.

'What word?'

'I spoke to you about a village . . .'

'Ah! Yes . . . I remember vaguely . . . It was somewhere in the Cantal . . .'

'Certainly not! In the Cher . . .'

'You think so? . . . I seem to remember it ended in "on" . . .'

It could not be helped! She did not remember either! He went down, thick-headed, still not fully awake, and his pipe did not have the same taste as on other mornings. He was surprised to find no one in the kitchen, or in the office, but, on the other hand, when he opened the dining-room door, he saw the whole house transfixed as if in the middle of some ceremony or posing for a photograph.

Mlle Otard had a dour, reproachful look on her face, no doubt because of his noisy return in the night. The sad lady, in her armchair, was already as far away as someone who was dying and no longer felt earthly ties. As for the Mosselets, they must have had their first argument that morning because they

166

avoided looking at each other and seemed to hold the whole world responsible for their estrangement.

Even the little Irma was no longer the same, and looked as if she had been dipped in vinegar.

'Good morning!'—Maigret flung out as good-humouredly as possible.

Nobody replied or made even the slightest gesture of acknowledgement of his greeting. However, the sitting-room door opened and the Superintendent of Police, not ashamed of being hale and hearty and even less ashamed of being himself, held out his hand to his illustrious colleague.

'Come in, I beg you . . . I suspected I'd find you in bed . . .'

The door was closed. They were alone in the sitting-room where the fire had only just been lit and was still smoking. Through the windows Maigret saw the grey, wind-swept quay, with clouds of spray after each great wave.

'Yes, I was tired . . .' he growled.

And, seeing the other's smile, he was compelled to prove immediately that he had not been deceived. He had not thought of the detail the day before, but it came to him now.

'Your Gustave Chipped-Tooth was there, sure enough! So there was a policeman on his tail! And this policeman told you that . . .'

'I assure you that I haven't any intention of making the slightest allusion . . .'

The fool! So he thought that the night before, if Maigret had spent the evening at the dance-hall with those two kids, it was for . . .

'I permitted myself to disturb you this morning, because the Dieppe police have made a discovery of, I dare say, a rather sensational nature . . .'

Maigret, out of habit, poked the fire. He would have liked something refreshing to drink, a lemon juice, for example.

'You didn't notice anything on your way down?' the other continued, who was as gleeful as an actor who has just been given an encore and prepares to deliver his best speech.

'You mean the people waiting in the dining-room?'

'As a matter of fact, it was me who insisted on having them gathered together and stopping their comings and goings . . . I am going to tell you some news which is going to surprise you:

the murderer or murderess of the young Jeanne Fénard lass is among them!'

It would have taken more than that to get a reaction from Maigret on that particular morning, and he merely looked dully, almost listlessly, at his colleague. And the latter would have been truly astounded to learn that, at that precise moment, the ex-Superintendent of the Police Judiciaire was pre-occupied with trying to remember the name of a village which ended in 'ois'.

'Look at this . . . Don't worry . . . The fingerprints, if there were any, were all washed off in the hours of rain.'

It was a small card which was already familiar to Maigret, a greyish, rectangular card, surrounded by flourishes, with the word 'Menu' printed on it.

The writing sketched on it in ink had almost been effaced by the rain, but one could still distinguish: *Soupe a l'oseille . . . Maquereaux sauce moutarde . . .*

'The menu of the day before yesterday . . .' he remarked, still without showing any surprise.

'So I've just been told. At least one thing is certain: this menu is a menu from the Otard guest-house, and a menu which had been used the evening before yesterday, that is to say, the day before the crime. Bear in mind now that it had been discovered this morning only by the greatest stroke of luck on the pave-ment of the Rue de la Digue, less than three yards from the place where Jeanne was killed . . .'

'Of course! . . .' growled Maigret.

'You agree with me, don't you? As you observed last night, I wasn't in a hurry to arrest Chipped-Tooth, in spite of his record, as some people might think I should have done. My method, as I explained to you, is to avoid rushing in at any cost. The presence of this menu at the scene of the crime proves, in my opinion, that the murderer is a regular frequenter of this house. And I'll go further. I tried, in the storm which was still raging this morning, to reconstitute the crime. Imagine that your hands are wet from the rain and that you have to fire accurately. What do you do? You take out your handkerchief to dry your fingers . . . And taking out that handkerchief, the murderer dropped . . .'

'I understand . . .' sighed Maigret as he lit his second pipe of

168

the day. 'And have you also deciphered the meaning of the numbers marked on the back of the card?'

'Not yet, I admit. Someone, who happened to be here in the evening the day before yesterday, used this menu to note something down. I make out, in pencil, "seventy-nine by a hundred and forty". And underneath, "a hundred and sixty by eighty". I thought at first that it might have been the score of some game, but I have dismissed this explanation. Neither is it a question of the times of a train or boat, as also had occurred to me. To this extent, the mystery still remains temporarily unsolved, but it is evident nonetheless that the murderer is a guest in the boarding-house. That is why I have gathered everybody in the dining-room, under the surveillance of one of my inspectors. I wanted, before anything else, to ask you this question: "Since you were here the day before yesterday, did you notice, in the course of the evening, someone making some notes in pencil on a menu? . . ."'

No! Maigret had not noticed anything like that. He remembered that M. and Mme Mosselet had been playing draughts on the card-table in the sitting-room, but he no longer remembered where you could have found the others. As for him, he had read his paper and gone to bed early.

'I believe,' went on the Superintendent of Police, satisfied with his little effect, 'that we can now question these ladies and gentlemen one at a time.'

And Maigret, continually looking for the famous word, more and more thirsty, sighed:

'Not before somebody has brought me something to drink, thank you.'

He opened the communicating door and saw Mme Maigret who had come to sit docilely with the others. In the grey light, the atmosphere was that of a waiting-room of a small town dentist: the half-drawn curtains, the glum faces, the legs which did not dare to stretch out, and the furtively exchanged looks of caution or distrust.

Mme Maigret obviously could have escaped from the irksomeness. But it was so completely in her character to do as the others did, to take her place in the queue—but not without providing herself with her knitting, which caused her to move her lips silently as she counted the stitches.

From politeness, the Superintendent of Police called her first, apologized for having disturbed her again, and showed her the menu, without trying to trip her up.

'This doesn't bring back any memories?'

Mme Maigret looked at her husband, shook her head, then re-read the figures, frowning like someone who hesitates to own up to a fanciful idea.

'Absolutely nothing!' she said at last.

'The night before last, you didn't see anyone writing on a menu?'

'I ought to tell you that, as I never stopped knitting, I hardly noticed what was going on around me . . .'

At the same time as she said this, she nodded to her husband. Though he understood that she had something to add which she wanted to say to him in private, he nevertheless said aloud:

'What is it?'

She was angry with him. She was always afraid of making a gaff. Consequently, she blushed, was intimidated, looked for her words, and continually apologized.

'I don't know . . . You must excuse me . . . I'm probably wrong . . . But, as soon as I saw those numbers, I thought . . .'

Her husband sighed as he thought that she would always be the same, humble enough to make you weep.

'. . . You're probably going to laugh at me . . . One metre forty, that's the width of the material . . . So is eighty centimetres . . . And the first number, seventy-nine, represents the length of a skirt . . .'

She was all pride when she beheld the gleam in Maigret's eyes, after which she went on volubly:

'The first two numbers, seventy-nine by a hundred and forty, tally exactly with the amount of material you would need for a pleated skirt . . . But not all materials come in lengths of a hundred and forty centimetres . . . With eighty centimetres, since you wouldn't have the right breadth any longer for the pleats, you would have to double the length . . . I don't know if I've made myself clear. . . .'

And, turning towards her husband, she exclaimed:

'You don't think it was in "ard"?'

Because she was still looking for the famous word that she was ashamed to have forgotten.

170

'It's one of my menus, that's true. But it wasn't me who wrote those numbers,' replied Mlle Otard to the Superintendent of Police's questions. 'And I must add that if my house continues to remain in a state of siege, I shall be obliged to . . .'

'You must excuse me, madame . . .'

'Mademoiselle!'

'You must excuse me, mademoiselle, and I will do my best to make sure that this state of siege, as you call it, lasts for no longer than is necessary. Allow me to inform you, however, that we are now convinced that the murderer is a guest in this house and that, under these circumstances, our presence here is quite justified . . .'

'I would really like to know who!' she retorted.

'I would really like to know as well and I hope it won't be long before we find out . . . In the meantime, I have some questions to ask you which didn't occur to me in the confusion yesterday . . . How long had Jeanne Fénard been in your service?'

'For six months!' Mlle Otard replied dryly, reluctantly.

'Can you tell me how she came to be with you?'

And, perhaps because she felt the weight of Maigret's malicious gaze on her, she let out:

'Like anybody else: through the door!'

'I can do without any clever remarks like that at the moment. Was the Fénard lass sent by an employment agency?'

'No!'

'She came of her own accord?'

'Yes.'

'You didn't know her?'

'Yes.'

She had now decided to reply, obstinately, with the least number of syllables strictly necessary.

'Where did you know her?'

'From home.'

'Meaning what?'

'She worked for years at the Anneau d'Or where I was cashier.'

'Is it a restaurant?'

'A hotel and restaurant.'

'In which region?'

'I've already told you: back home, Villecomtois . . .'

Maigret had to make an effort not to give a start. That was it, he had found the famous word at last: Villecomtois, in the Cher. This time, he forgot the promise he had made himself to remain in the background.

'Was Jeanne from Villecomtois?' he asked.

'No. She went there as maid of all works . . .'

'She already had a child?'

Mlle Otard retorted contemptuously:

'That was seven years ago and Ernest is four years old . . .'

'What was seven years ago?'

'That I left to set myself up here . . .'

'And she?'

'I don't know . . .'

'If I understand rightly, she stayed on there after you left?'

'I suppose so . . .'

'Thank you!' pronounced Maigret in the menacing tone of a lawyer in the Court of Assizes who had just finished examining a reluctant witness.

And, for the sake of appearance, the Superintendent of the Dieppe Police added:

'In short, she turned up here this summer and you engaged her because she was a girl from back home or, more precisely, a girl that you had known back home. I appreciate your gesture. And it was all the more generous, first of all because Jeanne had a child, but also because her bearing and conduct were not very much in keeping with the reputation of your establishment . . .'

'I did what I could,' Mlle Otard was content to reply.

Next it was Mosselet's turn to come in. He had a cigarette in the corner of his mouth and a shrewd, condescending look about him.

'This is still going on?' he asked, sitting down on the corner of the table. 'You must admit that as a honeymoon . . .'

'Did you write this?'

He turned the menu over and over between his fingers and asked:

'Why should I have drawn up the menus?'

'I refer to the pencil marks which are on the back . . .'

'I didn't see them . . . Sorry . . . No, it wasn't me . . . What do they mean?'

'Nothing . . . Of course, you didn't see anybody, the night

172

before last, engaged in writing on one of the establishment's menus?'

'I confess that I didn't pay any attention . . .'

'And you didn't know Jeanne?'

Jules Mosselet looked up and said simply:

'How couldn't I have known her?'

'I mean to say that you didn't know her before you came here . . .'

'I had already seen her . . .'

'In Dieppe?'

'No! Back home . . .'

That 'word' was going to crop up again! Maigret, though he was just a silent actor in this scene, exulted as if he had been the hero of it.

'Where is that, back home?'

'In Villecomtois!'

'You are from Villecomtois? Do you still live there?'

'Of course.'

'And you knew Jeanne Fénard there?'

'Like everybody else, seeing that she was the maid at the Anneau d'Or. I knew Mlle Otard too, who was the cashier. That's why my wife and I, when we were passing through Dieppe, thinking we would be better off here, with someone from back home . . .'

'Your wife is from Villecomtois as well?'

'From Herbemont, a village five miles away. It amounts to the same thing . . . When you are on holiday, you might as well give work to people that you know. Also, since Mlle Moulineau was recuperating here . . .'

Maigret had to look away so as not to smile and this action, he realized, nettled the Superintendent of Police who was not able to understand it. So then, this business in Dieppe had been acted out solely by people from Villecomtois, a village of which no one had heard before!

Maigret thought, 'No doubt the friend who gave this address to my wife was from Villecomtois too!'

As for the baffled Superintendent of Police, trying to preserve his dignity, he mumbled:

'Thank you . . . I will probably want to see you again . . . Will you ask your wife to come in . . .'

173

When his back was turned, Maigret took the menu, which was the only exhibit, from the table and slipped it in his pocket, putting his finger to his lips, as if to say to his colleague:

'Don't speak to her about that . . .'

Mme Mosselet took the place of her husband with the dignity of a woman who does not allow herself to be impressed by the law.

'What is it now?' she asked.

The Superintendent from Dieppe, deprived of his menu, no longer knew what to say. He began:

'You live in Villecomtois?'

'Villecomtois, in the Cher, yes. Three years ago my father bought up the Anneau d'Or hotel. When he died, since I was on my own and a man was needed to run the house, I got married . . . We closed for eight days for the honeymoon, but if it goes on like this . . .'

'Excuse me!' interrupted Maigret. 'You were married at Villecomtois?'

'Of course.'

'How far is it to the nearest large town?'

'Bourges is forty-three kilometres . . .'

'Then you bought your trousseau in Bourges?'

She looked at him for a moment in amazement. She was probably thinking: 'What has that got to do with him?'

Then she shrugged her shoulders imperceptibly, and decided to answer:

'No. My trousseau, I shall buy it in Paris . . .'

'Ah! Because you are going to continue your honeymoon in Paris?'

'We ought to have started from there. But I wanted to see the sea. Jules as well. We had never seen the sea, either of us. If it hadn't been for the exchange rate, we might have gone as far as London . . .'

'Then you brought as little luggage with you as possible . . . I understand . . . In Paris you will have every opportunity to build up your wardrobe . . .'

She did not understand why this man who was as large and solid as a battleship persisted in talking about such futile matters. Yet he went on, all the while puffing at his pipe:

'It's all the more to your advantage since you are nearly the shape of a model . . . I bet you take only a forty-two . . .'

'A large forty-two . . . It's just that, as I'm not very tall, the dresses have to be shortened . . .'

'Don't you do it yourself?'

'I have a seamstress who comes in daily whose work is as good as anyone's and whom I pay only . . .'

She was struck at last by the unusual character of the interrogation and looked up at the two men to see Maigret smiling and the other one, very much ill at ease, pretending to wash his hands of the whole affair.

'But what is all this about?' she asked suddenly.

'How much material with a width of one metre forty would you need to make a skirt?'

She did not want to reply. She no longer knew whether to laugh or be angry.

'The length, isn't it?' insinuated Maigret.

'So what?'

'In other words, seventy-eight or seventy-nine centi-metres?'

'And so?'

'Nothing . . . Don't worry about it . . . Just a thought . . . We were speaking about dresses with my wife and I claimed that you would be easier to dress than she was . . .'

'What else do you want to know?'

She looked at the door as if she was afraid that her husband would take advantage of her absence to go and get into mischief.

'You are completely at liberty . . . The Superintendent of Police is most grateful.'

She got up, still worried and uneasy, and with the suspicious air of those women who, because of their conviction in human perfidy, are unable to imagine that someone has told them the truth, even once, by accident.

'I can go out in the town?'

'If you like . . .'

When the door was closed, the Superintendent of Police got up as if he wanted to rush into the dining-room and order an inspector:

'Follow her . . .'

'What are you doing?' asked Maigret, as he went up to the stove which he had not poked for some time.

'But . . . I assume . . .'

'You assume what?'

'You are not telling me . . . Remember yesterday that she gave us the lamest evidence . . . According to her, she went out to follow her husband but mistook his silhouette and after following a stranger came back with nothing to show . . . And all this business of materials . . .'

'Exactly!'

'Exactly what?'

'I tell you that these marks on the menu prove that she isn't guilty, that not one of the women in the house is guilty, and it's for that reason that it isn't necessary to question the sad lady . . . That's what my wife and I call the teacher . . . You can take it that a woman bears her measurements sufficiently in mind and knows the sizes of materials well enough not to have to note them down . . . If, on the other hand, she entrusts a man to make a purchase of this kind, or if the man wants to give her a surprise . . .'

He indicated the back numbers of *La Mode du Jour* on the table.

'I bet,' he said, 'that we would find the pattern which delighted Mme Mosselet among them . . . They talked about it, she and her husband . . . The husband took notes with the idea of giving her a present . . . He rather needs to make himself pleasant to her, as we know it is she who has all the money, that's to say, the Anneau d'Or hotel . . . She took him because a man was needed about the house . . . Also perhaps because Mme Mosselet, late in life, had a vague yearning . . . But he had to be watched carefully . . . He was spied on . . . He turns up here at the home of a woman from the same village without suspecting that Mlle Otard has taken in a waif who used to live at Villecomtois . . .'

It was still raining . . . The transparent drops coursed down the windows. Now and then, a black oilskin went by on the pavement, hugging the wall.

'It's none of my business, is it?' Maigret went on. 'But the kids last night didn't always have something good to say about our Jeanne. She was a bad lot. She was embittered by her

176

misfortunes, and vicious. She hated the men that she held responsible for her downfall and she managed to make them pay for it . . . Because she was one of the few regulars at the dance-hall who was prepared to finish the night outside . . . The grogs end up making you sleepy, but not so much as it seems . . .'

The other man was embarrassed by his morning's attitude, his lewd, condescending smile when Maigret had come in.

'You can see the rest for yourself . . . You can see that Jeanne, back there, was the mistress of our good-for-nothing Mosselet . . . You can see that he is the father of the kid and that he has given the Fénard girl more trouble than notes of a thousand or even a hundred francs . . . Suddenly, she saw him turn up here with a wife loaded with money and as full of jealousy as a tigress . . . What does she do?'

'She blackmails him,' sighed reluctantly the Superintendent of Police.

And Maigret lit a new pipe, his third, and growled:

'It's no more difficult than that . . . She blackmailed him and since it wasn't his love he feared for but his daily bread . . .'

All the same, he opened the dining-room door and found everybody in their place, still the same as at the dentist's.

'You! In here!' he said in a different voice to Jules Mosselet, who was rolling a cigarette.

'But . . .'

'Get on with it!'

Then, to the Inspector, who was one metre eighty-five tall:

'You also . . . Come in . . .'

Finally, he looked at the Superintendent as if to say:

'With these characters, you know . . .'

Mosselet had less swank about him than in the morning, he was on the verge of lifting up his arms in anticipation of parrying the blows.

Maigret did not want to get himself involved. The women on the other side of the door shuddered as they heard the shouts, the vehement protestations, then the strange bumps.

Maigret, he looked out of the window. He thought that the boat for Newhaven might depart at two o'clock.

Then, by a strange chain of reasoning, thought to himself

that one day he would have to go and see what Villecomtois was like.

When someone touched his shoulder, he did not even look round.

'Is that it?' he asked.

'He has admitted it . . .'

And he was forced to remain a bit longer turned towards the window so as not to let the Superintendent of Police see his smile.

In some cases, it's better not to appear too . . .

# 6

# *JACQUES DECREST*
## *The Amethyst Fly*

'Hello? . . . M. Durand, of the *Echo de France*? . . . Will you take the call?'

'Yes, yes.'

There was the click of the switchboard, then the voice of a woman.

'Superintendent Gilles?'

'Yes.'

'Hold the line please.'

Gilles passed the receiver from his right hand to his left, opened the drawer in the desk to take out a cigarette.

'Hello? Hello, old man. What are you up to?'

The voice of Marcel Durand was terse, urgent.

'Nothing,' replied Gilles.

'We could meet for a drink?'

. 'Why not?'

'What time is it? . . . Five to five. Shall we say quarter past, at the Paix?'

'All right.'

'See you in a minute.'

Gilles lit his cigarette and inhaled.

It was nearly night already in his little office in the Quai des Orfèvres. He looked out of the window at the grey sky, heavy with rain, and the short stretch of the Seine which he could glimpse. It was higher than the day before.

If it goes on like this . . .

Grumbling to himself, he wrapped his woollen scarf round his neck and turned up the collar of his overcoat.

Superintendent Gilles detested the cold and rain which forced him to go around bundled up in a greatcoat. He felt himself only in the summer, when he did not have to bother even with a waistcoat. But what else could he do until man learnt to build his towns on movable platforms which could be taken to the South of France or returned to the North according to the seasons?

Luckily a bus was passing. He jumped on board. At the Opéra, he had only to cross the square to reach the Café de la Paix.

Durand raised his arm from the corner of the first *salle*. Well, well . . .

A young woman was sitting next to the journalist. A brunette, with a dark complexion under a bright hat, despite the bad weather.

'How are you, old chap? Sit down.'

Gilles took a chair opposite them and ordered tea and a brioche.

'What's the latest? Have you found your Chinaman yet?'

'No, that's still dragging on . . .'

'Do you know this young lady?'

She smiled. Her serious eyes slanted up slightly towards her narrow temples. How old was she? Twenty-five, perhaps?

'You could introduce me.'

'I've already told Irène Kiroff of you. She knows all about you. As a rule, she doesn't like the police. But she knows you aren't like the rest.'

Gilles smiled.

'That's a start anyway.'

'Isn't it? Better still, she has a Chinese boyfriend.'

'Well, hardly. You see, he isn't . . .'

Her sing-song voice was slightly muffled.

'Hush. I know what I'm talking about. Irène has been at the *Echo* for three months. She knocks up something or other for the women's page. That's not important. But she does know a Chinaman.'

This time the young woman started to laugh, and she seemed much younger. No more than twenty.

'Earlier on, she told me a most unusual story. That crime on the Rue Le Marois, you are all out of your depth over it at the P.J., aren't you? I think what she told me might help you.'

'Anything might help.'

Gilles looked at Irène Kiroff, whose face had become grave

again. She looked older when her mouth was set in its natural contours which no longer revealed any sign of the smile.

'Okay. Tell it to the Superintendent, Irène.'

'I'm listening to you, mademoiselle.'

'It all started with an insertion in the *Eclaireur de Nice*. Two lines advertising for a secretary. I saw it after lunch in the lounge of the small hotel on the Boulevard Carabacel where I was eking out an existence. My mother and I had left Russia with very little money and a few pieces of jewellery. We had enough money for about fifteen months, and the jewellery meant that my mother didn't have to go without anything during her last illness . . . You must excuse me . . .'

Gilles poured himself a second cup of tea.

'Not at all, mademoiselle. Please carry on.'

'Very well. I wanted you to understand . . .'

'Of course.'

'Finally, I had to look for a job. There was a telephone number with the advert so, without saying anything to the two friends who were with me, I crossed the hall and called it. You can't afford to lose any time when you answer adverts in the paper. It was a woman who picked up the receiver and she told me to come along the next morning. I was a bit anxious. A secretary of what, for whom? Anyway, at ten o'clock the following morning I was ringing the bell at the address I had been given. It was an apartment block, of course. In a large, new block next door to the Impérial. Do you know Nice at all?'

'Yes, mademoiselle. Boulevard du Tsaréwitch, isn't it?'

'That's right. The door was opened by a maid. I was told to wait for a moment in the sort of drawing-room you find in that area. Quite tasteless, but not gloomy because it was light and there was an enormous bunch of carnations in a crystal vase. I could hear children running around and laughing in the next room. After a couple of minutes, I saw the door slowly open and a man whose face took my breath away came in silently. A pair of round glasses with completely opaque black lenses hid his eyes; his hair was stuck down flat on his head; his mouth, which was weak, hung open, and his lips looked as if they were grey against the colour of his skin. He took a couple of faltering steps before feeling the back of an armchair and sitting down. 'Are you here, mademoiselle?' He spoke straight in front of him. His voice was flat and accentless, scarcely human. I hadn't moved, I was struck with fear and at the same time I was ashamed of my fear. Somehow I managed to murmur: "Yes, monsieur." He immediately turned his face in the direction of my voice. "An accident has deprived me of my sight," he explained, "that is why I need someone to be on hand." My work would not be demanding. Either I would accompany him in the afternoon to Monte Carlo or I would work on his collection of writings on roulette. I would always have the mornings to myself. The terms were nothing out of the ordinary but they would be of great help to me. I was not able to take my eyes off this man who could not see me. In the next room, the children had grown quiet or perhaps they had gone out. The man spoke with extreme deliberation but not hesitantly, his hands crossed on his knees, and his back was as straight as the sitting men you see in Chinese paintings.'

'How old was he?' interrupted Gilles brusquely.

'How can you tell? He certainly wasn't young. Forty, perhaps. I've hardly known any Orientals. I've no points of comparison.'

'Naturally.'

'Besides, I wasn't thinking about it, I was scarcely paying any attention. I was afraid. And I wanted to laugh. Secretary to a blind Chinaman! I would have given anything to turn it down. But I knew I would accept.'

'Yes,' said Gilles more gently.

Irène Kiroff leant her elbows on the yellow top of the table and, holding her hands together, cradled her chin on her thumbs. A caporal cigarette smouldered between her fingers, and the smoke formed a little cloud around her forehead. How had that devil Marcel Durand—who loved only his work, his little car, and baccarat—made friends with her?

'Sure enough, I accepted it,' she continued, 'and M. Ouang —I saw his name at the bottom of the stairs on the letter-box —asked me if I was able to start work that day. I had calmed down. For some reason, my confidence had suddenly returned and I promised to come back at half-past one. He got up and bowed his head to thank me, apologizing for not being able to have me seen to the door. "The chamber-maid has gone out with the children," he told me. He took a step forwards and knocked against the table. I offered to help him across the room but he stopped me by his gesture. "Don't trouble yourself," he said coldly, "I know where I'm going." As he didn't make any further move, I saw myself out.'

'He didn't tell you how long he'd been blind?' asked Gilles.

'No, I never found out.'

The young woman kept her eyes half-closed. Her cigarette, nearly finished, was close to burning her fingers.

'Go on, my dear,' coaxed Marcel Durand.

She looked at him and pulled over a green earthenware ashtray.

'Yes. But I don't know what to say now. Earlier on, I spoke to you spontaneously. I didn't have to think about it. Now I must search for the right words . . .'

Durand shrugged his shoulders.

'For God's sake don't try to do that. Women always have this habit. I can't remember what you told me earlier either, but something clicked since I immediately thought of the Chinese woman at Auteuil and telephoned Gilles. It was a reflex, but reflexes don't happen on their own.'

Irène Kiroff began to smile again.

'I think what struck you most were the sensations that I always felt in the presence of the Chinaman. That is what I tried to communicate to you in some way. I can't quite put my finger on anything he said or did. It's not something that can be put into words. But there was a sense of mystery about this man.'

She looked to Gilles and smoked more energetically.

'It was not because he was Chinese or because of his infirmity. His behaviour towards me was always perfectly correct and he was scrupulously polite. Sometimes we played all evening at Monte Carlo. He would sit beside me, a little further back, and ask me to describe the people around the table and tell me the bets I should place. For a long time I tried to figure out the system he followed, for he never explained it to me. Sometimes we won, sometimes we lost. He never showed any pleasure or displeasure. The sums he staked were never large, a couple of thousand old francs maximum.'

'Did he ever speak to anyone?'

183

'No. The croupiers knew us, but we changed table nearly every day. We usually left the casino between half-past six and seven o'clock. Sometimes we stayed later. On those days, Ouang would apologize and offer me some sandwiches at the bar. In the train, he talked to me respectfully but asked questions which made me wonder if he was altogether there. He would ask, for example, "How many bridges are there across the Seine in Paris?" or "What was the order of succession of the Kings of France?" If he hadn't paid so much attention or been quite so serious, I would have thought that he was making fun of me. He didn't seem to know much about Europe; perhaps he just wanted to gather some more knowledge. Once or twice I caught sight of the children who ran off down the corridors like cats as soon as they saw me. They were real Chinese dolls with their wax yellow faces and their slanting eyes which looked like marks left by a knife on the skin of an orange. The apartment didn't have the atmosphere of a woman about it except for the nurse . . . What did he do, this man? What did he want, with his stupid questions and his incompetent gambling. Not a word or gesture ever escaped him which didn't seem to me to be rehearsed.'

Durand, who had listened without saying a word, rested his finger against Irène Kiroff's wrist.

'Can I interrupt you for a second, Irène? . . . Have you seen the body, Gilles?'

'Yes.'

'A single stab wound?'

'Yes.'

'Death instantaneous?'

'Instantaneous. Doctor Pierre was quite positive after the autopsy. Besides, there was no sign of a struggle. Not that she had much chance of putting up a fight. Everything was in order on the tray of paraphernalia. She was still holding the needle with the ball of half-cooked opium in her hand.'

'Yes, that's what I was told. You can go on, my dear.'

The young woman shook her head.

'But I've nothing else to say! It went on like that for nearly ten weeks. And for ten weeks I lived in fear; a deep, irrational fear which nothing can explain. Right up until the day I fell ill. It was only a cold, a couple of hours in bed would have cured it. But it

184

was as if I'd been waiting for some excuse to be able to finish work. With the very first fluctuations of my pulse, the very first feeling of weakness in my legs, I wrote to Ouang that I was ill and that he should look for another secretary. That was the end.'

Gilles remained silent for a moment.

'And you haven't seen him since?'

'Yes.'

Irène Kiroff pulled her fur coat more tightly about her as if she had just shivered.

'When?'

'Yesterday.'

'In Paris?'

'Yes. Behind the church of Saint Thomas Aquinas. I recognized his slightly dumpy silhouette and the nape of his neck. A young woman was accompanying him. It was so peculiar, it gave me quite a shock. I immediately thought that I had been like this young woman, that I had *been* this young woman walking beside him.'

'You're certain it was Ouang?'

'Absolutely. I followed them for two or three minutes, then I quickened my pace to pass them. After a couple of yards I looked over my shoulder. But they had disappeared.'

'How?'

Irène Kiroff gave a little nervous laugh.

'Oh! There's no mystery about it. They had certainly gone into the big hotel on the corner of the Rue du Bac. Do you know it?'

'Yes, I know it.'

'It was the only door opening on to the street between us.'

Durand abruptly called the waiter.

'I'm stupid.'

'Why?'

'I've been wasting your time for the last hour. I don't know why, but this afternoon, when Irène told me this story, a phrase of hers stuck in my head, and all the pieces of the picture seemed to fit together. That's why I called you. She didn't use this expression when she told you about it, and I can't remember it now.'

Gilles looked at him.

185

'Are you sure?'

Durand counted his change. The sounds which regulated the traffic on the Place de l'Opéra came into the café as the revolving doors turned round.

'When shall I see you?'

'Telephone me.'

Durand stood up.

'I must get back to the rag. Are you coming, Irène?'

'No, no. I'm going home. Tomorrow's page is all set up.'

Irène Kiroff started to pull on her gloves.

'Where do you live, mademoiselle?' asked Gilles.

'Rue de Varenne.'

'May I come with you part of the way?'

'If you like.'

Durand left them outside.

The rain had stopped. A kind of icy fog muffled the lights and the noise. It was like walking in a different world, a world compact and empty at the same time, that the crowd thronging the boulevards did not manage to populate.

When she stood up, Irène was tall, almost as tall as Gilles.

'It's like being under a bell,' she murmured.

Had he heard her?

Instead of replying, he asked:

'Are you in a hurry?'

'No.'

He flagged down a taxi which was crawling along the kerb.

'Come with me.'

'When did he check out?'

'Yesterday evening, monsieur.'

'Was he on his own here?'

'He had his man-servant with him, monsieur. His secretary only came in the afternoons.'

'Do you know her name?'

'Yes, monsieur. I sent her name up every day: Mademoiselle Martin.'

Gilles smiled.

'Excellent. And her address?'

'I have no idea, monsieur. Perhaps the telephone reception-ist will have her number.'

186

'Would you inquire for me, please. You can send the reply to the bar. Are you coming, mademoiselle?'

Irène Kiroff did not reply but followed Gilles across the hall. She walked with a supple step but a little awkwardly.

'A whisky to chase out the fog?'

'Yes.'

She had hardly said anything in the car, not even to ask Gilles where he was driving her. He felt that she would stay with him until he himself left her.

The bar glowed mahogany and copper.

'Red Label?'

She nodded.

The barman looked South American. Gilles suddenly felt better, at his ease, because of the warmth.

He didn't wait for the drinks to be served.

'What are you afraid of?'

She stared at him intently for a second.

'You're right . . . I am afraid, but I didn't know it.'

'For heaven's sake . . .'

'How do you know?'

He offered her an open packet of cigarettes.

'Sorry. I only smoke Boyards.'

'That's all right.'

She took one of the fat cigarettes wrapped in maize paper and lit it.

'How do you know?' she repeated.

'Because you didn't tell me everything.'

She continued to look at him without flinching.

'It's all the same to me, you know,' he went on. 'Your Ouang can't be implicated in that business on the Rue Le Marois. Durand immediately understood that the crime couldn't have been committed by a blind man. As it is, it's difficult enough to kill someone even when you can see them clearly.'

'Then why? . . .'

'Why have I brought you here?'

'Yes.'

'To reassure you.'

A page-boy came in, studied the two Americans who drank without saying anything on the other side of the bar, and came towards Gilles.

187

'Excuse me, are you the gentleman who . . .'

'Yes.'

'The telephonist says that M. Ouang made very few calls, and that he hasn't any numbers noted down.'

'Very well. Thank you.'

Irène Kiroff drank three-quarters of her whisky in one go.

'Well then?' she said after a moment's silence.

'Nothing. You can go and eat your dinner peacefully and dream of the fashion page in the next *Echo de France*. As for me, I shall go back to work.'

'Which is?'

'I shall tell you that tomorrow.'

'Yes?'

'Yes. Shall we say seven o'clock here? It is not far from where you live.'

You could hardly make out the flow of the water under the cover of the fog.

Gilles went up to the parapet, saw the ash-grey trees on the bank rising up out of the flood. You could hardly see more than ten yards in front of you. He moved forwards in the yellow swirl. The night had turned yellow all around him.

If it rains again tomorrow . . .

He remembered the inundations of 1910, people crossing the Cour de Rome by boat. Tomorrow . . .

Under his heavy overcoat, he felt the Browning in his jacket pocket.

'They are dangerous, these sorts of animal.'

Why had he decided to walk to the Rue Le Marois? The Quai de Passy was never-ending, and he still had the length of the Avenue de Versailles to go . . . He was hardly thinking. He did not know what he would find or what he would say. The first thing was not to get on edge. Long walks at night relax your nerves. He had set off from the Place de l'Alma after dinner. 'I'll walk it off . . .' And then, he had not stopped since.

A strange woman, this Irène Kiroff with her washed-out eyes under her bright hat. What was she afraid of? What did she know? He only hoped that the Chinese students would still be living in the Rue Le Marois. They were as slippery as eels . . . Gilles remembered the first time he had gone there, the day

188

after the crime. They had been subdued, polite even. Yes, they had known Yama by sight, she lived in the same block, off the second courtyard. But they had never spoken to her. Had she been living with an Occidental? They swore they didn't know. Gilles had been certain that they were lying, that they knew all about Yama. But how do you get anything out of these people if they don't want to tell you? Nor had they heard or noticed anything unusual on the night of the crime. She had been found stretched out on her Cambodian mattress, stabbed through the heart, alone. There was no doubt that she had been smoking that night on her own. When the man with whom she lived had come in at dawn, the little lamp was blackened and had gone out through lack of oil. A large amethyst 'fly' was still balanced across the top of the glass of the lamp to shade the eye from the feeble flame. Everything had been left exactly as it was. They knew only what they'd read in the papers. Nothing else. Four students who shared a cheap but clean two-room flat so that it worked out even cheaper. Gilles was too familiar with the smell of cold opium not to have recognized it as soon as he came in. These four boys smoke, of course . . .

Gilles looked at the time on his wrist-watch. Eleven-thirty. There was a good chance he would find them around the salver . . . What would he say to them? There had been no fresh developments since he saw them last. Not the shadow of a lead. No footprints. The dagger still hadn't been found. The concierge hadn't noticed anything. But what could she have seen anyway, shuttered up in her lodge at two o'clock in the morning in a building which shelters a hundred and twenty tenants?

Why was Gilles so passionately pursuing this business which had made the headlines for a day or two before it had been quietly dropped a month ago? He couldn't explain it to himself. Perhaps it was something to do with the expression on the face of the corpse, a sad smile of resignation which he had seen once before on an ivory Kouanninh statuette in the collection of his friend Daniel d'Aulne. Perhaps because the total absence of any clues presented him with an absolute mystery . . . Superintendent Gilles liked the absolute, and he did not meet it very often in his work. But why Irène Kiroff . . .

A brusque screeching of brakes made him raise his head. The arches of the viaduct on the Boulevard Exelmans were

189

clearly outlined against the yellow swirl of the night by the lights of the café fronts and the neon sign of a neighbouring cinema.

Figures were running in front of him, forming a group in the middle of the road. There were shouts, explanations and swearing.

Gilles wanted to go on.

'Another one of them Chinks!'

He came closer.

The man was already being carried to the police station in the Rue Chardon-Lagache.

Some policemen dispersed the curious so that the taxi could manoeuvre enough to draw up alongside the pavement. On the ground, almost under the front wheel, there was a small dark stain. Gilles bent down and examined the greasy surface. Two yards away, he picked up the broken fragments of a pair of dark glasses.

At a quarter-past seven, Gilles ordered another whisky.

He was not impatient. He knew she would come. The same two Americans from the day before were drinking cocktails in the same corner without saying anything. It was as if they hadn't left, as if they lived there.

At twenty-past seven, the bright hat appeared above the curtains of the glass door.

Irène Kiroff was wearing the same coat, with a different scarf.

'Hello.'

Gilles held her delicate hand for a moment in his.

'I hope you haven't been dreaming of Chinamen.'

She smiled sadly.

'No.'

'You could have done. I found your M. Ouang last night at ten to twelve.'

The colour of her eyes changed a little.

'Where was that?'

'In the police station on the Rue Chardon-Lagache. Whisky?'

'Whisky.'

She was keeping quiet.

'What else do you know?' asked Gilles gently.

'Nothing.'

'He died at two o'clock in the morning. A taxi had knocked him over on the corner of the Avenue de Versailles and the Boulevard Exelmans. He never spoke to you about his wife?'

'No.'

Irène Kiroff smoked in the same way as the day before, supporting her chin on her hands.

'Not him,' she murmured.

And she saw two children's faces, two little dolls with level fringes in the sunlight.

'. . . But their nurse did. I only know that the mother was supposed to have gone off with a European, and that she lived somewhere in France.'

'Why didn't you tell me that before?'

She opened her eyes without moving.

'I couldn't bear to . . .'

'Inform against a man?'

'Yes.'

'That's good.'

A smile crept across Irène Kiroff's face.

'How did you guess?'

'The man who carried off Yama used to run a secret gambling den in Shanghai. I had learnt that he was up to the same trick here in France. When you spoke to me of Monte Carlo and gaming . . .'

'It wasn't very precise.'

'Certainly. Simple association of ideas. But there was something else . . .'

'What?'

This time Gilles did not reply.

'Did he make a confession before he died?'

'No.'

'He never regained consciousness?'

'Only for a moment.'

'Well . . . you don't have any proof?'

'Yes. I have two proofs. A fly . . .'

'What?'

Gilles pulled a small, brilliant object from his pocket and held it out to her.

'So that the light doesn't hurt their eyes, opium smokers

often hang a carving in some semi-precious stone on the glas
of the small lamps they use. These screens often take the form
of enormous insects. They call them "flies". If you look, you'll
see this one is made of amethyst. Last night, at the police
station, I was on my own with Ouang before the doctor arrived.
This was in his pocket.'

Irène turned the trinket over in her hand.

'And so?'

'The day after the crime, I saw it on the tray of smoker's
paraphernalia that Yama kept. It is very rare in Europe to find
such a beautiful example of craftsmanship. I suppose Ouang
had returned for it yesterday evening. He must have decided to
leave France, he had nothing else to do here. Your meeting
with him might have decided the matter if he was afraid that
you would betray his incognito.'

'But . . .'

'I don't know how much importance he attached to this
keepsake,' Gilles continued without pausing. 'As three o'clock
struck last night, the four young Chinese students who lived in
the same block as Yama paid me a visit. I had always suspected
that they knew the truth. When they learnt of the accident they
didn't deny that Ouang had come to see them in the evening.'

Gilles was quiet for a moment while he played with his
lighter and relit his cigarette which had gone out.

'Have no remorse, Mademoiselle Kiroff. I shall keep this
little discovery to myself. I shall do nothing to damage Ouang's
reputation. I think, besides, that his idea of honour has little in
common with ours . . . He was killed by a careless driver in the
fog.'

'Was he on his own? He can't have been walking about like
that, he hardly knows the quarter.'

'I told you that I had two proofs. Here is the second: Ouang
was alone *because he wasn't blind*. I was nearly certain of that
already because of something you had told me.'

'Me?'

'Yes. You told me that the first time you went to his house, he
knocked himself on a table. A blind man doesn't usually bump
into the furniture in his own apartment. I immediately suspected that he had done it on purpose, to prove to you that he
really couldn't see. It was a small mistake . . . Last night, when

ıe regained consciousness, he forgot that he was blind. When ıe opened his eyes, he looked around him like a man rediscovering the outside world. Just for a moment. Then he closed his eyes and died without opening them again.'

The young woman's hands trembled slightly.

'I am sure that it was this which made you frightened when you were alone with him, which gave you this mysterious sensation which you couldn't explain. He could see.'

As Irène Kiroff remained silent, Gilles added:

'I hope you won't mind if I ask you to keep this amethyst fly. It will bring to mind a singular period of your life. And it belonged to a man who loved a woman enough to kill her. There are few today who would go right to the bitter end of love.'

# 7

# *PIERRE VÉRY*

## *Watch the Red Balloons*

'Bertillon has nature in harness!' observed Prosper Lepicq, the barrister-detective, indicating to his host the moors covered in snow.

It was the beginning of January. A log fire gave out a feeling of well-being and security. On the occasion of the second wave of migration of woodcocks, Lepicq had come to spend a couple of days with his friend, M. Cousty, the mayor of a tiny hamlet lost on the edge of the army camp at Braconne. Maine-des-Amours, this hamlet was called. 'World's End' would have been a better name!

The two men, dressed for the shoot, were grabbing a generous bite to eat before going out to reconnoitre the scene of their impending exploits.

'No finer photograph than the snow,' said Lepicq, 'it registers everything: whether you were alone or if there were two of you; here, you ran, there, jumped; here, you came to a halt, and it tells for how long. If you were carrying a heavy load or if you disencumbered yourself of one, this gossip tells it. It reveals your weight and, should you take a fall, your build. In any case, the size of your footprint will suffice to betray your proportions. The snow divulges everything, the snow is the perfect informer!'

The Bohemian unraveller of enigmas had just reached this point in his discourse on detection when the dogs started to growl. The maid showed in a ridiculously bow-legged man, but one whose duties made him the terror of the local children playing truant from school: it was the rural policeman.

'What is it, old Célestin?'

'I've come, Your Honour,' stammered the old man, 'straight

from finding M. Beauregard murdered out on the moors. Begging your pardon, his throat had been slit like a pig's.'

They did, indeed, find the man dead on the snow. But, save for those of the rural policeman, there were no other footprints . . .
   Not even the footprints of the dead man.

Beauregard's house was a lonely, forlorn, tumble-down affair. The perpetually closed shutters gave it a blind aspect. Above the low roof floated an enormous balloon, tied to the main beam of the attic. The home of a crazy old Bogey Man or an alchemist escaped from some fantastic film . . .
   There was never a day that a boy did not come, furtively, to write on the walls in charcoal: 'M. Beauregard has the evil eye' – a joke which had come classic.
   'Little hooligan! Little rascal! I'll box your ears for you!' fumed the old man.
   The boy's father would immediately spring out, saying:
   'If you so much as lay a finger on my kid, I'll give you a kick in the pants, you old fool!'
   'You will, will you? I shall report you to the police! I shall have you dragged before the courts! There's such a thing as justice!'
   'If there was any justice, it would have shut you up long ago, you old trouble-maker!'
   Everyone at Maine-des-Amours detested the cantankerous old man. When Lepicq had met him two days before, Beauregard was returning from a long walk across the moors. He held, on the end of a string, three red balloons. His first words had been:
   'What's that, you're from Paris, *monsieur l'avocat*? Then it might interest you to know that I'm about to pursue an action in the City of Paris, where I own some apartment blocks!'
   He was bursting with pride and jubilation:
   'An action in the City of Paris, absolutely! . . .'
   A man had come along while this was going on. Beauregard had introduced them.
   'Doctor Vinson, Maître Lepicq, of the Paris bar.'
   'I came to give you your injection,' Vinson had said. 'But I'll call in again later. Are you feeling any better?'
   'Human nature will have to improve a good deal before my

health gets any better! And that won't happen tomorrow . . .' Beauregard had grumbled.

He had turned towards Lepicq: 'Everybody hates me! Everybody steals from me! It's a good thing the courts are there! I have four actions proceeding, one of which is against the council and another is against a journalist from Angoulême!'

Vinson smiled.

'You just cause yourself a lot of worry over nothing. You're rich, why bother . . .'

'And let myself be fleeced? No thank you! They'll find out that I'm no sheep!'

At this moment there was a loud bang: Beauregard was left holding only two balloons! The third had exploded, burst by a stone hurled by a boy with the help of a catapult.

'Little hooligan! Little rascal! I'll box your ears for you!'

The irascible old man dashed off in vain on the boy's heels.

Some little girls formed a circle and chanted caustically: 'M. Beauregard has the evil eye—the evil eye—the evil eye! . . . Voodoo! Voodoo! . . .' They mimed the casting of a spell.

Everyone laughed.

And now Beauregard, like a red and white snowman, was lying, his throat open, on the snow-covered moors.

On the completely white moors where, as far as the eye could see, there were no other footprints than those of the mayor, the policeman, Lepicq and Doctor Vinson.

'It looks as if he fell out of the sky!' said the mayor, stupid-ly.

Unconsciously, the rural policeman raised his eyes towards the clouds which the wind from the east was gently pushing in the direction of Coutras, towards the sea.

'It would be more usual to assume that he was murdered before the snow stopped falling!' commented Prosper Lepicq simply. 'The snow has covered his traces, as well as those of the murderer.'

Vinson stood up again after examining the body, brushing large patches of snow from his trousers.

'He hasn't been dead for more than two hours,' he declared.

It was now just after eight o'clock.

196

'What mischief was he up to out here at six o'clock in the morning?' grumbled the mayor.

Vinson had lit a Gauloise *bleue*. The mayor filled his pipe, then offered his packet of rough tobacco to the rural policeman, who rolled himself a thick, shapeless cigarette. The three of them stared across the flat open countryside.

Lepicq lit a cigar. He was looking at the body.

'Murder or suicide?' he mused out loud.

'Why should Beauregard want to kill himself,' answered the mayor. 'He was rich.'

The mayor was rich too, and felt no inclination towards self-destruction! He could imagine only with difficulty that after a certain age, and apart from certain incurable diseases which were very painful, there were any motives other than poverty capable of driving a human being to self-destruction (the despair caused by unrequited love being, thank God, the prerogative of youth).

'You looked after him, doctor. How was he?'

'Remarkably well. But his mind wasn't quite so good.'

'He was completely off his chump!' exclaimed the policeman bluntly.

Clearly, a sexagenarian who spent most of his time wandering about the countryside holding brightly coloured balloons on a string had set people talking . . .

'Now, now!' said the mayor. Then, to the barrister: 'You know, my dear maître, in the country you don't have to be very "original" before you're branded as being completely mad.'

'He was a right old hermit,' insisted the policeman, obstinately.

'What's your opinion, doctor?' asked the barrister.

'Persecution mania,' pronounced Vinson. 'Many a time he called me out on the flimsiest of pretexts or for no reason at all. He was agitated, saw nothing but threats in every snatch of conversation he overheard and, of course, thought it was all directed against him. He could read into the most harmless article in the paper some sly innuendo against himself, and get all worked up about it.'

A crow, wonderfully black against the snow, landed not far from the group.

The blast of a motor-horn frightened it away: a car appeared on the nearby road. The investigating magistrate from Angoulême, whom the mayor had telephoned, got out. The magistrate had set off at once. An inspector and two policemen accompanied him.

'It's simple enough,' the mayor concluded. 'If it was suicide we would inevitably have found the weapon. Unfortunately, we didn't find it, despite careful search of a large surrounding area. Hence—foul play . . .'

'Are there any suspects?' asked the magistrate. 'What's your guess as to the motive? Gain? Revenge?'

Gain and revenge were both equally plausible motives in the Beauregard case. As for suspects, you might as well say that there were as many as there were inhabitants of Maine-des-Amours: everybody hated the madman with his red balloons!

There was a long silence.

They were no longer four but eight now to study with perplexity the dismal moors, stretched out at the centre of which, like a terrifying riddle, was the old man with his throat cut.

While the magistrate questioned the neighbours, the inspector examined the house where the deceased had lived on his own, joylessly. Quickly impressed by Lepicq's 'truly Parisian' personality, and above all by his reputation as an unraveller of mysteries, the inspector had accepted warmly the barrister's offer to accompany him.

The house was furnished expensively, comfortably, cosily. Everything was arranged with meticulous care. Beauregard occupied by preference a sort of study, the walls of which were lined with books of forbidding appearance: scientific works without exception.

Surprise, surprise! One room was filled with children's balloons! Red, blue, yellow, green, pink, tied in clusters, their strings secured to the floor, they floated eighteen inches from the ceiling, agitated by the slightest draught. Like the vegetation of a dream, fantastic berries supported by incredibly supple stalks.

'The rural policeman was right,' said the inspector. 'He was a bit "deranged"!'

Lepicq did not reply. But he was of a different mind, having seen, in the library, a whole shelf of books dealing with meteorology.

*'You often saw him walking about the countryside holding a red balloon . . . Like a kid . . .'*

Why, of course! Beauregard was interested in atmospheric phenomena: he studied the currents, the force and the strength of winds, the variations of pressure.

Not long after, in Maine-des-Amours' unique auberge, Lepicq met up with Doctor Vinson again.

The latter was making his round of house-calls.

'To call it a "round" would be putting it a bit grandly,' said he, pointing at the innkeeper's son, busying himself blowing soap-bubbles. 'I came because of the kid, who was showing symptoms of a slight angina yesterday.'

'In such a climate,' said Lepicq, 'you wouldn't think that anybody would ever die!'

'People die here the same as everywhere else! Only . . .'

Lepicq noted a veiled bitterness in this 'only'.

'Only . . . they are never ill?' he finished.

'Never!' said Vinson.

They laughed. The proprietor came in to ask them what they would like to drink.

'I came to examine your little boy's throat,' said Vinson, rather dryly.

'Oh! It's not worth troubling yourself over, doctor,' replied the father with a furtive look of contrariety. 'It's cleared up! He got better on his own.'

'Delightful child!' groaned Vinson between his teeth.

He ordered some drinks.

'You see!' he said resentfully to Lepicq afterwards. 'Not only are they *never ill*, but if, by a thousand to one chance they are, *they get better on their own!*'

The barrister indicated the moors.

'It's amazing to think that Paris is only seven hours by train. You would think you were . . . on another planet!'

'That's exactly it, my dear Maître. I sometimes ask myself if Paris really exists.'

Through the open door they saw the magistrate and the inspector pass by, in deeply animated conversation with the mayor. This naturally brought their thoughts back to the Beauregard case once more.

'Personally, I don't believe in a crime,' said Lepicq. 'I am convinced that Beauregard killed himself. Consequently, I would like to ask you a question professionally, doctor. Beauregard, you told me, had a persecution complex. He was pursuaded that someone wanted to make an attempt on his life. In your opinion, could the species of reasoning I am about to put to you have sprung up in his unhealthy mind: "If I wait until my enemies strike, they are quite capable of making my murder look like suicide—so much so that I won't even be revenged! But if I kill myself, I can make my death look like a crime so that the police will accuse my enemies of my death." Could Beauregard have been capable of such a line of argument?'

Vinson turned it over in his mind.

'Perfectly plausible,' he declared at last. 'Absurd Machiavellian logic of this kind is exactly what you would expect from a paranoiac. Similar cases have been recorded in numerous studies. It's a classic case of persecuted-persecutor. All the same,' he qualified himself, 'I don't share your opinion: it seems to me that the suicide hypothesis can't be admitted. In reality, how could he dress up his suicide to make it look like murder?'

'Bah!' said Lepicq. 'The only clever move was to make the weapon he used disappear.'

'That goes without saying,' said Vinson. 'But how was he able to perform this incredible feat?'

'Easily enough!'

'Easily enough?' repeated the doctor in amazement.

The barrister smiled.

'That posed a pretty little problem: how could a man slit his throat with a razor and then make the razor disappear, so that it would look like a crime? Really, my good doctor, it's childish! Childish is the word! Look . . .'

He pointed to the innkeeper's son, who was making soap-bubbles.

'The balloons . . .'

'The balloons?' repeated Vinson.

'Why yes! . . . Beauregard fastened five or six balloons to the blade of the razor which he had, first of all, detached from the handle so as to obtain the least weight. Alone on the moors, certain of not being seen, he cut his throat. What happened next? The bloodstained razor slipped from his fingers . . . and flew off, carried away by the balloons! There you have the problem solved! . . .'

'It's the wildest fantasy, my dear maître.'

'Ha! The insane are great fantasists, my dear doctor! That explains why Beauregard didn't put a bullet in his head: the uplift of the balloons would have been insufficient to carry away the gun. The same remark applies to a dagger: it would have remained anchored to the ground. Whereas a thin razor blade . . .'

Vinson remained silent: he visualized a man stretched out on the moors with a dagger in his heart, and, tied to this dagger, some colourful balloons, bobbing gracefully according to the wind, above the corpse . . . The image of a bloodstained razor being conveyed into the air by a cluster of balloons was no less startling!

He protested:

'Beauregard would have known that the balloons, weighed down by humidity, at dusk, would fall to earth: that they would be discovered and that then . . .'

'Certainly! But he could also have hoped that they would burst in the heat at the middle of the day. Or that they got lost and were destroyed a long way off in the Braconne Forest . . . How should I know? And we shouldn't forget that he was mad.'

'It's an idea,' said Vinson at last. 'What do you intend to do?'

'The wind is blowing from the west, that is to say, from the same direction as this morning, towards Angoulême. If my theory isn't hare-brained, it isn't completely out of the question to hope to find our suicide's balloons, stuck in the branches, given that the weight of the razor would have prevented them from gaining very much height.'

'An outside chance at most!'

'But a chance all the same! For want of something better to do . . . I intend to set off on an expedition after lunch. If you would care to come along? . . .'

'Gladly.'

Lepicq emptied his glass.

'Not a word to the magistrate or the inspector. In the

case—which is only too likely—that I don't succeed, I will be made for all time ridiculous in their eyes ... But I intend to bring a hunting dog with me.'

'A hunting dog?'

Lepicq's only response was a smile.

At two o'clock in the afternoon, they met out on the moors, at the place where the corpse had been discovered. Lepicq was carrying a hat box.

'Here is my hunting dog!' he said, laughing.

The box contained a red balloon ...

'We could have let ourselves be guided by the smoke of our cigars, or have adopted Tom Thumb's method: throwing leaves of cigarette papers to the wind, and following them. But a balloon will be more practical.'

'A red balloon ... Tom Thumb ... This line of inquiry,' said Vinson, 'has something ... something ...'

'Childish about it?'

'No. Fairy-like.'

'It's the same thing,' said the barrister. 'Besides, I have my own style of conducting an investigation, it is well known!'

He released the balloon which was caught by the wind. Holding it by the end of a string some sixty feet long, they advanced, in this way, towards the forest.

They jumped over streams, skirted round thickets, and crossed fields lying fallow. From time to time, Lepicq pulled lightly on the line like an angler drawing the fish.

In the forest, it was necessary to shorten the line considerably, though it risked upsetting the experiment. Even then, the line became continually snagged. Nevertheless, the balloon continued to guide them.

'Look here,' said the doctor, just after they had made some more zigzags, 'this is ludicrous. We're not going to find anything!'

'Really?' replied Lepicq, in such a strange tone that the other, surprised, looked at him, then followed the direction of the barrister's gaze.

'Over there,' murmured Lepicq. 'You see them?'

On their right, forty yards away, four balloons were caught half-way up a young oak.

They approached on tiptoe, speaking in whispers—in the way you approach birds, fearful that the slightest noise will scare them away.

Hanging from the string binding the balloons together was a razor blade with a brown stain of dry blood on it.

'Bravo!' said Vinson. 'There is the proof that he committed suicide. It is a pity you didn't bring the magistrate and the inspector along!'

'I'm not a detective, I'm a lawyer,' replied Lepicq. 'I seek out murderers not to deliver them to justice but to make certain of their patronage! If I chance to discover them before the police—and that has happened more than once,' he slipped in maliciously, '—I endeavour to make them understand that their best interests lie in entrusting me with the commission for the care of their defence at the Assizes. The long and the short of it is that I am trying,' he concluded sarcastically, 'to cut the grass from under my colleagues' feet. I am, if you like, a salesman in crime! Times are hard: one recruits one's clientele where one can.'

The doctor laughed heartily.

'It's very clever! This time, unfortunately, all your troubles have been for nothing!'

'I think not!'

'How's that? After all, it was a suicide. You have proved it yourself!'

'I have never believed in Beauregard's suicide!' replied Lepicq pensively. Then he went on in a different tone: 'Come along, doctor,' he said, 'don't be a bad loser! You have fallen into the trap I laid for you. Beauregard was murdered. Murdered by you! . . .'

'Have you gone mad?' said Vinson, stepping backwards.

'These balloons provide the irrefutable proof of your guilt.'

'How's that?'

'For the simple reason that if Beauregard had committed suicide in the extravagant and childishly complicated manner that I outlined to you, *the balloons would not have come to grief here, but in the diametrically opposite direction.*'

'And why is that?'

'*Because this morning the wind wasn't blowing towards Angoulême but, contrary to what I told you, towards Coutras,*'

*towards the sea. It wasn't coming from the west but from the east.*
Consequently, it necessarily follows that the balloons were
brought here and hitched on the tree. By whom, if not by the
murderer anxious to give countenance to the suicide hypothesis? Now, you were the only person aware of my astounding
balloon theory. Hence you must be the murderer. In the dinner
hour, you came here with these four balloons and this old
handleless razor—following my suggestions to the letter! You
can see the little scratches you made on the trunk and on the
lower branches when you climbed the tree . . . While we were
walking, I watched your little game; you were leading me,
cautiously, without appearing to do so. And I am sure,' he
concluded, 'that, if you were made to take off your clothes, we
would find the trace of a puncture somewhere on your skin: the
mark left by the needle of the syringe with which you took your
own blood to stain the blade of the razor. Ah! Don't try the
rough stuff with me!' he exclaimed, hastily drawing his revolver
on Vinson who, recovering from his stupefaction and carried
away by anger, was preparing to knock him down.

'I am not your enemy,' said Lepicq mildly. 'Otherwise I would
have brought along the magistrate and the inspector.'

'That's all right!' murmured Vinson. 'I was tired of brooding
on my disappointed dreams, my dreams of being buried alive,
in this lost country.'

Vinson had been an intern for two years at a hospital in Paris.
An exceptional student, he seemed destined for a brilliant
career. Unfortunately, some foolish speculations of his father's
and, as a result, a passed-up chance of an advantageous
marriage had prevented him from sitting 'the prize exam'. The
need to start earning a living immediately had compelled him to
set up a less than modest practice in Maine-des-Amours with
no other prospect than of vegetating miserably until the end of
his days.

'I killed Beauregard to rob him. I knew he kept a large sum in
gold coins in his house—a fortune, in fact.'

'And you benefited from the numerous visits you paid him
while you were looking after him to try to find out where he hid
his treasure?'

'I found out yesterday.'

'But Beauregard immediately suspected you when he realized that he had been robbed?'

'Yes. This morning, at dawn, he telephoned me and said he had taken a turn for the worse. When I got to his house, he wasn't in. I surmised that he had telephoned only to get me out of my house long enough for him to have a look round on his own. (I live alone and my maid goes home to her husband.) Thus, he had every opportunity to discover the money-box I had stolen from him.'

'You rushed back home and met Beauregard on the moors?'

'He had found the box and taken it with him. You can imagine what happened. I knew it was all up: in a moment of panic . . .'

'What did you kill him with?'

'When I make house-calls, I always carry a scalpel in my medical kit . . .'

'I see.'

'Afterwards, I took to my heels. The snow was still falling and covered all the footprints.'

There was a long silence.

'To lay a trap like the one with the red balloons, you must have already suspected me?'

'Do you remember,' said the barrister, 'when I asked you if the idea of disguising a suicide as a murder could have occurred to someone suffering from persecution mania? It was your reply which aroused my suspicions. You willingly endorsed the suicide theory which suited you so well. You told me that it was frequently the case, and often cited in the studies. Now, I have read a great many studies of delusions, doctor, and I am on friendly terms with a good number of psychiatrists, and I know that this is not the ordinary course of events with this type of aberration. *As a general rule, paranoiacs do not kill themselves. On the contrary, they cling to life . . . to annoy their fellow-citizens for as long as possible!* From that moment, these were the questions which had to be answered: "Is Dr Vinson ignorant . . . or is he lying?" Now, I only needed a few minutes of conversation with you to judge that you were a very gifted man!'

'I could have made a career for myself . . . a brilliant career,' said Vinson with a bitter smile. 'I had the ability, the necessary courage to . . .'

'I'm sorry, doctor,' said Lepicq.

'What are you going to do?' asked the other man. 'Turn me in?'

'That is contrary to my principles. So that . . . So that I find myself in rather a difficult position,' admitted Lepicq, jiggling the revolver in the palm of his hand. 'You could give yourself up, for example. That would be best from every point of view. I would find it a joy to put my talents at the service of your head . . . Be that as it may, it is up to you to resolve the situation.'

On these words, with a singular look towards the red balloons, he walked away.

Some time later, when he was not far from Maine-des-Amours, he saw a red balloon scurry past, high in the sky, then another, then two more.

He immediately started to run as fast as he could towards the village to inform the magistrate and the inspector. Because this passage of balloons seemed to him to indicate, without any doubt, that Beauregard's murderer had found a means of resolving the situation. A solution which was lugubrious but radical.

An hour later, Lepicq, flanked by the mayor, the magistrate and the inspector, found the body of the doctor at the foot of the oak tree.

After writing a short note of confession, Vinson had cut his throat with the razor, so staining it with his blood for the second time.

# 8

## PIERRE VÉRY
### The Lady of the Museums

In Prosper Lepicq's imagination dangled the silhouette of the
wretch who had hung himself, swaying—one is tempted to say,
vulgarly!—under the hook of the light fixture in this commonplace dining-room.

This was taking place on the fourth floor of an ageing
apartment block, Rue Jean-Jacques-Rousseau, in Paris.

'And to think that this poor devil . . .' muttered Inspector
Camard, point vaguely towards the fireplace.

Then he walked across to the window that was being
violently lashed by the rain.

The barrister-detective remained motionless, right under
the hook of the light fixture. His broad forehead, the curiously
steady yellow pupils of his eyes, and his small, restless mouth
made one think of a bird of the night, at ease in the half-light.

'What was his name?'—he asked.

'Moulinet. Jules Moulinet. Damn it!'

The body had been found the day before (Sunday 26 June), at
seven o'clock in the morning, by a Mme Baudry, a likeable
widow, the neighbour of the deceased. Each morning, she
brought him the paper, made him a cup of coffee, and did a
little cleaning. According to the concierge, she entertained
hopes of marriage, because, for just over a year, Moulinet also
had been a widower.

'Oh, very good!' said Lepicq. 'I'm astonished too! The idea
of killing yourself when you have the luck to . . .'

'What luck?'

Lepicq indicated a photograph on the wall; the Inspector
laughed thickly, then went on with his account:

'When Mme Baudrey came in yesterday morning, she had to

switch on the lights as it was still dark. It was chucking it down outside, if you remember . . . At this point, she saw the body. A chair had been knocked over on the floor. The deceased was still wearing outdoor clothes, shoes, detachable collar, tie, and the bed had not been disturbed. Moulinet hadn't been to sleep that night.'

'What was the time of death?'

'About midnight, according to the police pathologist.'

'Any signs of a struggle?'

'None.'

The corpse exhibited no other bruises than those left by the rope around his neck. In the apartment, the disorder was only what one would expect to find in the home of a man living alone. There were no fingerprints besides those of Moulinet and Mme Baudry. As for the latter, nothing had been stolen.

However, there was one curious detail: a heap of ashes in the fireplace. Another curious detail: his right hand, which had been opened only with the greatest difficulty, was clenched round a five hundred franc note.

'These histories of people who hang themselves,' said the Inspector, 'you can't usually make head or tail of them . . . In a criminal case, the *mise en scène* is easy . . . And when the rope is as common as the one our man used in this case, it can be quite a job to find the stockist! Nonetheless,' he concluded conceitedly, 'found him I have! An ironmonger on the Rue Croix-des-Petits-Champs. He sold Moulinet a length of this type of rope early on Saturday afternoon.'

The rain, which the wind plastered against the window panes . . . This interior, so grey, so forlorn . . . Three rooms backing on to a courtyard: Furniture worse than poor, hideous: in modern bargain basement style, mass-produced . . . The wallpaper, equally 'modern' . . . And not a book, not a picture! . . . Just, on one wall, this photograph which had inspired the barrister to say: 'The idea of killing yourself when you have the luck to . . .'

*The luck!* . . . The luck of a Jules Moulinet! . . .

In Lepicq's imagination, the poor devil was still swaying, dressed in an off-the-peg suit of indifferent hue, shiny from the cuffs to the knees. In real life, Moulinet ought to have worn dubious shirts and luminous black ties. A stale, depressing odour seemed to emanate from the apartment, from the wallpaper, from each object: the smell of the widower! . . .

The jovial voice of the corpulent Camard:

'All the same, you've got to consider every angle, so we made inquiries about Mme Baudry . . . But she has an alibi: she spent the night at the bedside of a sick relative.

'Furthermore, it doesn't look as if Moulinet had any enemies. This was confirmed by the concierge, his neighbours, his colleagues and his superiors—for the last seven years he has been working on the securities counter of the Banque de France.

'Hence: suicide. But what was the motive for the suicide? By nature, Moulinet was mild-tempered and discreet, almost timid. His family are all dead. And he doesn't have a mistress. No vices (that we've heard of, but we always end up hearing about them). He was in good health. He had few wants and less ambition.

'What's left? . . . Neurasthenia? Tiredness of living alone?

'What intrigued us most was this five hundred franc note that was found between his fingers.'

Lepicq was holding the same note in his hand at that moment. The barrister felt a sensation which he couldn't put into words or dismiss from his mind. He would like to have been able to shout at Camard: 'Can't you shut up, there's a good chap? Just for a minute! So I can give it a bit of thought . . .'

Thought? All he could do was to turn over the words he had heard: 'The doctor established the time of death as around midnight. There was a pile of ashes in the fireplace . . . It was chucking it down outside.' He could see Moulinet burning his papers. From time to time, the widower would stop for a moment and go over to the window to cool his forehead against the glass and muse to himself, face to face with the rainy night. Then he would continue to burn his old papers.

'These papers, guess what they were?' exclaimed Camard. 'My dear fellow, they were bank-notes! Quite so . . . According to the report of the forensic laboratory that we received early yesterday afternoon, those papers consisted entirely of the most recent issue of five hundred franc notes. And the bally idiot had burnt a famous number of them.'

Lepicq gave a start.

'False?'

'That's what we said. Crime or suicide, his death could be accounted for if the notes were false. But not a bit of it! Chemical analysis of the unburnt fragments has clearly shown that they were genuine notes!'

If that was the case, Moulinet, who earned four thousand francs a month, had burnt a fortune by midnight. And after fulfilling this fantasy of a tycoon, he had brought his dull existence to a cheerless conclusion: a rope, a light fitting, and that, on a windy, wet midnight hour, under the eye of . . .

'This young woman? . . . The late Mrs Moulinet?'

'In person! She was called Gloria.'

He laughed heavily:

'Gloria Moulinet! . . . Comical, isn't it?'

She must have been extremely beautiful, this Gloria. A cold beauty, 'marmoreal', so to speak. But what perfection! What delicacy of feature! . . . What nobility in the perfect half-moon of her lips, in the straight line of her nose, in the sweep of her brow . . . The classical beauty of the Greeks. A mythological allure. Truly, a Diana . . . How had the pitiful Jules Moulinet won her . . . O unfathomable heart of woman! . . .

'And where did Moulinet obtain this fortune?' continued Camard relentlessly. 'The answer was child's play . . .'

'The Banque de France,' interrupted Lepicq. 'Stolen bank-notes.'

'The Banque de France, of course. At the end of Saturday morning, Moulinet, the ideal employee, appropriated four million francs of the bank's money in five hundred franc notes. Eight thousand notes . . . His colleagues remarked that he was carrying a parcel wrapped up in newspaper under his arm, but who would have thought . . .

'A woman is the cause of it, probably. As always . . . One day—one evening!—this devil Moulinet meets an attractive woman . . . He, the wrong side of forty; she, a right little tart. She enflames our humble, honest Moulinet who grows hot and loses his head. (A Moulinet is hardly difficult to enflame!) He steals four millions!

'But this was only a little man! . . .

'The same evening, his passion cools. Horrified, Moulinet

realizes what he's done, and that he will inevitably be found out, and that retribution does not tarry far behind discovery . . .

'So, there comes this stupid episode of burning the notes; the hook on the ceiling, the rope . . .

'*Cherchez la femme* . . . We've looked for her; we'll find her before long. In any event, it's an open and shut case!'

'Excellent!' said Lepicq. 'Only . . . there is one objection . . .'

'And what is that?'

'Why did Moulinet choose notes of five hundred francs when he could have stolen notes of ten thousand francs, five thousand francs, or even one thousand francs? Eight thousand notes don't exactly do up into an unobtrusive packet.'

'I suppose that he hadn't any choice.'

'Hmm! . . . Very well, let us admit that. But explain to me why he burnt only seven thousand, nine-hundred and ninety-nine notes?'

'Seven thousand, nine hundred and ninety-nine?'

'Why, yes, because this one makes the eight thousandth!'

The barrister produced the five hundred franc note which had been found between the fingers of the dead man.

'Oh! You're always splitting hairs,' replied Camard complacently, shrugging his shoulders.

Lepicq smiled:

'According to you, it was just before midnight that Moulinet decided to hang himself?'

'What of it?'

'In that case, *why did he buy at the beginning of the afternoon – that is to say, straight after committing the theft—the rope with which he would only decide to hang himself towards midnight?*'

'Oh, you know! . . .' said Camard with a gesture of indifference. 'In any event, you're bound to admit that it was suicide! I've told you all along that you wouln't find yourself a client in this case! Come on! I'll buy you a drink to console you.'

The barrister folded and unfolded the five hundred franc note.

'If it's all right with you, I would prefer to stay here a bit longer.'

'As you like! I'll wait for you downstairs, in the Chope.'

Lepicq was extremely intrigued. He thought to himself: 'It

can't be possible! Camard's explanation holds good . . . but why *ought* it to be false! I'm sure that it's wrong! A man who commits a theft and runs off *immediately* to buy the rope with which to hang himself! . . . It just won't do! Besides, if he regretted what he'd done, why make things worse by burning the notes instead of returning them?' The rain came on worse than ever, deepening the shadows in the room. The barrister-detective turned on the electric light. It shone squarely on the beautiful and serious face of Mme Moulinet. Lepicq sat lost in contemplation of the bank-note, the eight thousandth, that Moulinet hadn't burnt. Hadn't been able to bring himself to burn . . .

Camard was on his third aperitif when Lepicq rejoined him on the inside terrace of the bar. The barrister, squeezing a flat parcel under his overcoat, came in soaked.

'It's a mystery!' said the Inspector. 'But where have you been?'

'I have just been making a few inquiries amongst the local tradesmen. And I have become convinced that Moulinet had decided to kill himself *even before the time he committed the theft!*'

He took out the eight thousandth five hundred franc note.

'Has it ever struck you, my dear Camard, that no one ever *really* looks at bank-notes? I mean, as works of art. We only look at them to ascertain their value of exchange. Well, one day, Moulinet had the imprudence to examine a bank-note carefully: and he died of it!'

'Oh! First rate!' Camard burst out laughing. 'You really are a rum chap, you know . . .' The barrister got up. '. . . Now where are you off to?'

'Finish your drink. We're leaving.'

'Where are we going?'

'To M. Marc-Augustin Verrier's.'

'Who is that?'

'The man who designs the bank-notes on behalf of the Banque de France.'

In the taxi, Lepicq furnished the Inspector with some further details. His brief investigation had shown that Moulinet was possessed by an incredible aversion to the new issue of five hundred franc notes. In the local stores, when he paid for his purchases with a thousand franc note, he refused the new design of five hundred francs. He insisted on one of the old designs, or, in their absence, small change. Once, in a sudden fit of pique, he had been on the verge of ripping up one of the new notes when, coming to himself, he had given it to a beggar!

'Curious! . . .' said Camard. 'But, all the same, you're not going to pretend that Moulinet stole eight million francs for the sole pleasure of burning them!'

'For *the sole pleasure of burning them*, yes!' the barrister affirmed gravely.

'Because their ugliness offended his aesthetic standards?'

'Not at all! Moulinet didn't know the first thing about art, the poor devil! Hadn't the least interest in art! *It's for that reason above all that he's dead!*'

At Passy, in the private town-house of the painter and official draughtsman, Marc-Augustin Verrier, they found only a valet. The artist was accustomed to spending the end of the week (Saturday and Sunday) in his studio on the Rue de Tournon. There, in complete solitude, he worked. 'It's very nearly the only time Monsieur does work, as well!' The rest of the time, Verrier received calls, or rendered them himself: he was very worldly.

Lepicq showed the valet a photograph of Moulinet: hadn't M. Verrier received a visit from this individual recently?

'Yes, monsieur. I remember him clearly. This character called about two weeks ago. The meeting was bizarre: you wouldn't believe it, but he didn't say a word!'

'Not a word?'

'Absolutely nothing! He stared fixedly at M. Verrier. He would have liked to speak to him, but no sound came out. He was almost trembling. The excitement, surely . . . The fact that he was in the presence of such a famous artist! At last, he withdrew. Escaped, more like it! He was very comical!'

'Comical! . . .' repeated the barrister-detective, pensively.

Twenty minutes later, Camard and Lepicq rang the door-bell of the studio on the Rue de Tournon. There was no answer.

'Marc-Augustin Verrier is dead, I fear!' said the barrister-detective, much to Camard's astonishment.

It was necessary to summon the services of a locksmith. And, in fact, the official draughtsman of the Banque de France was discovered with his head slumped across his drawing board, a bullet hole in his left temple. He couldn't have heard his murderer enter the room: death had struck him in the middle of his work. The blood flowing from his temple had left a large stain on his papers, and half-covered a project for a new bank-note.

'I admire your flair ... but I don't understand it!' said Camard.

'The explanation is here,' said Lepicq, handing him the eight thousandth five hundred franc note.

The Inspector bent over the note, he held it up to his eyes, then he held it out at arms' length. First, he scrutinized, in the bottom left-hand corner, the credit: *Marc-Augustin Verrier (delineavit)*, then, in the bottom right-hand corner, the name of the engraver: *L. Barthelemy, sc*; next, the signature of the chief cashier, and that of the secretary-general; then, the serial number, the text of the statute deterring counterfeiters and forgers, and, finally, the designs: on the left, a blacksmith resting his hammer on an anvil; on the right, standing up, a thick-set woman carrying a platter of fruits—quinces, or something like them. Between these two figures there was a white circle. On the reverse, two young children engaged in the harvest and looking after animals. Between them, the same white circle.

'I still don't understand!'

Lepicq had a melancholy smile.

'In a man's heart, there is always a woman,' he said. 'If she is not alive, she is dead ... "*Cherchez la femme,*" you said. You were right ... But you didn't search for her in the right place! ...'

He held the bank-note in the light, *and Camard, in the white circle, perceived, in the watermark, a woman's head, very beautiful, a cold beauty, 'marmoreal'. Her lips formed a perfect half-moon. A straight nose. A high forehead. The classical beauty of the Greeks ... A mythological allure ... Truly, a Diana ...*

'Gloria Moulinet!'

Lepicq opened the flat packet he carried beneath his overcoat: it was the photograph of Mme Moulinet which he had taken from the apartment in the Rue Servandoni.

'Well I never!' stammered Camard. 'If I go by that, Gloria Moulinet cheated her husband with Marc-Augustin Verrier! . . .

'From the minute Moulinet, out of curiosity, looked through the transparency of a bank-note and made this discovery, he can never have known another minute's peace of mind. The collapse of his illusions . . . All his fervour for them destroyed in a second . . . The dead woman he adored, whom he had never wished to replace in his heart, was only a woman like all the others! . . .

'From there came his change of attitude, his strange behaviour, his eccentricities: he can't bear the sight of these bank-notes which remind him of the time when his wife posed, with bare shoulders, in front of her lover! He refuses these notes! A beggar passes: he throws him one of these notes! Then, carried away by his hate, the timid employee goes to ring the bell at Marc-Augustin Verrier's door. But in the artist's presence (such a famous man!) his courage deserts him, he stays speechless, he runs away, ashamed, distraught . . .

'Strange tormented soul: when Moulinet sees one of these five hundred franc notes between a man's fingers, a rage possesses him. He is the same in every way as someone who has seen, in the hands of a stranger, the photograph of a cherished woman! Photographs: that's the word! . . . For Moulinet, these are no longer bank-notes, but photographs! And each one cruelly reminds him of his misfortune . . . It is then that he gives in to his worst extravagances: he steals some bundles of notes! To burn them! . . . Finally, there was nothing more for him to do except hang himself. But not before having killed the other . . .'

'And to think,' sighed Lepicq, 'that Moulinet was mistaken! There had never been anything between his wife and Marc-Augustin Verrier!'

'What? . . . But, damn it all! This portrait . . . You think it's a simple friendship, a Platonic friendship . . .'

'Not even that!'

'A chance meeting, then?'

215

'Gloria Moulinet and Verrier certainly never met each other!'

'Well, something is needed . . . At least . . . What about this, then. A photograph, that Mme Moulinet had lost . . . Verrier found it, and . . . No, no: it's ridiculous!'

'Ridiculous, indeed!' repeated the barrister-detective placidly. 'Verrier hadn't any need to meet Mme Moulinet, nor to possess a photograph of her.'

'I've got it!' interrupted Camard. 'A model bearing an astonishing resemblance to . . .'

'. . . To Gloria Moulinet. That's it. More precisely, it is Gloria who resembled the model. And it doesn't happen to be a living model! And it doesn't happen to be a particular model! But thousands of models! Come on, my dear chap, think it over! . . . Gloria Moulinet's beauty, undeniable certainly, was not original at all! On the contrary, it was classical! Classical to the point of becoming impersonal! The beauty of the Greeks . . . A Diana . . . And so, aren't the art text-books and the museums full of similar examples of Greek or Roman beauty? The goddesses, the Dianas, the Venuses, the Junos are legion. If the unfortunate Moulinet so much as once visited a museum, he would have recognized his wife nearly everywhere, on canvas, in marble, in alabaster! . . .'

'But Marc-Augustin Verrier . . .'

'This type of classical beauty was precisely what Marc-Augustin Verrier, by instinct, tried to reproduce. An artist neither by talent nor by temperament, but an "official" artist, an academic, just good enough to copy the ancient masters! The funniest thing—or the saddest,' concluded Lepicq comically, 'is that the Musée du Louvre is situated only a couple of hundred yards from where Jules Moulinet lived . . . and Moulinet never went there!'

# 9

# JYPÉ CARRAUD

## For Piano and Vocal Accompaniment

### 1. INTRODUCTIONS

'Monsieur Snowdrop?'

'Monsieur Manneville?'

Manneville (Hubert Alphonse Amédée), forty-seven years old, musician, belated disciple of Erik Satie, composer of the *Pavane for a Defunct Tax-collector*, disarmingly able, large patrimony, town-house Avenue Foch, villa at Biarritz, country seat near Etretat, racing stables. By appearance: a pale blond giant with narrow shoulders, striking eyes of blue or faded green, heavy eyelids, a short but damp moustache, two wrinkles on his forehead like a contented smile. A knitted waistcoat contrasts with his excellently cut suit. His voice is pleasant because restrained. His attitude is that of a good pupil brought by mistake before the school authorities.

They shake hands.

'Allow me to introduce you to Madame d'Huez-Romanche.'

Thirty years old, brunette, tall, thin, greyhound-like: a model of fashion draped over an armchair; baroness.

He kisses her hand.

Stanislas Snowdrop sits down, crosses his legs, lights a cigarette, contemplates his smoke.

Hubert Manneville walks up and down, enervated and fretful.

Mme d'Huez-Romanche mechanically chips the red varnish off her nails.

Complete silence.

The hotel bedroom is banal. Banal also is the fall of the rain: the shiny promenade where some shiny townspeople hurry in shorts and waterproofs; the wide beach of drab sand; the grey-green sky. This could be Deauville, Paris-Plage or the

Sands of Olonne, a day on which the tides have wrecked the Indian summer. Three details alone place the scene in England: the sash-windows, the Bible on the bedside table, the gas fire in front of the false chimney.

Suddenly, Hubert Manneville stops, swallows his saliva, chokes, asks:

'You had a good trip?'

'Not bad.'

'Did you go via Calais?'

'Via Dieppe.'

'The ship wasn't tossed too badly?'

'I've no idea. I stayed in the bar.'

'It's a pity that, for your arrival in Westcliff-on-Sea, you haven't profited by more clement weather. The least ray of sunshine . . .'

Stanislas Snowdrop takes his cigarette between two fingers, yawns behind them.

'One would think that one was on the Riviera rather than at the mouth of the Thames . . .'

Stanislas Snowdrop stands up.

'What is it all about?'

'I beg your pardon?'

'You summoned me by telegram. Your telegram spoke of a danger. What is this danger?'

'It's . . .'

'The danger of arrest? If I judge by the plainclothes policemen that I met in the hall.'

'I . . .'

'What are you accused of?'

'I . . . Have you read the papers?'

'I only read them at the barber's.'

Hubert Manneville chokes a second time. Then, humbly:

'I am suspected of murder.'

'And you are?'

'I beg your pardon?'

'Guilty? Innocent?'

'Innocent, of course!'

Stanislas Snowdrop sits down again, crosses his legs once more, throws his cigarette end in the fire, and lights another.

'I'm listening to you.'

## 2. TROUBLES OF LOST LOVE

'As you can imagine,' said Hubert Manneville, 'Solange . . . Madame d'Huez-Romanche . . . and myself . . .'

He interrupts himself to clear his throat.

He continues:

'We met each other ten years ago at the Schola Cantorum. It was love at first sight for both of us. Unfortunately, she was already engaged and comes from a family whose regard for their word once given . . .'

'So she married the Baron d'Huez-Romanche, then?'

'Five months later. At Sainte-Clotilde.'

'You as well, you got married?'

'Out of . . . convenience.'

'With the only daughter of a rich Northern textile industrialist?'

'I . . .'

'Nonetheless, you have continued to see the baroness?'

'Only with the best and most honourable intentions.'

'At first, yes. Teas at Rumpelmayer's, dances at Claridge's, recitals, concerts, exhibitions, museums, rose-gardens, parks and public gardens.'

'Certainly.'

'Then, little five to seven o'clocks at hotels of assignation.'

'The baron abandoned her.'

'Liaison style 1880, discreet, convenient, correct, which may last a year, a couple of years, which can last a whole lifetime if . . .'

'If?'

'If one wasn't possessed by the desire to live, at least for a few days, as husband and wife, to pass the nights together, to wake up in the same bed. Whence this classic trip abroad. One leaves separately. One meets in an hotel. Oh! Two separate rooms. Not even communicating. An hotel, it isn't only the guests; it is also—above all—the chambermaids, the boots, the receptionists, the lift-attendants, the doormen, the page-boys, the flunkeys who watch you, read you, unmask you, despise you. So many precautions to take! You must not forget to leave your shoes outside your door! To creep down the corridors like a thief, always ready to make for the W.C. if somebody happens to pass by! Not to make your fondness for each other too obvious! Not to rumple the sheets! To have returned to your room before the *maid* arrives who brings the *breakfast*! And one realizes that, in this hotel, in a town and a country where no one knows you, it is even more difficult to safeguard appearances than in Paris.'

'You . . .'

'The preamble is accurate?'

'Alas!'

'Very well, go on. I've had enough of restoring the Diplodocus.'

'Eh?'

'Like Cuvier. With a fragment of vertebrae.'

'I . . . I continue. It is only outside, a good distance from the hotel, that we feel really free. Free, for example, to talk to each other, to walk arm in arm, to kiss each other. Last Thursday, we decided to go as far as the casino at Southend, following the sea. The weather was . . . well, certainly not like today. The sky was blue; light and clear. The air was warm and perfumed by pollen. You would have thought that you were . . .'

'On the Riviera, I know.'

'Suddenly, a scruffy young man, almost in rags, plants himself in front of us, gives us a wry smile, makes the vague gesture of a military salute, and says to us in a horrible cockney accent: *Prints delivered tomorrow morning . . . Les épreuves vous seront remises demain matin.*'

'I had understood . . . *J'avais compris.*'

'He holds out a card to me. I took it. I read there a handwritten number and the printed address of a photographer called Aelfric Chalkwell. Turning around, I see a man—Mr Chalkwell without any doubt—pointing his Leica at a group of students in gaudy caps. You'll find photographers like this on every beach. Nevertheless, our day was spoilt. What was most paradoxical about it was that I had brought my Kodak for the same purpose. I tried to be sensible about our worries. What difference could there be between my photographs and those of Mr Chalkwell? The *amour-propre* of the author or the sensitivity of the lover? Not even that. After further thought, only one thing mattered: the possession of the negative. Was it in the hands of an honest and trustworthy artist, respectful of

professional secrets, a negative like this, where a doubly adulterous couple could be seen entwined, represented a grave danger. So I resolved to go and find Mr Chalkwell first thing next morning to demand its return.

'After a restless night, I put my plan into action. I was received by Mrs Chalkwell. A captivating young blonde. Child-like. Immaterial. A heroine out of Dickens. I told her the number written on my card. She handed over to me two photographs printed side by side on a postcard. By a sort of irony, or rather because of the strong sunlight which accentuates the contrasts and hardens the features, the photographs were at the same time a good likeness and horribly grotesque. Mrs Chalkwell informed me that they would cost me three shillings. I handed them over to her, asking her if, for what I'd paid, I had the right to the film. She replied that she would pass on my request to her husband. She went into the next room. A moment later, she ushered me in, then returned to the bouti-que. I found myself in the laboratory of the establishment, in the presence of Mr Chalkwell and his assistant, one trimming some proofs in a guillotine, the other rinsing them in a tank. Without interrupting what he was doing, Mr Chalkwell claimed that it was impossible for him to surrender the negative that interested me because it was part of a roll of thirty-six exposures. He added, very helpfully, that if on another occasion I wanted any more prints I would just have to tell him the reference number and he would bill me and send them to me. I pursed my lips. He smiled at me. That gave me confidence. I related my story to him, my troubles. Next he said that, to be kind to me, he would consent, against a small indemnification, to cut up the compromising roll. I held out a ten shilling note to him and asked, in the hope that he would give me back some change, if that seemed sufficient to him. He made a sign, and his assistant slipped out of the room. He remained silent for a few more seconds, as if he was engaged in a calculation in his head. Then he informed me: *One thousand pounds . . . Mille livres.*'

'Understood.'

'I didn't need anything else to realize that I had fallen into the hands of a blackmailer.'

'You have a very quick understanding.'

'I could feel my anger mounting. Mr Chalkwell told me, still in a very friendly way, that he sympathized with me over my disappointment and consented to allow me the rest of the afternoon to think over his proposition. He suggested that I should come back to see him about six o'clock. More than a suggestion, it was well and truly an ultimatum. I went back to the hotel. I couldn't refrain from putting Madame d'Huez-Romanche *au courant*. Like me, she didn't know what to do. Going down to the hall, we surprised Mr Chalkwell's assistant conversing with the receptionist. The net was drawing in on us: Mr Chalkwell would know our names, our addresses, our positions—and the marketable value of his discretion.

'A thousand pounds was nothing to either of us. But should we give in to blackmail? I had read, in the professional manuals, that blackmailers, as a rule, were never satisfied by the amount agreed upon; that they always kept some proof in their possession and that they never stopped exacting fresh payments; that their victims ran the risk of spending their whole lives without being able to escape from the sword of Damocles suspended above their heads. Inform the police? A strange way of avoiding a scandal! But to blackmail the blackmailer? To extort his piece of film from him by using whatever threat necessary? That seemed the most expedient course to me. I bought a clasp-knife. A Sheffield steel blade. And I waited resolutely for the hour of the rendezvous. My resolve was strengthened, I admit, by drinking a good few gins.

'At last, I went to Mr Chalkwell's. Mrs Chalkwell was out. The assistant was in charge of the shop. He told me to go through to the laboratory, without going in himself. As soon as the door was closed, I threw myself on Mr Chalkwell, my knife in my hand, open, and demanded the unconditional surrender of the negative. Mr Chalkwell, looking very calm, pointed out to me that he had enough sense to have put such a document in a safe place.'

'Plausible.'

'It was so plausible that I was completely dumbfounded. Letting go of my knife, I could only revile Mr Chalkwell in an outburst of extreme bad temper. I shouted, I yelled, I stamped my feet. Mr Chalkwell confined himself to repeating to me placidly that, in view of my position and my attitude, a thousand

pounds was no longer enough, but that it was now two thousand. At one point, I saw the look on his face alter. I thought that he was becoming more humane, that he was so smitten with remorse that he would give me my due, and might even apologize. But he enjoined me to leave him in a voice so harsh that I obeyed him automatically. I asked him to inform me as to his intentions. He replied that we would speak of that later. I can only compare the state he was in with that of someone about to have a heart attack. I left the laboratory. I went through the shop, which was empty. By seven o'clock I had reached the hotel. In my excitement, I had forgotten my knife at Mr Chalkwell's. At quarter past seven his assistant, returning from a round of deliveries, found him dead, with this same knife driven into his heart.'

'Struck from in front or behind?'

'In front. The blade had entered the third intercostal cavity, an inch from the sternum.'

'The ownership of the knife has been established?'

'I recognized it as mine.'

'Fingerprints?'

'The handle had been wiped.'

'Was it the victim's assistant who pointed the suspicions at you?'

'At the same time as he managed to keep out of the blackmailing.'

'When is the jury convened?'

'The day after tomorrow.'

'The delay will be sufficient time for me.'

'To establish my innocence?'

'To uncover the truth.'

'You . . .'

Stanislas Snowdrop gets up, goes to open the window, throws out his cigarette butt, breathes in the damp air.

Then:

'One last small matter. I don't live on air; I have a wife, a secretary, and a tax-collector; they all have the best of appetites . . .'

Hubert Manneville's crowning misfortune.

Mme d'Huez-Romanche, without appearing to be paying attention, looks vaguely disdainful.

# 3. MOSES MACMORAY

Neither tall nor short, chubby, bloated indeed, with the head of a goldfish fallen in the water-pump, the Chief Constable, Moses MacMoray.

On his desk, mixed up with the files of the County Police, are strewn the French dailies, a photograph of Sacha Guitry, the Michelin guide, some tickets for the Metro (not the Tube but for the stations Saint-Lazare, Montparnasse and Pigalle), a souvenir album of the Folies-Bergère, a novel by Ch. de Richter in the *la Cagoule* edition, a packet of Gauloises *bleues*.

His francophilia manifests itself even in his greeting.

'Glad to meet you, Monsieur Snowdrop. I've read a lot about you. I hunt out the Parisian newspapers, V Magazine, the works of Curnonsky, the patriotic poems of M. Aragon. You come for the Manneville affair? A very sad business! You think that he isn't guilty? I wish it were so. His Concerto on the Entente Cordiale is very . . . *how do you say?* . . . picturesque! It was inspired by Scottish and Auvergnat themes. I heard it, last year, in the Salle Pleyel. A real triumph. Everybody was whistling. Do you smoke? Can I offer you a . . . er . . . a . . . *dash it!* . . . a *cibiche*? A good old Gauloise? I've also got Gitanes, Celtiques, Elégantes. That's real tobacco. English are just weed. You must be thirsty? Would you like cognac? Perrier?'

He speaks French quickly, too quickly, in a monotonous drone. He stutters, doesn't pronounce his 'r's', but on the other hand, pronounces his 'u's' correctly, rolls his humble eyes with satisfaction.

Stanislas Snowdrop accepts a Gauloise, several fingers of cognac. (It is humid outside.)

Then, one gets down to the case.

'The victim,' says Moses MacMoray, 'was a blackmailer. In French . . .'

'*Maître-chanteur.*'

'That's right.'

'Have you known it for long?'

'No. This Mr Chalkwell has lived in Westcliff for ten years, and no one has ever made a complaint against him. We learnt about it from M. Manneville when we interrogated him. Then, we made sure of it by . . . er . . .'

'By corroboration. What were they?'

'*First*, Mr Chalkwell's expenditure was disproportionate with the earnings of his trade. *Second*, his wife and his employee have made statements to the effect that, when a client claims the negative of a photograph taken on the beach, Mr Chalkwell locks himself in the laboratory with the client to discuss the . . . er . . . conditions of sale. *Third*, the employee has made it clear that only in these cases did Mr Chalkwell . . . er . . . insist that he follow the client to find out where he lived and what was his name.'

'Mr Chalkwell, what sort of man was he?'

'Here's his photograph.'

A man in his fifties, spruce, pomaded, dyed. Hard eyes under tired eyelids.

'His wife was younger than him?'

'Twenty-five years younger.'

'Pretty?'

'Very pretty.'

'Her morals?'

'She comes from an excellent family. She is a practising Methodist. She is very well regarded.'

'The assistant?'

'What do you say?'

'The employee?'

'His name is Slim Burton. He isn't a very respectable person. He lives in one of the house-boats at Leigh-on-Sea. A mile from here. These are a sort of barge where the poor live.'

'How old is he?'

'Thirty perhaps. But he doesn't look any older than sixteen or seventeen. He's got red hair and his face is scarred all over from smallpox.'

'Any convictions?'

'One for prostitution.'

'Pimp?'

'No. He was prostituting himself.'

'Charming.'

'Twice for larceny.'

'Good. And what is M. Manneville doing mixed up in all this?'

Moses MacMoray nearly chokes himself.

225

'*By the dickens!* What is he doing? But he is the murderer!'
'Why?'
'*First*, he was the only one who would benefit by the murder.'
'The only one that you know of.'
'*Second*, he was the last person to go into Mr Chalkwell's while he was still alive.'
'The proof?'
'A spinster . . . *une vieille fille* . . . who lives opposite. She saw no one go in after M. Manneville.'
'Not even Slim Burton?'
'Yes. But it was too late for Slim Burton to have been able to commit the murder. The pathologist was categorical.'
'I envy him.'
'Of course, he didn't base his conclusions on the rigidity of the corpse but on the coagulation of blood.'
'Mrs Chalkwell? She didn't see anything? Hear anything?'
'No.'
'She was out?'
'She was on the first floor of the house. In the *lounge*. She was reading the *Pilgrim's Progress*.'
'Funny idea to read Bunyan while someone is killing your husband!'
'She didn't know that he was being killed. *Third*, M. Manneville admitted that he had had a violent argument with Mr Chalkwell.'
'Then M. Manneville must be remarkably obtuse . . . Do you think that, if he was guilty, he would have told you about this argument?'
'*Fourth*, the knife belonged to him.'
'So he would have committed two errors: one, leaving his weapon on the scene; two, reclaiming his property.'
'*Fifth*, the film that he wished to destroy has disappeared.'
'Has it been found on him or in his room?'
'Certainly not. It's probable that he would have thrown it away or burnt it somewhere.'
'A probability is not a proof.'
'When you were a judge, wouldn't you have sentenced someone on a probability?'
'Perhaps. But I realized my mistake and changed my profession. You see, you don't have anything against my *zigoto* . . .'

*'Zigoto?'*
'In English: guy.'
'That's not English. It's American.'
*'Never mind!* As I say, you haven't anything against M. Manneville except presumptions. I grant you that, although they are neither precise nor serious, they are, all the same, corroborating. But to assert that a man is guilty of murder, you must nonetheless be certain that he has the requisite moral strength. You've seen M. Manneville . . . You've questioned him . . . Haven't you weighed him up as well? He's a Colossus, but he's soft, spineless and weak! Him, kill someone? Not even with a ball-point pen!'
'I don't blame you for considering the facts from your client's point of view.'
'You, do you want me to tell you from what point of view you see them? Not from that of the sheriff, oh no! But well and truly from Mr Slim Burton's personal little point of view.'
'What do you mean?'
'Who is this Slim Burton? A thief. A queer. A blackmailer's accomplice.'
'His complicity isn't legally proved.'
'And if I prove it?'
'He will be protected by the law. As a witness for the Crown.'
'Why not like a policeman!'
'I'm sorry?'
'Who is the *flic* in this affair? You or him? Who found the body? Who informed the authorities? Who spoke to you about M. Manneville? And about the photograph?'
'Then you suspect him?'
'For the moment, I suspect nobody. Not even M. Manneville.'


## 4. MRS CHALKWELL

A street where all the houses look alike. Each little sandstone house with its little garden of roses or rhododendrons in front.
'When you're drunk,' Stanislas Snowdrop mutters, 'it must be hard to find your digs.'
Here and there, a discreet sign: *Insurance, Tea-room, Hair-Dresser, Guest-House.*

It rains.

A fine Anglo-Norman rain, that you scarcely feel falling, but which cuts right through you, soaks you.

Stanislas Snowdrop rings the late Mr Chalkwell's bell.

Mrs Chalkwell comes to answer the door. With her long, blond hair, her lithe body, her diaphanous skin, one would have said that, in the grey light, she was more than a character from Dickens, a fairy from the bard Ossian. She is sad, and her sadness seems shadowed by fear.

She stammers:

'The house isn't taking on any work for the moment. My husband . . .'

'I know,' says Stanislas Snowdrop. 'I would just like to have a chat with you about the affair.'

'You are? . . .'

'A private investigator. M. Manneville has engaged me to look after his interests.'

She hesitates. Then:

'Come in.'

She shows him to the lounge. On the way, he checks the lay-out of the place. On the ground floor, the hall, the shop and the laboratory—the latter on the right of the hall with which it communicates. On the first floor, in addition to the lounge (right above the shop), a bedroom and a kitchen.

The lounge is smartly furnished, luxuriously indeed; club chairs in light leather, a baby grand piano, glass-topped pedestal tables, a deep wool pile carpet, a chimney made of painted bricks.

'You were here when the crime was committed?'

'Yes.'

'Wouldn't you usually have been in the shop?'

'No. We close at six p.m. and I go up immediately. I have dinner to prepare.'

'However, an hour and a quarter after closing, you still hadn't started cooking?'

'I felt tired.'

'That explains why you started to read. You don't find Bunyan's work too difficult?'

'I always find a great consolation there.'

'You didn't leave the lounge?'

'No.'

'You didn't hear anything?'

'No.'

'Not even M. Manneville arguing with your husband?'

'The laboratory walls are covered with thick drapes.'

'Is it possible that someone could have come in without you seeing them?'

'No. Both the garden door and that of the shop set off a bell when they are opened.'

'You heard those bells a couple of times, then: one, when M. Manneville came in; two, when Slim Burton went out; three, when M. Manneville went out again; four, when Slim Burton returned. Four times in all.'

'Yes. Four times.'

'Do you remember exactly what time it was on each occasion?'

'No. I remember only that Slim Burton probably went out very soon after the arrival of M. Manneville.'

'Did you notice a suspicious lapse of time between the sound of the garden bell and that of the shop?'

'No.'

'Then Slim Burton informed you of the murder?'

'Yes.'

'How much longer was it after you heard him come in?'

'Perhaps five minutes later. More rather than less.'

'Were you aware of . . . your husband's strange activities.'

'If I had known about them, I would have left him on the spot.'

'Never had any suspicions?'

'N-no.'

She hesitated for a fraction of a second. Her cheeks colouring slightly.

'Last question: do you believe solemnly and sincerely that M. Manneville is the murderer?'

'I . . . I really don't know.'


## 5. SLIM BURTON

'Damn it all! Mr Chalkwell (Aelfric to the ladies) can't have been very generous.'

In the rain, Stanislas Snowdrop walked along the sea for half an hour. Careful to avoid the puddles, his collar transformed into a damp poultice, he glanced but distractedly at the Thames estuary, sombre, and blurred like a Turner.

Here are the house-boats. *Kerquois*, barges, long-boats. The wrecks on which a maladroit Robinson Crusoe might have built, here a belvedere, and there a verandah, everything out of soap-boxes. They are blackish, agglutinous, sinister. They lie on a smooth surface of slime, surrounded by slack moorings, seaweed, crabs, old rusty tin cans, pollution. It is amongst all this, Moses MacMoray said, that the poor live.

A female, dragging along her squelching brood, points out Slim Burton's house-boat to Stanislas Snowdrop.

'Slim is in town,' she says, 'but you're nearly sure to find him if you go round the pubs.'

Slanislas Snowdrop sets off again, flounders across a boatyard cluttered with little white sailing boats, samples two saucers of boiled cockles at a stall, tramps at last, between the Tudor façades, the historic cobblestones of Leigh-on-Sea.

The pubs still aren't open yet, but their customers are already queuing up.

Slim Burton, red-haired, thin, with the face of a young ruffian, is slouching against the King George's Inn. He appears annoyed when Stanislas Snowdrop introduces himself to him. Then, he quips:

'If you want me to open my heart to you, buy a bottle of gin at the grocer's and we'll go back and drink it at my place.'

Five minutes later, Slim Burton on his right, the gin on his left, Stanislas Snowdrop turns back towards the house-boats.

On the way, Slim Burton turns up his nose at the stalls selling shell-fish.

'Whatever you do, don't eat them. They're fished out of the muck. They are not allowed to sell them raw because of the typhoid.'

Slim Burton's house-boat. A letter-box is nailed to the entry of the gangway. The deck is rotten, littered with old planks, buckets, laid out washing. The cabin, to which one gains entry by a steep flight of steps, is dark, crudely furnished in pine, varnished with filth, smelling of tar, fish, mildew. Slim Burton lights a lantern. A flickering yellow light spills out. He gets out the glasses. Stanislas Snowdrop discreetly wipes his, opens the bottle. The gin flows, a spangled glimmer of Danzig alcohol.

'What exactly was your job at Mr Chalkwell's?'

'I helped him do everything.'

'Laboratory work; outdoor photography; I know. But what else?'

Slim Burton smiles slyly.

'I did what he told me to do.'

Stanislas Snowdrop lights a cigarette, swallows a large gulp.

'You were out when Mr Chalkwell was murdered?'

'Fortunately.'

'You were, I believe, delivering some photographs?'

'Right.'

'Where?'

'Fifty-six Crowstone Avenue, six Manor Road, nine Satanita Road.

'Was it so urgent?'

'Not especially . . .'

Slim Burton breaks off to refill his glass, recovers his puny, carnivorous smile, and goes on:

'The boss told me to go off as soon as M. Manneville arrived.'

'You weren't intrigued by that?'

'I've a very docile nature.'

Stanislas Snowdrop suppresses an epithet, blows a smoke-ring, drums his fingers on the table, soils them and wipes them in his pocket.

'You returned to Mr Chalkwell's about seven-fifteen p.m.?'

'Right.'

'You immediately went into the laboratory?'

'Right.'

'You discovered the body?'

'Right.'

'You informed Mrs Chalkwell at once?'

'Of course.'

'She doesn't say that.'

'What?'

'She says that it was more than five minutes after you returned before you came up to the lounge.'

'She's wrong.'

Slim Burton's look grew mean; his voice, strained.

'Wrong about what?'

His voice softens again, becomes almost gentle:

'She's wrong to be so positive. You would need a stop-watch to . . .'

'Even without a stop-watch, you can guess how long passed between the sound of the door and the appearance of Mr Slim Burton without fear of being too far out.'

'Really, I don't remember it at all. The sight of a corpse . . . I hadn't seen one since my poor mother's death . . . Yes! I remember that I deliberated for a while whether I ought to warn the police first or . . . the widow.'

'A commendable precaution.'

Stanislas Snowdrop coughs slightly.

'And you really didn't know that Mr Chalkwell was a blackmailer?'

'Really.'

'You never guessed why he had you follow certain customers? Why he had you gather all the available information about them?'

'I'm not a great thinker.'

'But I am. For example, here is a problem which I would like you to solve for me: You owed ten pounds and a few odd shillings to your grocer . . . How come you paid this debt the very next morning after Mr Chalkwell's murder?'

Slim Burton turns green, sucks in his lips and part of his cheeks. He stammers:

'You don't have to be broke to keep your creditors waiting.'

## 6. SIMPLE QUESTION

It is night. The rain is iridescent in the lamplight.

The Chief Constable, Moses MacMoray, is on the point of leaving his office.

Stanislas Snowdrop asks him:

'When you searched Mr Chalkwell's body, did he have any money on him?'

'Fifteen pounds or so.'

'It didn't look as if his pockets had been rifled?'

'His wife assured us that he usually carried less spending money on him.'

## 7. SUPPER OF THE LOVERS

In the dining-room of the hotel, Stanislas Snowdrop joins Hubert Manneville and Mme d'Huez-Romanche. He sits at their table, exchanges some commonplace remarks, attacks his soup.

More than once, Hubert Manneville attempts to question him, breaks off, looks slavishly at his mistress, remains silent. This little comedy does not fail to amuse Stanislas Snowdrop. Eventually, as he clears his plate swimming with fillets of plaice, he begins to talk about the affair.

'There are three possible hypotheses: one, you are the murderer . . .'

'My thanks for this priority.'

'I'm not speaking in order of preference. Two, the murderer is Slim Burton . . . the assistant . . .'

'That wouldn't surprise me.'

'Three, it is Mrs Chalkwell . . .'

'Such a decent woman!'

'Each of these three has a plausible motive. You . . . unnecessary to hark back on that. Slim Burton? The lucre: he might have thought that his boss had got his hands on your thousand pounds. Otherwise, revenge: the accomplice of an opulent blackmailer, he himself had remained poor. Mrs Chalkwell? The disgust which could have pushed a puritanical little wife to take the law into her own hands when she learnt what her husband really was.'

'Do you think she could have known before . . . the accident?'

'Yes. But only for a short while, I would swear to it.'

'Anyway, it makes me think of the murder of Buckingham.'

'Eh?'

'Of Cromwell's Roundheads, of the Mayflower Pilgrims . . .'

Weary of the erudition, Stanislas Snowdrop calls the waiter:

'There is nothing else to drink except water?'

'We serve a very good tea.'

'No beer? Pale Ale? Stout?'
'We haven't a licence.'
'You want a kick in the pants.'
'Would you care for anything?'
'Nothing.'
'Some tea?'
'No. Nothing.'
'If I trust to the only clue that I have been able to glean today, the murderer must be either Slim Burton or Mrs Chalkwell.'
'Why?'
'Up until recently, Slim Burton *a tiré le diable par la queue.* In English: to be stone broke. He had incurred a lot of debts. Well then, he repaid them all the day after the crime.'
'And what do you deduce from that?'
'An alternative. Either Slim Burton is guilty, and robbed his victim of a certain amount of money. Or he is innocent, but knows who the murderer is, and has already started to blackmail him. According to my inquiries, you haven't come into contact with Slim Burton since six p.m. last Friday . . .'
'I appreciate your confidence in me!'
'Then it's Mrs Chalkwell who is guilty?'
'The logic seems impeccable to me.'
Hubert Manneville's appetite returns, he finishes his piece of plaice.
Mme d'Huez-Romanche, who has not said anything, continues not to say anything. But she did not stop staring at Hubert Manneville—with a certain measure of scorn—and Stanislas Snowdrop—with a look of complicity.


## 8. NOCTURNE

Eleven p.m. or so.
In pyjamas, bare feet, a slipper in his hand, Stanislas Snowdrop is hunting mosquitoes. Twenty or so corpses are scattered across the walls.
Then, he pisses in the wash-stand. Both out of convenience and to revenge himself for having had to drink water over dinner.
A knock on the door.
Softly, but insistently.

He groans, straightens his clothes, goes to open it.

Mme d'Huez-Romanche, in a wrapper trimmed with gold buttons, comes in and closes the door behind her. Smiling, she holds out a bottle of beer.

'I had to bribe the night porter to procure it. It's Guinness.'

'Extremely grateful.'

He fetches his tooth-mug, fills it up precipitately, puts it to his lips, stops.

'Perhaps you are thirsty too?'

'I beg you. Drink.'

While Stanislas Snowdrop drinks, Mme d'Huez-Romanche sits down in an armchair. Her dressing-gown, opening, reveals thin, well-shaped legs as far as her knees. Although she is wearing bedroom slippers, she has kept on her stockings.

She murmurs:

'Can you spare me ten minutes?'

'With pleasure.'

She glances at the door.

'Would you mind pushing the catch? If M. Manneville surprises us, he will suppose something.'

'I don't see him having such imagination.'

All the same, he does as he is asked, sits on the edge of the bed, waits.

She turns her legs towards him and begins hesitantly, in a warm but subdued voice:

'I wouldn't like . . .'

'What wouldn't you like?'

'You to think that he was guilty.'

'Think that he was guilty! Why?'

'Because, earlier on, he fell into your trap.'

'My trap?'

She sways in her armchair. Her wrapper opens slightly further.

'In principle, you posed the following alternative: either Slim Burton killed to steal; or he knows the murderer and is blackmailing him. You know very well that it is possible to formulate a third hypothesis—this one: Slim Burton found Mr Chalkwell dead and robbed him.'

'In point of fact that comes immediately to mind.'

'Of course.'

235

'Even to the mind of M. Manneville.'

'The contrary *would* surprise me.'

'As for this hypothesis, M. Manneville well and truly avoided pointing it out to you, and it was the only one unfavourable to him. Someone who was guilty would not act in any other way.'

'Yeah.'

'That leaves you cold?'

'The hypothesis, yes.'

'But M. Manneville's attitude?'

'Ever since the beginning of the affair, M. Manneville has always acted as if he was guilty.'

'In other words?'

'I think that he is innocent.'

She seems disappointed, upset.

She says, ironically:

'Innocent . . . in every sense of the word?'

He consents by a nod of the head.

A silence.

Long enough for him to sink two glasses of beer and come to a definite opinion on the legs displayed for him.

She gets up abruptly, comes to stand in front of him, and, with a fierce, contracted expression, on the verge of stamping her feet, sobbing, and scratching out with her fingers, she snarls:

'All right! Yes! I shall be frank. I was hoping that he was guilty. The scandal? The divorce for my sins? The loss of all the rights to my children? My ruin? Of no importance. I would have risked everything for him, because he would have risked everything for me. But now! All these insults! All this muck-raking! For what? For nothing! Thanks to what? Thanks to the gaffes of monsieur! To his stupidity! To his cowardice! A coward . . . I realize it now, but he has always been one. Otherwise, would he have allowed my marriage to take place? Would he himself have married? Would he have prostituted our love by furtive little five to seven o'clocks? A blackguard and a coward!'

He coughs evasively.

'Well say something!'

He remains silent.

She straightens her back, rips off her wrapper, runs to turn out the light.

And, ravished, Stanislas Snowdrop remembers the sight of a pale, thin body, dressed only in a wasp-waist corset and two stockings, one of which, undone, coils round her ankle.


## 9. WALTZ IN THREE-PART TIME

Midnight. In front of Mme d'Huez-Romanche's bedroom.
'Solange! Why have you locked your door on me?'
Footsteps. The large almond-green silhouette slips away.

Two o'clock. Hubert Manneville's bedroom.
In his almond-green pyjamas, the man himself is yellowy-green.
'To suffer! And there isn't even a piano!'

Five o'clock. Stanislas Snowdrop's door half-opens.
'All clear.'
'One last embrace?'
'And one will forget everything.'


## 10. PRIORY PARK

In the vicinity of Westcliff-on-Sea.
A park and an old house.
The house serves as the museum. The park is adorned by a stretch of water where the reflections of trees and sky are criss-crossed by the wakes of swans and ducks.
The weather is warm and fine.
While, in the museum, Stanislas Snowdrop lingers in front of stuffed birds, old maps in the Treasure Island style, blunderbusses, polished stones and sculptured stone, in the park, Hubert Manneville and Mme d'Huez-Romanche stroll around the stretch of water, a yard apart from each other.
He whines:
'Have I done something wrong?'

She smiles nervously.

'Perhaps.'

He insists conceitedly:

'You would think that you didn't love me any more.'

She exclaims, at once, coldly:

'And even if that were true?'

He leans against a pine tree, pants:

'I would ask you the reason.'

'It's this. You are nothing but an egoist and a scoundrel.'

He looks up at the hazy blue sky.

'After what I've done for you!'

'Look who is talking!'

'Are you insinuating that . . .'

He hesitates, looks around him, sticks out his stomach:

'So much the worse for you! I'll tell you then! It was me who did it!'

She avoids his eyes, contemplates the water speckled with floating leaves, and murmurs:

'Would you dare say it in front of the police?'

'Absolutely. I generally know what I am doing and what I say.'

'If you know what you were doing so well, why did you leave your knife in Mr Chalkwell's third intercostal cavity?'

It takes him a moment to find the reply.

'A crime . . . is never perfect. The cleverest thing to do is never to look completely innocent.'

From behind a clump of shrubs, a few yards away, emerges a well-known face like a colourless goldfish: the Chief Constable, Moses MacMoray.

'Monsieur Manneville, I have warned you earlier that everything you say will be taken down and used in evidence against you . . .'

Hubert Manneville dives into the stretch of water, crosses it in a frantic crawl, and is met on the other side by two plainclothes policemen.

Mme d'Huez-Romanche follows a squirrel high up with her eyes.

Moses MacMoray doesn't know what to say.

Behind another clump of shrubs, Stanislas Snowdrop laughs—until he is fairly fit to burst.

## 11. FACTS AND MEMORY

*'For h'is a jolly good fellow . . .'*

The high-pitched nasal voice comes from a house across the street from the late Mr Chalkwell's. On the first floor, chained to his window, round-eyed, open-mouthed, flapping its wings, a parrot surveys Stanislas Snowdrop.

Stanislas Snowdrop throws away his cigarette, crosses the carriage-way, and introduces himself to the adoptive mother of the parrot—an old spinster with big teeth, big feet, and very black hair cut in a fringe. She bids him come into the lounge and offers him a cup of tea.

They talk.

The night of the crime, she didn't see anyone go in except Hubert Manneville and Slim Burton. She does not remember anything unusual.

The parrot, meanwhile, carries on his repertoire:

*'For h'is a jolly good fellow . . .'*

The conversation falters. There is nothing left to do except take his leave. But an instinct keeps Stanislas Snowdrop nailed to his armchair.

'That's a very pretty bird you have there . . .'

As if flattered, the parrot resumes:

*'For h'is a jolly good fellow . . .'*

Night falls.

Opposite, the lounge of Mrs Chalkwell lights up. A slender silhouette festooned with light can be seen bustling around.

The parrot breaks off, watches, starts to repeat:

*'Why those baggages? Why those baggages? Why those baggages?'*

Stanislas Snowdrop asks:

'Earlier on, your parrot regaled us with an old popular song; and now, he only talks about baggage! Why?'

The old spinster racks her brains a moment.

'One evening, when the electric light was turned on at Mrs Chalkwell's, we saw her packing some bags. I said: Why those baggages? And Jacky must have remembered it.'

'One evening . . . which one would that be?'

Another plunge into thought:

239

'It was . . . My word! It was the night Mr Chalkwell was murdered.'

'What time?'

'My Westminster was just striking seven o'clock.'

'What an idiot I am!'

'Pardon?'

'You didn't see anything else?'

'Twenty minutes later, Slim Burton came into the lounge and said something. Mrs Chalkwell looked extremely agitated. They went out, switching off the light behind them.'

## 12. WHY THOSE BAGGAGES?

'Mrs Chalkwell . . .'

'M. Snowdrop . . .'

'Would you like to tell me why, last Friday, at seven o'clock, you started to pack your suitcases?'

She becomes confused.

'Friday last?'

'Yes. The night of the crime.'

She bursts into tears.

He leans towards her, takes her avuncularly by the shoulders.

'Don't cry, my dear. I know you are not guilty. Come along! Tell me what happened.'

She bows her head, sniffs.

He insists.

'Did you want to leave? You had found your husband's body? You were scared of being compromised?'

She shakes her head.

'Well then?'

She stammers:

'I had just learnt that my husband was unworthy of me.'

'How?'

'I lied when I said that I never suspected anything, that I had never heard anything when my husband was arguing with M. Manneville. Actually, I had come down and half-opened the door of the laboratory. I listened and, once I was sure, I pushed it fully open. My husband saw me. The look on his face changed . . .'

240

'M. Manneville didn't see you?'
'No. He had his back to the door.'
'Next?'
'I closed it again. I went upstairs to the lounge.'
'Night was falling?'
'I turned on the lights, and then I started to pack my bags.'
'Where would you have gone?'
'I don't know. I couldn't stay with him any longer.'
'Why didn't you admit all this?'
'Because I was interrupted by Slim Burton when he came to tell me of the murder. He told me that my behaviour would be interpreted as a proof of guilt. I thought that he was right.'
'And?'
'He has already borrowed a hundred pounds from me since then.'
'In other words, he's blackmailing you?'
'He didn't threaten me in any way.'
'That wasn't necessary.'
A pause.
'You have nothing else to tell me?'
'I don't think so.'
'You are sure that your husband saw you in the laboratory door?'
'Absolutely certain.'
'You continue to insist that Slim Burton had been back for more than five minutes before he told you of the murder?'
'At least five minutes.'
Another pause. Then, she asks, timidly:
'Just now, you said that you knew I was innocent. How?
He smiles.
'Because if you had been guilty, you would not have neglected closing the shutters before packing your suitcases.'
She goes to close the shutters, comes back to him.
Against him.

## 13. OFF THE POINT

It is not without trouble that Stanislas Snowdrop is able to procure the address of Moses MacMoray.

He finds him in the middle of eating some hot cross buns.

He asks him:

'Do you remember if Mr Chalkwell had his pen on him?'

'When we came to take the depositions?'

'Naturally.'

'His pen was lying on a table, in the laboratory.'

'The cap was screwed up?'

'Yes.'

'Was there a chair in front of the table?'

'Yes. But . . .'

'I'll explain it all to you tomorrow.'


Mme d'Huez-Romanche dines alone.

Stanislas Snowdrop sits in front of her and asks:

'M. Mannevilie?'

She smiles.

'In bed.'

'With a fever?'

'No. The excitement.' •

She asks a question in her turn:

'The investigation is making progress?'

'I think I shall have it finished tomorrow.'

She inclines her head towards him.

'Why this long face, those tired eyes . . . You are working too hard . . .'

He did not dare to say anything.

His back was aching.


## 14. 'A LA MANIÈRE DE EDGAR ALLAN POE'

Midnight. The hour of illegal perquisitions.

The moonlight makes the silt around the house-boats gleam.

Stanislas Snowdrop, wearing crêpe shoes, a cosh in his pocket, halts in front of the residence of Slim Burton.

There is no light burning.

'If I am to believe Edgar Allan Poe, the best hiding-place is the one most obvious, most ordinary, and most accessible. Before we render ourself up to the regrettable caprices of fate, let us make sure of one thing first.'

He switches on his torch and rummages through the letter-box. He extracts an envelope, opens it, reads the contents, whistles, departs.

One o'clock in the morning.

At the entrance of the late Mr Chalkwell's establishment is fixed a large yellow box in which, when the shop is closed, customers may leave their films to be developed.

Calmly, Stanislas Snowdrop forces it.

Two o'clock in the morning.

Regaining his bedroom, Stanislas Snowdrop discovers Mme d'Huez-Romanche stretched out on the bed.

She smiles at him.

'I thought that, since we would be taking leave of each other tomorrow . . .'

'Not tomorrow. Sooner.'

'All the more reason . . .'

He holds out to her a roll of film.

'A goodbye present.'

She unrolls it.

'But . . .'

'Exactly. The photograph which preoccupies you bears the number seventeen.'

## 15. WHERE VIRTUE IS REWARDED AND VICE PUNISHED

The following day.

At Stanislas Snowdrop's request, the Chief Constable, Moses MacMoray, has assembled in his office Hubert Manneville, Mme d'Huez-Romanche, Mrs Chalkwell, Slim Burton, and the old spinister with the parrot.

Stanislas Snowdrop details:

'The case hangs on three propositions: Mr Chalkwell was a blackmailer; Slim Burton is his worthy pupil . . .'

Slim Burton interrupts him:

'I shall bring an action for defamation.'

'You can tell that to the jury,' replies Stanislas Snowdrop.

And he continues:

'The third proposition: Mrs Chalkwell has some principles.'

Mrs Chalkwell blushes.

'Having established that, the case becomes as clear as crystal. Mr Chalkwell was blackmailing M. Manneville and is found dead after an interview with him. Only three people had the actual opportunity to kill him: M. Manneville, Mrs Chalkwell, Slim Burton.

Slim Burton almost lets out a yelp. Stanislas Snowdrop ignores it.

'Now none of these three people killed Mr Chalkwell.'

Sensation.

'During their discussion, M. Manneville kicked up a rumpus with Mr Chalkwell. This brought down Mrs Chalkwell who came to listen and opened the laboratory door. Mr Chalkwell caught sight of her, was dumbfounded, and dismissed M. Manneville immediately. He knew his wife's severity. He was sure that she would leave him. He committed suicide with the knife which M. Manneville left behind him.'

'But,' says Moses MacMoray, 'all the same, it was not Mr Chalkwell who wiped his fingerprints off the handle of the knife!'

'No. Here Slim Burton intervenes. He returns soon after, discovers the body and, nearby, on the table, a letter in which Mr Chalkwell explains the reasons for his suicide. He quickly foresees the possibility of blackmail. He steals the letter, wipes off the fingerprints, directs the suspicion on to M. Manneville. When M. Manneville was well and truly compromised and on his way to the gallows, Slim Burton would only have to call on him and sell at a good price the letter which would prove his innocence. I have this letter here. I found it, simply enough, in Slim Burton's letter-box. *My darling wife, Try to forgive me. Everything I did was for you, to secure for you the luxuries which your youth deserved. I shall kill myself because you will not be able to love me any more.*'

Moses MacMoray grabs the letter and asks Slim Burton:

'Do you deny it?'

Slim Burton makes a wry face.

'It's not worth the trouble.'

Moses MacMoray turns to Hubert Manneville.

'Provisional on the confirmation of the handwriting, I can assure you that the jury will dismiss the case against you.'

Hubert Manneville thanks him with a condescending smile.

Moses MacMoray puts his hand on Stanislas Snowdrop's shoulder.

'My warmest congratulations, *my dear fellow*. Unfortunately . . .'

He fingers his collar. The words stick in his throat. At last, he says very quickly:

'I am obliged to place you under arrest.'

Stanislas Snowdrop bursts into laughter.

'What is the charge?'

'No one, in the United Kingdom, has the right to interfere with the letter-box of a British citizen without a search warrant. However . . .'

'However . . .'

'Given your standing, you will no doubt be able to obtain your liberty on the payment of a fine.'

'How much?'

'It's usually two hundred pounds.'

To Hubert Manneville:

'Naturally, you will pay the fine on his behalf?'

Hubert Manneville sticks up his chin.

'Not for the life of me! There are insurance policies which cover professional risks. Are you coming, Solange?'

He leaves. After a moment's hesitation, Mme d'Huez-Romanche follows him.

Stanislas Snowdrop murmurs:

'Go, flirt!'

# 10

# LÉO MALET
## The Haulage Company

It was a quiet street and really countrified. The Normandy-style villa stood far enough away from its less prosperous looking neighbours to show that oil and water don't mix. There was a park at the back, a lawn at the front, and a small garage on the side. Two plaques of different sizes were set into one of the concrete pillars of the drive. They gleamed in the clear morning sunlight. The larger was an engraved copper affair bearing the name of André Pellerin; the other, enamelled, stuck just below, warned: *fierce dog*, without specifying the relationship between the two. In fact, there wasn't a dog, fierce or otherwise, and the plaque was there only because it was a compulsory item of a suburban villa's traditional decor. Men aren't the only ones to have their little ways.

I say that because the man with whom I had an appointment, a director of a haulage company, was, if I was to believe my friend Marc Covet, an eccentric of the first water. The soak-journalist had been in my office the day before when my potential client had telephoned to ask me to come out and see him at his private residence. As soon as I hung up, Covet had said:

'André Pellerin? Haulage company? If it is the one I know, I hope you enjoy yourself.'

I had protested that the world was full of Pellerins.

'All right, but if this one lives on the Rue Charles-Haget at Fontenay-aux-Roses'—which was the address I had been given—'he's the one I know. You remember my accident last year? He was the man who ran into me. Strangely enough, we got to know each other quite well after our rather violent encounter. Not for long though! The man's afflicted with problems which soon make all dealings with him unbearable.

You know the sort. He falls ill on the day he puts his matches in the pocket reserved for his cigarettes and vice versa. He's just like that. I wonder why he needs a private investigator? I can't see you two as bed mates. You'll have him constantly on your back if you work for him, and if you upset his routine in the least bit . . .'

In short, more finicky and pernicious than, as a Christian, he had any right to be, Pellerin, in the words of the reporter from the *Crépuscule*, would not make any job he had for me easier by sticking his spokes in my wheels. I'd find out for myself before long. By my watch, I was slightly early for our appointment. Actually, I must have been even earlier than my watch— advertised as a precision instrument—indicated because the shutters of the house were closed and there was no sign of life round the back. I decided to wait a bit before going in. I filled my pipe and smoked and read the paper as I waited, leaning my back up against the gate. It was in this relaxed pose that Pellerin's maid caught me. She was middle-aged and had about as much sex-appeal as the shopping basket folded up under her arm. Absorbed as I was in my reading, I didn't see her coming up until she said a haughty, *'Pardon me,'* before introducing the key she already held in her hand into the lock. As she pushed open the gate, she looked me over. I held my pipe in one hand and my hat in the other.

I gave a friendly smile and introduced myself: 'My name is Nestor Burma. I have an appointment with M. Pellerin.'

She looked me over again without replying. I was clean-shaven and I had brushed my teeth. She didn't start to scream for help so I suppose she reckoned I was telling the truth.

'I noticed the shutters were closed,' I explained, 'so I didn't ring the bell. Perhaps you could tell M. Pellerin that I'm here.'

She twisted her eyes round in the direction of the windows and a flicker of surprise crossed her dour features. Right from the time she had growled at me to get out of her way she hadn't said a word. She made up for it now:

'Well, how about that! It's impossible. There must be something wrong sòmewhere. My watch must be out or some-thing. M. Pellerin is always up by now. He's as reliable as clockwork. Have you got the time?'

I said that I had and told her. Apparently, it tallied with what

247

her own watch said and, after some quick mental arithmetic, with her alarm-clock, the town hall clock at Fontenay, the speaking-clock, and several other instruments used for slicing up time. This fact seemed to plunge the good woman into dismay.

'Well, how about that!' she repeated.

And without another thought for me, she hurried towards the house and disappeared. I followed her. The deserted vestibule was furnished only by an antique rococo hall-stand on which there was a memorandum book. I opened it. Every day, the old crank Pellerin left ludicrous detailed instructions for his housekeeper—whose name, Mme Chevalier, was written on the cover—listing all the small ancillary jobs that he wanted her to attend to. For the day before, the directions were for her to clean the back of the 'little room', to call at the cleaners for his blue trousers which ought to be ready, and not to forget the rose cuttings, etc. The page bearing this day's date was blank. I was just beginning to ask myself if the maid, in the absence of clear instructions, would be able to manage the vacuum cleaner properly when I heard her coming down the stairs.

'Well . . . how . . . about . . . that!' she stammered. 'It's incr-cr-credible but I've looked in his room. Monsieur hasn't s-s-slept here . . .'

It took a lot of getting out. Especially that last part. Up to then she had been coughing it out with all the natural expansiveness of a machine gun. Now she took her time over it. For all that, we weren't getting very far. Besides, I was starting to feel that it was embarrassing either way. I pointed to the notebook.

'And he hasn't left you any instructions,' I said, thinking that that would knock her flat.

It didn't knock her flat but she at least managed to speak normally again. That was something.

'I don't understand it at all. I've been in M. Pellerin's service for five years and this is the first time anything like this has happened,' she explained, after checking out my credentials.

'Everything has to start somewhere,' I said philosophically. Then I added, as if Fontenay was the back-end of beyond, 'But he could have chosen another day to drag me out of Paris.'

'That's true. You have an appointment with him. Don't you think that makes it all the more peculiar?'

248

'I don't know. Can I wait?'

She nodded mechanically and, in a dream, showed me into a drawing-room. She opened the french windows wide. The furniture was symmetrically arranged. The room looked out on the park and I was left alone with my pipe for five minutes at the most. Then Mme Chevalier came back.

'I have just been in the garage,' she informed me. 'The car is there.'

I nodded my head non-committally. She departed again, dragging her feet. I lit my pipe, which had gone out, and lost myself in contemplation of the park. I saw the woman cross it with a rake in her hand, slowly making for a sort of pigeon-house built at the far end. A lost soul in every respect. As I had suspected, she was suffering cruelly in the absence of instructions. She opened the door of the pigeon-house, went in . . . and didn't waste any time coming out again, screaming her head off.

I sprang through the window. I was too late to gather her up in my arms. I wouldn't have wanted her there anyway. Stretched out on the ground, she just managed to whisper before she fainted:

'In there!'

I burst into what now clearly was a pigeon-house. It had needed cleaning out for a long time. Broken chairs were stacked in one corner, garden tools in the other. And in the middle of all this, a man was swaying gently. He wasn't on a child's swing either.

There was no risk that the hanged man would leave nor that he would be the object of the unhealthy curiosity of his neighbours because no one in the area seemed to have heard the scream of the housekeeper. All the same, it didn't stop me shutting the door on him. Then I busied myself with . . . his victim; I brought her round without too much difficulty and helped her back to the house. I asked her only one question: was it her employer who was drying out in the abandoned pigeon-house? She answered in the affirmative. I left her in front of a potion and, out of habit, went upstairs to see if I could pick up anything from the deceased's bedroom. The same symmetry reigned there that was to be seen in every room of the house. The bed hadn't been disturbed and didn't display any suspicious creases. On the subject of creases, I didn't learn anything from the pillows either.

Without any precise reason for it, I looked in the adjoining closet. It contained clothes and footwear, all meticulously arranged—the contrary *would* have been surprising—but nothing else. Not another body, for example. Not that I expected to find anything else, in the absence of a corpse, other than his jackets, neatly wrapped up in protective covers, hung up in there on coat-hangers. His shoes, all equipped with boot-trees and securely laced up left to right, were laid out on a small shelf. At that point I considered it time to allow the law to benefit from my macabre discovery. I descended the stairs to look for a telephone. There was one in a small study. I dialled the number of the Police Judiciaire and had the luck to get my old friend, Superintendent Florimond Faroux, on the other end of the line.

'Nestor Burma here. I'm calling from Fontenay. Which division is it in?'

'Sceaux. Why?'

'To find out if you know anybody there. I've been served up a corpse for breakfast, and it's always a delicate matter to break to the police if you haven't been introduced to them.'

'Ah, ah! A corpse? Well, well! It's been a long time . . .'

'Yes. I thought the gods had forsaken me. But everything's getting back to normal.'

'Of course! Knife? Revolver?'

'Rope.'

'You lucky devil!'

We kidded each other around for another five minutes like this, at the end of which I promised him that I would give the alarm to one of his colleagues at Sceaux, Edouard Pascot, whom he knew slightly. Before following this advice, I foresaw that I would probably be detained by this business longer than I thought and telephoned Hélène Chatelain, my secretary, to make certain that nothing important had cropped up which needed my attention at the Agency.

'The answering service,' I was told by the beautiful child, 'reports a call last night from an André Pellerin.'

'Really? At what time?'

'Midnight. He gave his name but didn't leave a message and didn't say if he would call back.'

I said: 'He won't be calling back.'

I hung up and, without shirking my duty further, informed Chief Inspector Pascot of the job awaiting him on the Rue Charles-Haget.

'Don't move,' this worthy (at least, I suppose so) officer told me.

I didn't follow his order to the letter. I shifted myself just as far as the gate to wait for the arrival of the law. They didn't take long. A police car and an ambulance pulled up in a pointless but spectacular swarm of sirens and flashing lights which only managed to produce a tousled head at the window of the closest villa and delay a housewife for two minutes on her way to market. That was the extent of the tribute paid to curiosity —curiosity didn't seem to rate highly in this corner of suburbia. Five characters got out of the car, the first couple as if they were bailing out of a plane: three policemen in uniform and two civilians dressed like ordinary folk. One of the civvies looked like a doctor picked up on the way. The other, elegant, had a conceited look about him which was aggravated by his lady-killer moustache. He was one of the policemen you find nowadays—he went to school and for him there would be only facts which remained to be verified. He didn't attract me particularly, but I went towards him and put out my hand all the same. He seemed too young to be an officer so I inquired:

'Chief Inspector Pascot?'

'Inspector Lepetit,' he corrected me.

He shook my hand. He was a lot less warm than Jane Russell.

'Was it you who telephoned?'

'Yes, it was me.'

'An acquaintance of Superintendent Faroux?'

'A friend.'

'What's this case got to do with Superintendent Faroux?'

'Nothing. But as I'm a private investigator, I thought it worth while to take out insurance.'

I smiled. He didn't smile.

'So you're a private detective . . . Nestor Burma, if I understood correctly?'

I nodded my head. That was to tell him that he had

251

understood correctly. Then he nodded his head. I preferred not to understand the significance of that movement.

'Well then?'

'Well then what?'

'What were you doing here?'

'M. Pellerin had made an appointment with me. I don't know why.'

'A client?'

'Not any longer, anyway.'

'How did he make the appointment?'

'By telephone.'

'When?'

'Yesterday afternoon.'

'What time?'

'About four o'clock.'

'Okay.'

The terse style. Everything about him was terse. I added:

'He tried to reach me in the night. Again by telephone.'

'Why?'

'I've no idea. The answering service took the call.'

'Okay. Where is it?'

He meant the body.

'This way.'

He gestured a pair of policemen and the doctor to follow us. We skirted round the house. Old mother Chevalier appeared at the kitchen window to let out a piercing scream before staggering back to her chair.

'That's the housekeeper,' I explained.

'Understood,' grunted Lepetit, as if to say: 'You teach me nothing. I see it all. I'm the sort that understands fast.'

Faster than a horse, certainly, but not so sturdy. And if he saw everything as fast as that, I asked myself what he was doing wasting his time at a suburban police station when he could have been Commissioner of the whole French police force in Paris. With such fast understanding, he only needed to glance at the corpse to reach a conclusion:

'Hanged,' he said.

You couldn't hide anything from him. There was something to be said for education after all.

They proceeded to work after this. André Pellerin was taken

down and laid out on the stretcher which the ambulance driver had brought in meanwhile. He looked shorter stretched out than strung up. He was of medium build, grizzled, about fifty years old and tipping the scales at around sixty kilos in round figures. He had been dead a long time and if I had seen him swinging on the end of the rope, it was simply because the Chevalier woman had bumped into his feet as she had gone into the pigeon-house. Those feet, swathed in their expensive shoes with neatly crossed laces, seemed to symbolize appropriately the motive of this unexpected suicide. Because it *was* a question of suicide, the combined reports of the forensic scientists and the police were categorical about that point.

Nevertheless, the next of kin, and especially his sister—he had a sister, a son who worked with him, and a partner; but not a wife, he was a widower—when they passed by later on, were stunned by the news. But as Inspector Lepetit insisted on repeating to them, 'Facts are facts.' And from the evidence he had accumulated, it was as clear as daylight to him that the preceding night, André Pellerin, after putting his car in the garage, had directed his footsteps towards the old pigeonry and hanged himself there. It was difficult to account for the reason he should have chosen such a place, but it didn't matter. Strictly speaking, you could understand that the garage was too small for the sort of aerial gymnastics he had in mind. The body didn't exhibit any signs of violence to support a theory that he had somehow been killed before being hanged. On an overturned pair of step-ladders, there were footprints clearly made by the shoes of the dead man, especially an imprint of the right sole, still smeared with oil picked up in the garage, that had resisted the walk across the park. A heavy-duty torch which Mme Chevalier recognized as belonging to her employer was found on the scene. The pigeon-house wasn't connected to the mains, so the deceased had probably used it whilst making his macabre preparations and had left it burning until the batteries went flat. The corpse's pockets contained only what you would expect the pockets of an upright and conscientious citizen to contain. Identity papers and the membership cards of one or two associations. Some other insignificant documents, a packet of cigarettes, a cigarette lighter, jumbled up with a key-ring

carefully sheathed in a leather case. The deceased's finger-prints were found nearly everywhere—on the steering-wheel and the door of the car, and on the torch. They would have been found on the door-handle of the pigeon-house except that those of the maid and myself had been superimposed.

Inspector Lepetit didn't get upset about that. He had decided already that it was suicide and nothing seemed to contradict his theory. It stood out a mile, in other words. All the same, something about it struck in the throat. For example, I wondered how it was that a perfectionist like André Pellerin didn't leave a note of some kind in the traditional way. After that, I got to thinking of how Pierre de Fabregues had once inflicted the trip from Paris to Cannes on me for the sole reason that he wanted me to witness his suicide.* That sort of thing didn't happen to you twice. And you mustn't forget this point: Pellerin had seemed to need the services of a private detective the day before. I pointed that out.

'Of course,' growled the Inspector. 'But facts are facts. And what is there to show that you haven't been making it all up? Private detectives, you know . . .'

I knew. But I retorted that even though facts actually *were* facts, he could always check them out. From the time of the call, Pellerin must have made it from his office. If the girl on the switchboard shared the same meticulous habits as her employer . . . Lepetit slid over to the telephone without replying. I followed him. And perhaps because he was certain of his fact (one more), he let me listen in on the conversation.

'Hello! Pellerin Haulage and Co.?' he asked with his eyes on the open telephone directory. 'Is that the switchboard?'

'Yes, monsieur.'

'Police here. Inspector Lepetit. I need some information.'

'Inspector? The police?'

'Yes.'

'Very well, monsieur.'

She couldn't get over it.

'About four o'clock yesterday afternoon, did your employer ask to be put through to . . .'

* A reference to the Nestor Burma story entitled 'L'homme au sang bleu' (SEPE).

254

He looked questioningly at me.

'Alésia two seven o nine,' I said.

'. . . Alésia two seven o nine?'

'I'll look for you, monsieur . . . I'll probably have it written down . . . I'm just looking . . . Yes, monsieur,' she said a few seconds later.

'Thank you. One other question. I see that you trade under the name Pellerin and Co. Is the son the associate or is there another partner?'

'I think it would be best if you spoke to M. Godard,' said the receptionist, who had started to feel that this was all a bit beyond her.

'Who is this M. Godard?'

'M. Pellerin's partner.'

She put him through and Lepetit didn't beat about the bush.

'Inspector Lepetit of the Sceaux subdivision here. I am telephoning from M. André Pellerin's residence. He is dead and I shall require your presence here and that of his son if you are able to contact him . . .'

He hung up.

'He really did telephone you,' he said, thoughtfully.

I replied: 'I sometimes tell the truth.'

'It's a suicide, all the same,' he carped on. 'Facts are facts. Other than that, it's a perfect crime. And I haven't a lot of confidence in perfect crimes. I leave them to novelists and private detectives . . .'

I smiled: 'You've made your point. Just let me work on that angle.'

'I absolutely forbid you to do anything of the sort,' he bellowed. 'I . . .'

He changed brusquely from severity to friendliness. For the first time, a smile blossomed under his dandy little mustache.

'All right. So he telephoned you. And probably not just once but twice . . . Think about that call last night. Very likely it came from here. Just before he hung himself . . .' His smile broadened into ill-concealed scorn. 'You enjoy a certain reputation, don't you? I wonder whether you still deserve it. Haven't you guessed the reason for that second telephone call yet? It was to dispense with your services, of course!'

'That's possible. But it doesn't alter anything.'

'You know what I think? I think there's a woman mixed up in it. He wanted you to watch her. That's what you freelances do most of the time, isn't it? Only something more serious turned up later on which made him commit suicide. So he tried to contact you and prevent you sticking your nose in his business. Is your private number in the directory?'

'No. Only the office.'

'Then it's clear to me . . .'

'Except for the reasons why he killed himself,' I objected.

'Don't you bother about that,' he cut in. 'His friends and relations will fill us in with the details.'

But as I had already supposed, they hadn't any idea. The three of them soon arrived. They parked right behind the ambulance. The peaceful Rue Charles-Haget began to take on the congested look of a car park without losing any of its calmness.

The late André Pellerin must have conceived his son in a fit of megalomania when he mistook himself for Rocky Marciano. Lucien Pellerin was a twenty-five-year-old giant with tree trunks for legs and battering rams where other people have arms. But perhaps it was all appearance. The mug balanced on his broad shoulders had the leadened features typical of someone who doesn't get enough sleep. Since he drove one of the lorries belonging to the parental concern, the nights he spent at the wheel probably accounted for his papier-mâché complexion and red eyelids. My name, when it cropped up, didn't seem to mean much to him; but he frowned when he heard the profession I exercise.

Pellerin's partner, Robert Godard, belied the sober dress of a provincial solicitor he affected by his friendly, bustling manner. It didn't suit the age he looked anyway. He was the same build as the deceased, a little more thickset perhaps, and held out a hand which left me supposing that the whole work-force at Pellerin & Co., including the management, helped from time to time loading and unloading the lorries.

The deceased's sister, Aunt Annie, showed all the signs, from her bi-focals down, of being a strait-laced old spinster. She had been dragged along by the other two who probably intended it as some kind of unpleasant joke on her. I strongly

suspected she would manifest the same obsessions as her brother; or, at any rate, carry on the tradition brilliantly.

Inspector Lepetit, in his usual forceful manner, explained everything to them down to the last detail, not forgetting to mention that the deceased had arranged an appointment with me, the purpose of which was unknown. Did they know? They did not and neither could they come up with a plausible explanation to account for his suicide. Aunt Annie mouthed the principal part, whining that it was inconceivable that he should have killed himself, a whole life of rectitude, etc. being opposed to such a course. Godard and the son took up the chorus; they just didn't understand it, not one bit . . .

Lepetit didn't let all these protestations upset him. It wasn't the first time he knew a man do away with himself, eaten up by a secret mental anguish of which his friends and acquaintances were ignorant. He wasn't wrong, for once.

'Pellerin,' ventured Godard timidly, stammering badly, 'didn't have an enemy in the world . . . at least, not to my knowledge . . . but, of course, one can't be expected to know everything . . . what I'm trying to say . . . look here, Inspector! If we rule out suicide, what other possibilities are open to us . . .'

'There is no doubt that it was suicide,' broke in Lepetit. 'An inquiry, should one be conducted, will confirm it.'

Godard sighed and kept quiet.

'It's inconceivable,' repeated Aunt Annie.

Lepetit shrugged his shoulders and repeated his favourite expression: 'Facts are facts.'

He was right. Facts *were* facts. And you could conclude from them that Pellerin had hanged himself. He had explained all that to me from beginning to end. There were numerous factors militating in favour of the suicide hypothesis. There was only one small, insignificant clue, almost invisible to the naked eye, which left the way open to suspect foul play and, indeed, proved it. But this detail, overlooked by Lepetit, I kept to myself. If the Inspector had been less arrogant in my respect, or if he had more or less promised to shave off his moustache in exchange, I would have imparted it to him. But that moustache —he seemed too fond of it to accept any deal, and then, in any case, I hadn't any right to lead a parallel inquiry to the official one.

I wasn't working on the case, but I could arrange it so that I was. To make up the loss caused by Pellerin's inconvenient death, there was nothing to prevent me from offering my services to his family.

The day after my trip to Fontenay, I wound up all the business on hand at the Agency, and the day after that I started my campaign.

My first visit was to Aunt Annie, who had seemed far and away the most shocked by Lepetit's conclusions. She received me rather coldly in the small, dingy apartment that she shared with a couple of cats at the end of a back street in the 7th *arrondissement*. She obviously wasn't rolling in money and I told myself that if I was engaged by her, it would be just as well not to bank on lining my pockets sufficiently to go twice round the world with an actress. I didn't have to worry about fixing a retainer commensurate with my dignity but still appropriate to the old girl's finances. She couldn't admit that it was suicide. Agreed! But as for murder—and what other alternative was there?—that wasn't a comforting thought either and she preferred to let the matter drop at that point without stirring up any more scandal. In short, she didn't throw me out of the door. But it was a near thing.

I buzzed along to the son next, not in the hope of finding him at home—he must have had to return to work at the haulage company—but out of curiosity to see where he lived. I was secretly surprised that he didn't live at Fontenay, for the villa was large enough to house quite a crowd before they would start getting in each other's way. It was a long way from the luxury villa of his father to the sort of slum where he lived now. Contrary to my expectations, he was in. And not alone. A slut who turned out to be his wife answered the door of their ugly apartment.

'How much this time and who for?' she sneered.

'I would like to see M. Lucien Pellerin. It's not about any bills.'

She looked surprised. She showed me to her husband, whose hand was swathed in a thick bandage, and went off to deal with a brat bawling in the next room. I could hear her singing softly and, with the exceptions of the child and the decor, it looked a happy little hole. The young man sat sunk in a

shabby armchair right in front of me, smoking—unbelievably
—a fragrant cigar which must have cost the earth and frowning
in exactly the same way as on our first meeting the day before
yesterday. An idiosyncrasy, perhaps. Or maybe my face or my
profession—one of them on their own or the two together
—didn't much meet with his approval.

'What do you want again?' he asked, without moving from his
seat or acknowledging my greeting. (Hostilely, on the whole.)

'I'm not happy about this suicide story,' I began. 'As you
know, your father had asked me to call on him which is how I
happened to discover the tragedy. He must have had an
assignment for me. He didn't get a chance to tell me what it
was, but . . .'

'All right! Me, I know.' With his chin, he indicated the room
where his wife was. 'It didn't go down well with him when I
married Martha; he wanted you to nose around in our private
life.' He laughed. 'I can understand how you grieve over . . . the
loss of a client, especially one from whom you hadn't had time
to extract a commission, but don't expect me to settle up for
your expenses. For the last forty-eight hours, I've done nothing
but pay up. But this one? Not a chance.'

I said: 'You don't owe me anything.'

'That's lucky. And if the old man had owed you anything, it
would have been the same. Now you can get out.'

'With pleasure. I only came to put you a proposition but we
might as well forget about it.'

'What proposition?'

The door-bell rang at that moment. His wife went to answer
it.

'Mornin', Madame Pellerin,' said a young voice. 'The
guv'nor sent me because he heard that you'd settled with
Madame Plantier and . . .'

'Come here for your money,' bawled out the injured man
defiantly.

The woman escorted in a cheeky youth.

'How much do I owe your guv'nor? He can't wait, eh?'

'Oh, you know,' said the youth, taking a piece of paper from
his pocket and handing it over. 'I've had enough of this
business. I just do as I'm told. As for can't wait, you can't blame
the boss. You've been owing for more than six months.'

259

'That's enough!'

On a sign from her husband, the woman took out a thick envelope full of banknotes and started to count some out.

'Thanks,' said the youth. 'Until the next time, then.'

'There won't be a next time,' laughed Lucien Pellerin. 'It won't be long before I'm off out of this dump. Here, catch your tip.' He threw him one of his family-sized cigars. 'Show that to your guv'nor before smoking it so that he sees once in his life, at least, what a Henry Clay looks like. Hundred and fifty francs each,' he crowed.

The errand-boy looked at the cigar respectfully, slipped it in his pocket and went out.

'What's all that?' I said, indicating the envelope his wife was putting away. 'Part of the inheritance already or your first child allowance?'

'What's that got to do with you?'

'Nothing. I'll be off then. Goodbye, M. Pellerin.'

'Just a minute. You were telling me about a proposition.'

'Never mind that. You don't seem disposed to accept it.'

'Tell me anyway.'

'I repeat that I'm not convinced it was suicide. I'm sorry, but your father might have been murdered. I could . . .'

'. . . Investigate the possibility and squeeze me for some money?'

'All work deserves to be rewarded.'

'Well, you keep your work and I'll save myself some money. Look here, Brahma . . .'

'Burma.'

'Look here, Burma. You make me laugh.' He did as he said. 'Murdered! That's a good one! My father didn't have a lot of reasons to kill himself, but more than anyone had to murder him. I'm not forking out any fat fees to make an out-of-practice detective happy.'

'Okay. But you admit that this suicide theory doesn't hold water?'

'Like loads of suicides. You'd have to be able to look inside their heads to know what was going on in there. My father was completely cuckoo, they don't come any madder. When I started to drive a lorry for the firm, I used to live at Fontenay. But my work made me get back at odd hours; he couldn't stand it and I had to go and live in a hotel. You get it? He was off his head, I tell you. After all, it's possible that he killed himself because he didn't find something in its usual place. It's possible. But murdered? No. You make me laugh. You'd better find an easier way of making money.'

'You didn't like him much, eh?'

'What's that got to do with you?'

'Nothing. Just asking, that's all.'

'In passing, eh? Out of routine? Well, think what you like, I didn't hate him either—if you want to know. It was just that his obsessions made life practically impossible with him.'

'The figure of speech is appropriate.'

'Yeah! That gives me an idea. Murdered!' He roared with laughter. 'Perhaps by someone even madder than he was. Someone who wanted to be the only one of his kind on the face of the earth. Investigate that, detective!'

I said: 'He wasn't killed by a madman.'

'Oh, oh! Some clues already, Sherlock?'

'So-so.'

'No joking. Well, take it easy. I wouldn't want to know them even if you'd been a hundred times more mysterious.'

'Too bad . . .'

I didn't have to stand up to take my leave. I had been standing up all the time. I put a finger to the rim of my hat.

'So long, then.'

'Cheers,' replied Pellerin. 'Tell me one thing, though . . .'

'Yes?'

'Wouldn't you like to know how I did this?' he asked sarcastically. 'I thought that you detectives—received your first child allowance, eh? and did you get on well with your father, eh? and have you been inoculated, eh?—asked questions without rhyme or reason?'

'Not when they already know the answers,' I smirked. 'You sprained your wrist counting your pile of money. Lack of practice.'

'You haven't quite got it,' he sneered. 'I had to knock an errand-boy on the head to steal his money bag. Like most errand-boys, he was a bit thick-skulled . . . Now try to find someone to employ you to investigate it. You might make yourself a bit of pocket money . . .'

When I got outside, I reviewed the situation. Aunt Annie: zero. The son: likewise. That left the partner. I went to try and sell him my story. He wasn't alone either. In the director's office at Pellerin Haulage & Co. that had been shared formerly by the man who had hanged himself at Fontenay, someone was just finishing a chat about the affair when I announced myself. It was Inspector Lepetit: still elegant, still sure of himself, still in possession of his moustache, and still—no, a little bit better disposed to Nestor Burma, or so it seemed. Humouring me, no doubt.

'Well, look who it is! The man who gives the mystery a knock-out punch' he exclaimed jovially when he saw me. 'What brings you here?' He didn't wait for a reply. 'I thought I'd warned you off the case, but it seems that was too much to ask a private detective.' He said it playfully, without acrimony. 'Don't tell me, you've discovered he was killed with an axe?'

M. Godard acknowledged this little joke with a discreet bleat of laughter, flattering to the Inspector without being upsetting for me.

'Not yet,' I smiled. I fired a sally back at Lepetit: 'The motive for the suicide is still unclear.'

'You think so?' he chuckled. 'There have been some fresh developments, Monsieur Nestor Burma. M. Godard informs me that . . .'

'Inspector!' he interrupted with embarrassment. 'Do we really have to go into that . . .'

'Definitely. If you knew what a persistent breed they are, you would realize that it was better to point out their mistakes than to leave them something for their imagination to play with. You can't get rid of them otherwise. You'd have them for ever under your feet.'

'As you like, Inspector. But it's already a painful enough subject . . .'

'So,' I said. 'You hold the motive?'

'Yes. That is, if you can get hold of a hole. The hole is in the company's finances and was only discovered by M. Godard yesterday. A hole dug by Pellerin. Of course, the business belonged to him, but he's siphoned off so much without telling anyone that the firm is on the brink of bankruptcy . . .'

'Perhaps not bankruptcy,' the partner interrupted timidly.

'But, well . . . there have been some withdrawals . . . quite a lot of withdrawals . . .'

'You see that I was right to keep a hold on the facts and not waste my time trying to find complications, eh, Burma?'

I asked: 'Why should he have needed to dip his fingers in the till? To satisfy an obsession?'

'That's about the size of it. Have you heard of Lola Garigue?' I shook my head. 'You've probably seen her photo on the cover of certain magazines. Didn't I tell you the other day that there would be a woman at the bottom of it?'

'And that's where Lola comes in?'

'In the flesh.' He drew a figure of eight in the air. 'He was maintaining her. Now do you get it?'

'I'm only a simple private investigator. I give the mystery a knock-out punch, but only after a certain degree of difficulty. I'm all at sea when it's too easy.'

'You see what they're like!' roared my detractor, asking Godard to be a witness. (The latter smiled. The smile was a bit thin. He was probably thinking to himself that it was all very well that Lepetit, happy to have found at last a motive for the mysterious suicide which justified his conclusions, should take the opportunity to rub a private detective's face in the dirt, but that wouldn't repair the hole in his company's capital.) 'There's always a skirt in it. With these facts, Burma, you'll need to pull more than a wry face.' He decided to take me more seriously and added: 'Pellerin, despite his money, couldn't hope for the exclusive rights to the affections of the lady in question. She probably told him something recently which made him a bit uneasy. His intention was to have her followed by you. But the very same night, knowing that it was his fault that the company was about to collapse'—Godard raised his hand—'he decided to throw it all in, tried to dispense with your services, and hanged himself . . . Yes, all right,' he went on to meet Godard's silent objection, 'to say that he ruined the firm is putting it too strongly. All the same, he had misappropriated funds belonging to the company and he would have been obliged to account for it. Everything would have been fixed up in private, of course, except that he lost his head. Suicides are strange people.'

It was well said and it held. By more than a thread. And if

263

there hadn't been something, somewhere, which looked like a thread, I would have been convinced as Godard seemed to be by it. There didn't seem to be any point now in asking him if he would like to engage me to make inquiries in other directions.

I had the luck to see Faroux the same evening.

'Well then,' he said, 'it seems this business the other day has given you the chance to cross swords with Inspector Lepetit.'

'Who is that fellow?' I asked. 'He appears to think a lot of himself. I would really enjoy taking him down a peg or two.'

'He's a bit green and tends to be high and mighty, but he isn't a bad chap and he's a good policeman.'

'My opinion is that he's completely bungled the case. It's not his fault. He lacks flair and imagination.'

'And you, you've got more than your share, haven't you? But don't overdo it. As you were on the job, I thought I'd sneak a look at the file. Lepetit is what he is and you're free not to like him. You're not the only one, by the way. But his report didn't leave any loose ends. If there wasn't any apparent motive at the start of the inquiry, that's not the case now. But you're still not satisfied, are you? Perhaps you still think the fellow was murdered?'

'Something like that.'

'By a really clever murderer, eh? You and he would make a right pair.'

'Not so clever. He forgot one detail . . . and Lepetit over-looked it.'

'What detail was that?'

I told him. Faroux laughed derisively, shook his head and nearly dropped his chocolate-coloured felt hat on the floor.

'You've got your obsessions too, I tell you.'

'Precisely. And by this remark I take it you realize that you can't get rid of them so easily. I can't interfere personally now. I tried but didn't get anywhere. For this reason, I saw the son. He married against his father's wishes and works for the firm as an ordinary employee, without receiving any share in the profits. He's on a basic wage and lives from hand-to-mouth. In fact, up until these last couple of days, he's been stone broke. Now he's paid off his debts and smokes Henry Clay cigars which cost a hundred and fifty francs each.'

'And he's the murderer?' asked the Superintendent, ironically.

'No. I tell you that just to show that nothing escapes me.'

'And nothing escapes Lepetit either. You shouldn't take him for an idiot. Young Pellerin's change of fortune reached his ears and he looked into it. It is established that he hit the jack-pot on the National Lottery recently.'

'The Lottery has a lot to answer for,' I declared. 'Me, I've never won anything on it.'

All the same, some folding stuff fell at my feet two days later. Lucien Pellerin telephoned me, all smiles, to apologize for his previous bad manners and invite me to come and see him and Aunt Annie urgently at the latter's apartment. I asked what it was about—with this family it was just as well to make certain from the outset. I had already been in trouble with one appointment.

'Oh well,' he stammered, 'we would like you to take up the inquiry again . . . from the presumption . . . of murder . . .'

'Good. I'll be right over. Try not to hang each other before I get there or the police will end up suspecting me.'

I found them both, aunt and nephew, in good health when I arrived at the old girl's place. In good health, except for the young man's injured hand which was still buried beneath its dressing.

'What's happened that suddenly makes you resort to my services?' I asked, deciding to play rough because of the washed-out tea which was being poured into the cups.

Dumbly—she didn't open her mouth the whole time I was there, and the only contribution she made was to indicate her approval, and even that was done without enthusiasm—Aunt Annie thrust some documents under my nose. I recognized that they were life insurance policies.

'Ah, ah!' I said. 'There's a clause which excludes suicide, eh?'

'Don't think us any meaner and more heartless than we are,' whined Lucien Pellerin. 'For us, suicide is as inexplicable as murder, but if it was proved . . .'

'Officially, it is.'

'Then you were bluffing us the other day?'

'No. There was one piece of evidence fighting alone against the facts. A tiny clue which has most probably since been destroyed. If there is a criminal, don't expect me to unmask him tonight. He's clever.'

'Unmask him when you can . . . It strikes me that if Father took out life insurance, he wouldn't have done anything like commit suicide which would cause us to lose the premium. Me, I wasn't on good terms with him, but Aunt Annie . . . I can understand that when you're about to hang yourself, perhaps you don't think of all these things, but, all the same . . . If there is any possibility of proving that he was murdered and, consequently, claiming the premium of the insurance I . . . There won't be much to come from the firm which, it seems, is on the verge of bankruptcy. From now on, this is our last resort. Do you understand?'

'And the National Lottery?'

'So you inquired about it?' He shrugged his shoulders. 'Five hundred thousand francs. It's not the earth.'

'It's the National Lottery though, isn't it?' I pointed to his injured hand. 'You told me about some errand-boy.'

'Forget about it. Sylvio, one of the drivers at work, did it the day that father's death was discovered. He accidentally reversed and trapped my hand against the wall. A bit more and it would have had to be amputated. And Godard hopes to rebuild the company with raw recruits like that . . .'

'I get the impression that it wasn't an auspicious day for the Pellerin family.'

'Yes. I'm lucky that I have enough to live on while I'm getting better. As you know, it's only to the Lottery that I owe my present affluence. I'd lost the ticket but got the tobacconist's where I'd bought it to issue me a note that they'd sold it to me. That's the accepted practice.'

'Talking of notes,' I said, 'how much can I expect as my fee?'

'You agree to . . .'

'Give me fifty thousand francs as a retainer,' I said. In a roundabout manner that meant precisely, *yes*.

'There's a driver called Sylvio at Pellerin Haulage. I want a complete run-down on him,' I said a little later to my assistant, Reboul. 'Perhaps he's just careless. It might be something

266

else.' I repeated the story of the accident he had caused. 'If he was trying to kill the son, it opens up possibilities. From what Pellerin told me, I infer that he only joined the firm recently.'

Reboul went off to work on Sylvio—who ought to be just accident-prone—and I went to call on Lola Garigue with the first excuse which came into my head. I got the better deal. Lepetit was right. I knew her saucy little face from having seen it on the cover of *Lace and Black Stockings*, though this wasn't the view of the star that was usually on display in this type of publication.

I pulled her leg—so to speak—for a good half hour and left convinced that even if she was getting long in the tooth (due to the toothpaste she once advertised perhaps), she hadn't anything to do with her benefactor's death.

Next I set to work checking that this Lottery business was on the level. I soon put my mind to rest on that score. After that, I telephoned Faroux to tell him in which direction my inquiries were leading. Out of politeness. He didn't give me any encouragement but he didn't lay into me over the phone either. Also out of politeness, I suppose. I returned to the office hesitating between some tobacco and something to wet my throat. The theory I had *afoot*—you will see later that that's the word—held, but was difficult to prove.

Late in the evening, Reboul came in with his report. He had had some lucky breaks and brought home a whole crop of leads.

'Someone gave you a good tip,' he started.

'The accident was attempted murder, eh?'

'No. It was stupid and careless like all accidents, but our client's life was never in danger for a moment. Only, this Sylvio is an odd type of body. An odd type of body-guard, as well. That's more or less what he was before he started wrecking lorries. You were right: he hasn't been there long.'

'Body-guard for whom?'

'Salvetti. Another one of those Corsicans from Montmartre, recently suspected of arms trafficking. Does that mean anything to you?'

'No. It isn't an arms dealer I'm after, although you never know. After all, there might be a lead there. Stay close to Sylvio, old fellow.'

'Difficult for the time being. He's on his way to Tourcoing at the moment, where he's gone to make a delivery. Nothing unusual about that.'

'Don't let him out of your sight when he returns.'

Reboul went off to bed and I returned home to do the same. I couldn't sleep and got up again almost immediately. I fell on the telephone and called Pellerin who, having carried out his promise to desert the slums, was living for the moment at Fontenay:

'Nestor Burma here. If you hadn't injured your hand, would you have been making any trips, amongst others, to Tourcoing this week?'

'Yes. Why?'

'What load?'

'Hides.'

'Destined for where?'

'Decatoire and Co. Why?'

'No reason.'

'I should hope not,' he grumbled. 'Damn it! The real Sherlock has got nothing on you. I start to get the idea that even if you can't find out anything to satisfy your clients, you know how to give them the impression they're getting their money's worth . . .'

I hung up without getting annoyed and dialled Marc Covet's number.

'Hello, Covet. Get out your car and come round here. I'm taking you to Tourcoing. You can expect enough copy for a really sensational "Exclusive".'

Not to get out of the habit, the soak-journalist swore at me. But he didn't refuse.

At Tourcoing, the next morning, I had no difficulty finding the premises of Decatoire & Co. and had the satisfaction of seeing a lorry parked outside with Pellerin Haulage & Co. written in large letters on the tarpaulin.

I said to Covet: 'My instincts tell me that, in order to defray some of the costs of the trip, this lorry won't be going back to Paris empty. I want a front row seat, Nestor Burma's usual place, so I shall jump on the back when I think they're ready to leave. I want you to tag along behind in case anything happens. It won't be before nightfall.'

268

I watched the lorry discreetly all day, in case it should disappear from under my nose. I got a couple of opportunities to study the driver. Under his leather jacket, the famous Sylvio looked as if he was in disguise. He was accompanied by some kind of co-driver, an abject, nervous character with dried-up features and timid eyes. The lorry driver get-up didn't seem to suit him either.

In the afternoon, they went to a factory and loaded up bails of cloth, then they halted for a long time on the outskirts of the town before setting off back to Paris. I took the chance to take my leave of Covet and slip under the canvas cover while the two lascars were drinking in a nearby café.

Not long after that, night fell, a night which promised blackness and infamy—but that depended on what use it was put to. The lorry started up. Out of sight in my niche, half-suffocated by the strong smell given off by the bails of new fabric, I grinned. If the five tonner didn't pick up some other merchandise en route, little Nestor wouldn't be looking too good.

Suddenly, I thought that we had teetered into the ditch. The heavy lorry staggered first to one side and then to the other. We had abandoned the highway some time ago in favour of a rutted dirt-track. My hopes revived that I hadn't been wasting my time. One poetic thought following another, I checked the mechanism of my gun and stowed it away where it would be handy should the occasion arise. We lurched on for a good while, then the lorry stopped, the back-end still lost in a thicket. I had hidden myself in the damp undergrowth—it was raining in this god-forsaken hole—before either of the men had stepped down from the cabin. One of the customers up front stayed where he was and played with the headlights, turning them on and off, before finally cutting the engine. A voice greeted them out of the darkness and told them to pull up a bit because it wasn't feathers they had to load up.

'Merde!' swore the co-driver. 'We could have chosen better weather for our last trip. It's all right for Salvetti, eh?'

'Something wrong?'

I didn't hear the reply. The engine fired, the wheels spun in the mud for a moment before gripping, and the lorry advanced, jolting more than ever. I waited awhile, then started to work my way round to it carefully. A whole army was milling round the vehicle. I heard someone give an order to move the bails of cloth to make room to put the other goods underneath. It was more than an hour before it looked as if nothing else could be crammed on the trailer. The canvas was tied down and some realist suggested returning to the house before they split up.

'Just for a minute, then.'

'That's right. Just time for you to tell us the business, Sylvio . . .'

I watched the group making for a house which had all the subtle allure of a death-trap. A weak light flickered in one of the windows as if bothered by the rain. I made certain that they hadn't left a guard and slipped back, soaked to the skin, to my hiding place. I had even less room to stretch out in than before, but I wasn't complaining. Not long after, the lorry set off for Paris carrying a clandestine passenger who was thoroughly determined that it wasn't going to reach the capital.

I had formulated a plan in which Covet and his car had a part to play, but it looked, for the moment, as if the journalist had lost track of the lorry. I decided to take my chances when we were going through a large market-town which I had seen, on the way out, was provided with a police station.

I crept up to the window giving on to the cabin and shattered the glass with the butt of my gun. There was another noise in reply, more breaking glass. Sylvio, surprised, had momentarily lost control of the wheel and smashed another window. But he quickly regained control, swearing madly, and pressed his foot down on the accelerator. That didn't much suit me. The co-driver had been asleep, but he woke up with all this going on around him and started to look aggressive. So I took the opportunity to let off a shot. Legitimate self-defence, in other words. I didn't hit the co-driver, I got Sylvio in the top of the arm. This made him throw the lorry into a swerve. We hit a fountain. I threw myself back and let myself roll when I hit the ground, still clenching my gun in my hand, just as the co-driver let rip through the rear window. I loosed off a volley and some windows opened. The lorry was just about to disappear round a bend when one of the bullets struck a tyre. It exploded like a bomb.

After that, I've no idea what happened. When I started to see straight again, I was in the police station and Sylvio, his mate, and even Covet were keeping me company. Covet explained to me that he had lost the trail and, war weary from driving up and down, had decided to return peacefully to Paris when, passing through a place which seemed in the throes of revolution, he had realized that I couldn't be very far away. I told the police what it was all about and they replied that they had actually found a cache of arms on the lorry. They let me call up Faroux. I announced the news to the Superintendent that I had just rendered a service, if not to Pellerin Haulage, then to society at large in a triumphant tone. Then I had some more serious things to tell him.

A couple of hours later, Covet on my heels, and me on my knees, I went into Faroux's office at the Tour Pointue.

'I see you were right, Burma!' he exclaimed. 'But, God Almighty, it only held together by a thread.'

'A boot-lace,' I corrected him. 'Have you informed Lepetit?'

'Don't be too hard on him. I doubt if he could prove his suicide theory now without arresting the whole of the deceased's family . . .'

'Good. Did you find any evidence at our friend's?'

'The mark of a large bolt which had been fixed to the moulding of the ceiling. The poor fellow was taken by surprise —the same technique used by Eyraud in the Gouffé business.'

'And Thibert, the master of the rope. You'll find that one in Professor's Balthazard's *Shorter Forensic Medicine*. Obviously, he had a mistress? But who helped him?'

'We don't know anything. She's absconded.'

'Ah, ah! Or dead, perhaps? In these circles, that can happen quickly if it's necessary.'

'I hope we can put our hands on her because . . . well, that johnny we arrested doesn't look as if he has any intention of making a confession and we haven't any material evidence of the crime. Of course, even if he doesn't admit it we can still charge him with trafficking in arms. But he could plead ignorance to that all the same.'

'Let's go and try to refresh his memory. Everyone will be there.'

'Even Lepetit,' smiled Faroux.

That pleased me.

'My dear Godard,' I said, 'would you like to explain your perfect crime to everyone or would you prefer me to do it for you? You're not answering? So much the better. I love making speeches. Here you are then. You've been in league with Salvetti, the arms dealer, for some time. Under the cover of an honest firm, you shipped his highly illegal merchandise for him. At the same time, you have a very demanding mistress and you were dipping your fingers in the till. Pellerin realized this was going on but he didn't suspect you. He suspected his son who, just then, had been spending money as if it was water. Wanting to avoid a scandal, he decided to engage a private investigator. He rang me from the office you shared with him, which is how you came to know that he had called me. Or he might have even told you himself. The intrusion of an honest tax-payer such as myself into the firm's business was full of consequences. Because it wasn't just a question of the stolen money, there was this matter of the shipping of arms as well. In the hours which followed Pellerin's telephone call, you had plenty of time to contact Salvetti and hatch a plot to silence the old fool. In the arms trade, human life is cheap. The same evening, using some pretext or other, perhaps that of discussing the deficit, you lured him to your house. There everything was ready to surprise him and hang him. You pulled so hard on the rope that you blistered the palm of your hand—I noticed that the next day when I shook hands with you. But what mattered was Pellerin's body, and that showed no signs of violence. It was exactly as if he had hanged himself.

You drove him in his car—Messieurs Pellerin and Godard, haulage contractors in every sense—back to his villa. That was a risk you had to run. But you were right because nothing happened on the way. When you arrived at Fontenay, you parked the car in the garage and put on your victim's shoes —you both took more or less the same size—to make it look as if it was Pellerin's footsteps which led to the neglected pigeon-house. You put your foot in the patch of oil intentionally to carry it over there. Another sample of Pellerin Haulage. You suspended the body, returned his shoes to him, and left. Finally, you telephoned my office. Another risk you had to run. If it had been Nestor Burma who had answered, you would have pretended it was the wrong number. But if, as you supposed, I didn't like being disturbed in the night but still wanted to know first thing in the morning what calls I had had in the night and I used an answering service, you would leave Pellerin's name and everyone would presume that, before committing suicide, he had tried to dispense with my services. That went all right, too. The suicide theory came into existence above all, though, because you managed to link the disappearance of the money with the death of the deceased. It isn't necessary to add that you were careful not to leave your finger-prints anywhere. None were found. You returned home with an easy mind. On foot, probably. But it doesn't matter. In short, everything had gone perfectly according to plan. And if he hadn't taken out some life insurance policies which his relatives were eager to get their hands on . . . And this trip to Tourcoing, as well, which Lucien Pellerin had probably decided to make despite his father's death . . . That didn't fit in with your plans. So Sylvio, the dreamy driver, straightens it out for himself by injuring the young man. Does that all fit together, my dear fellow?'

He damned me to hell and mouthed off about there not being any evidence. There wasn't, in fact. But Faroux and his crowd, not forgetting Lepetit, who took that to heart, had uncovered a first-class witness in the afternoon. They found Godard's mistress as a result of poking around Salvetti's connections. She was a pin-up à la Lola Garigue, but less classy. The villains had kidnapped her more or less to keep her from opening her mouth. She opened it all right when they took her to the station. She had been present at the murder. They had needed someone to distract his attention while they put the rope over his neck. The Gouffé business, second take. After this testimony, Godard didn't bother denying it any more.

'It doesn't matter, Nestor Burma,' he said as he signed his confession, 'but I'm wondering what put you on the track. I thought I was fire-proof. Was there something I forgot then?'

'Nestor Burma's theory held on a thread,' laughed Faroux,

while Lepetit, on hand at the interview, gloomily stroked his moustache.

'A shoe-lace,' I corrected him once more. 'Yes, the next time *that you put on a perfectionist's shoes for him, you won't forget to see that the laces are done up in his usual fashion.* Otherwise you run the risk of shocking the imagination of a shock-detective, should one be strolling in the area.'

For luck, he spat out: *'Merde!'* It didn't bring him any.

# APPENDIX
# EUGÈNE-FRANÇOIS VIDOCQ
## The Cheek of Judas

One day, in the summer of 1812, a man named Hotot, a former
agent of the Préfecture before my appointment as chief of the
Sûreté, came to see me. For some time he had been anxious to
return to police duties and, on this occasion, he offered me his
services for the Fête de Saint-Cloud.

I was all the more astonished by this step, as I had previously
laid information against him which had led to his being brought
before the court of assizes. Though my suspicions were
aroused, I received him kindly all the same. By acting in this
way, I was able to read his mind without him realizing. It was
agreed between us that he should station himself near the main
ornamental lake in order to point out to me the numerous
pickpockets which the festival never fails to attract in this spot.

On the appointed day, I went with two of my agents to the
designated place. But it was in vain that I looked for Hotot. He
was not to be seen amongst the crowds which thronged the
edges of the lake. After walking up and down for some time,
hoping to come across him, I decided to send one of my men to
find him. After scouring every corner of the park and its
gardens, my agent returned, admitting defeat. No sign of
Hotot. The rogue himself turned up at this moment, announc-
ing enigmatically that he had been just about to 'reel in six of
the light-fingered gentry' when they had caught sight of Vidocq
and scuttled off—though he did not despair of meeting up with
them later and once more 'baiting the hook'.

I pretended to swallow this story; and Hotot, thinking he had
duped me neatly, seemed to be secretly congratulating himself.
We spent the rest of the day in each other's company. In the
evening, after I had left him, I learnt that several thefts had
been committed on the other side to the one which Hotot had

indicated to us was being 'worked' by the pickpockets. I realized immediately that the ingenious fellow had brought one side of the district to my attention only so as to be free to work in another. Resolved to nail him at the first opportunity, I let this go unremarked and, so as not to arouse his suspicions, acted as if I was especially well disposed toward him. An opportunity was not long in presenting itself.

I was on my way home after spending a night on duty with Gaffré, a fellow agent, when I realized that we were not far away from where Hotot lived. On the spur of the moment I suggested to Gaffré that we should pay him an unexpected visit. Gaffré agreed. Hotot was still in bed when we knocked at the door.

'Oh! It's you!' exclaimed Hotot, clearly surprised to see us. 'What miracle brings you here so early in the morning?'

'Just passing,' I replied, 'so we thought we'd drop in and offer you a glass of something.'

'Now you're talking! Lead me to it.'

'Gaffré's going for it.'

'Good for him.'

Gaffré went out and Hotot climbed back into bed.

While my agent was away, I gave Hotot's apartment a searching appraisal. Hotot's undisguised weariness, his wet clothes and muddy boots, and the disorder in his bedroom made it obvious that he had retired very late. I was suspicious but did not say anything. Gaffré returned with a bottle and, after a few glasses, Gaffré and I left together.

As soon as I was alone with Gaffré, I told him what I had noticed. He replied that he had been about to raise the subject himself. We exchanged thoughts and agreed on this point: Hotot had been out on some nocturnal ramble or other. At midday we reported to M. Henry who told us that during a sudden downpour in the night more than four hundred pounds of lead had been stolen from a half-built house on the Boulevard Saint-Martin. The watchman, who was certain he had seen the thieves, had declared that there were four of them.

'I know one of them,' I said, 'and as for the rest, I shall have them before long.'

'How is that?' asked M. Henry.

276

I recounted to him what I had seen in Hotot's bedroom, and the Head of the Second Division was convinced that Hotot was no stranger to this theft.

At once I went to visit the scene of the crime with the Commissaire of Police of the district. We saw, in one place, the clear imprint of studded boots and where the earth had been depressed by a man's weight. Convinced that these marks had been made by Hotot, I gave orders that the ground was not to be disturbed. Then I went to buy a cooked chicken and, once again accompanied by Gaffré, returned to Hotot's.

For Hotot's benefit, we were unsteady on our feet as we came in and put on a show of being slightly drunk. Producing the cooked bird from underneath my frock-coat, I said we had come to have dinner with him. While Hotot, still in bed, went into ecstasies over the savoury aroma of the fowl, Gaffré stooped down and hid Hotot's shoes in his hat without Hotot remarking it. I shouted across the road to the wine shop to send up a flagon and, as there was no table, we ate around Hotot's bed.

When Gaffré had finished eating, I gave him a pretext to leave us by asking him to step round to my house and advise them that I should not be home for dinner.

When we were alone, Hotot reminded me of his repeated requests to return to police work. He enlisted me to speak in his favour with M. Henry and added that, to persuade me to make use of my influence, soon after the nomination he would give me some useful leads. He even mentioned the names of a few thieves to me, amongst others, Berchier, called Bicêtre (no doubt because of his long acquaintance with that prison), Caffin and Linois—with the single stipulation that I should take them red-handed.

To encourage these revelations further, I said that it was the only way of impressing M. Henry. Consequently, Hotot told me that these three characters had recently stolen the lead off a roof and that an old scrap-metal dealer, Bellemont, in the Rue de la Tannerie, was acting as receiver for them.

At this moment Gaffré came back with half a bottle of brandy which Annette had given him. As he replaced Hotot's shoes, he launched me a glance which left me in no doubt that Hotot was implicated in the theft committed on the Boulevard Saint-Martin. We drained the bottle and left. On the pavement Gaffré confirmed the signal he had given me: Hotot's shoes had exactly matched the footprints. I had known they would.

If you consider this behaviour towards his friends, you can realize what an unprincipled rogue he was. He thought nothing of selling his friends in an attempt to buy the consideration of M. Henry and so purchase his own immunity. Armed with this insight into his nature, I knew him for a greater villain than those he planned to denounce, and it struck me that he was probably the instigator of the crime.

I obtained some fresh information which further convinced me that this was the truth of the matter, and I resolved to purge society of such a monster. As a result, I instructed my agents to watch him. And knowing that he had two mistresses, Emilie Simonet and Félicité Renaud, I thought it would only be in the interests of justice that I should try to excite the jealousy of these two women.

After making all my arrangements, I hastened off to a rendezvous I had with Hotot on the Champs-Elysées. I told him that I had an assignment for him—to obtain the confession of a man about to be arrested. If Hotot was already in the cell when the man was brought in, he should have no difficulty in winning his confidence. Hotot agreed eagerly, asking only that he could first have a few words with Félicité, who adored him.

'Go on,' I said, 'but don't be all day about it. When you've finished, go straight to the little café-tabac across the road from the Théâtre des Variétés on the Boulevard Montmartre. Ask for a bottle of beer and go and drink it at the back of the bar. Two policemen accompanied by an officer will come in looking for someone, signal your presence to them by lifting your little finger. They will arrest you and take you to the post at the Lycée. Once there, they have instructions to leave you alone for two or three hours before the suspect is brought in; that way there won't be any doubts about you when you start asking questions.'

'That's a good scheme,' replied Hotot. 'Don't worry about me. I'll fool him well and truly. You won't be disappointed in me. Thieves' honour . . .'

We parted on this exchange. While Hotot went to say goodbye to his mistress, I hurried to the Préfecture and instructed two inspectors to effect his arrest in the café-tabac. To assure myself that everything went according to plan, I followed him. And soon I had the satisfaction of watching Hotot, with his hands tied together, marching out triumphantly between those two gentlemen.

I left Hotot in the lock-up. He celebrated his good fortune at first, but lively scenes ensued later as he failed to convince the corporal, the sergeant, and the officer of the post, each in turn, that he was really a police spy, and that they should allow him out to get something to eat.

Faithful to my plan, I went to the Place du Châtelet where Emilie lived. I found her at Mère Bariole's, one of those wretched taverns where the riff-raff of prostitution collect under the pretext of having a drink.

As she knew me for a gay dog, Emilie willingly accepted a few drinks from me. When I saw the wine was starting to fuddle her brain, I burst out that she was too good for the likes of Hotot. She asked me what had made me say that. I pretended reticence, the more to arouse her curiosity. She insisted so vehemently that I was forced to admit that I had met Hotot with Félicité Renaud on the Champs-Elysées. They had been quarrelling, but had made up again and gone off together.

'Did they, indeed!' said Emilie. 'And I was stupid enough to believe him when he told me he didn't see her any more.'

'You're too trusting ... They're certainly friends at the moment, and from what I heard I bet they spent last night together as well, somewhere near the Palais-Royal, I expect.'

'Oh! Not last night, Jules.* He spent last night with some friends.'

'That's right. I remember now. He was with Linois, Bicêtre and Caffin, wasn't he?'

'Who told you that?'

'Why, Hotot himself!'

* Vidocq was a master of disguise and alias, as Holmes would be later. Jules was one of the names he used to pass amongst the underworld.

279

'He did? That's just like him. He told me not to breathe a word about it to anyone. But tell me, Jules dear, do you know where he's gone with Félicité?'

'Yes, to Bicêtre's, but don't ask me where he lives because I forgot to ask his address.'

'Oh, I know it all right—Rue du Bon-Puits, he lives at Lahire's on the fourth floor. I'm going to go round there now and teach him a lesson. Come with me and you'll see.'

'That's not the way to go about it, Emilie. You want to make certain that they are there before you start kicking up a rumpus. I've a better idea. Why don't you wait at the bottom of the stairs while I go up. If I come down immediately, it means the birds have flown, but if I'm a long time, you can come up when you're ready.'

'You're right: it's better to be sure before making a row.'

I took Emilie by the arm and we made our way to the Rue du Bon-Puits. I went in on my own. After I had made certain that Bicêtre lived there, I rejoined Emilie in the street.

'We're out of luck,' I said. 'Lahire, Bicêtre and his wife have gone to Linois' for supper. Do you know where he lives, Linois?'

'Yes. He lives with his mother in the Rue Joquelet. Come on, it's this way.'

'I'm worn out, Emilie. Let's give it up.'

'No. You wouldn't refuse me a little thing like this would you, my pet?' coaxed Emilie. And to decide me, she lent over and gave me a peck on the lips. I pretended to yield to her entreaties.

In the Rue Joquelet, I went up to Linois' on my own again. As he knew me only by name, I knocked on his door and asked him where I could find Hotot. When he said he did not know, I descended the stairs, wishing him good night, to where Emilie was waiting for me.

'Our luck's against us,' I told her. 'Caffin owes them all a drink and they went round to call on him twenty minutes ago.'

Emilie did not know Caffin's address but she thought one of the 'ladies of the night' in the Place aux Veaux would know it. I protested. Emilie insisted. And we bent our steps towards the

Place aux Veaux because it was essential to my plans to discover the whereabouts of Caffin.

On the way I managed to aggravate my companion's ill-humour until she became so communicative that she told me everything I wanted to know about Hotot. Indeed, he had been the wretch who had urged his friends to commit the theft the night before.

A good-time girl, Louison la Blagueuse, whom we met *en route*, when asked by Emilie for news of Caffin, said that he ought to be with Emilie Taquet either at Mère Bariole's or La Blondin's. Another prostitute, further down the street, said that he was at Mère Bariole's. And that was where we went.

We had stopped off for a drink at least a dozen times in the course of the evening. Emilie was, by now, rolling drunk. She threatened to start a fight if the Madame did not promptly produce her lover. Quite reasonably, La Bariole protested that he was not there but added she was welcome to look for him upstairs. A minute later she came back down again and said she had seen only Caffin.

Emilie was of no more use to me. Moreover, she might let slip some chance remark which would upset all my plans. Consequently, knowing she would go to the ends of the earth to scratch out the eyes of her unfaithful lover, I suggested we tried the Hôtel d'Angleterre.

We left together. But not surprisingly there was no sign of him at this thieves' kitchen either. It was time I disencumbered myself of Emilie. I told her to stay where she was while I went to see if Félicité had returned to her apartment. Instead of carrying out this commission however, which would have been the last word in complaisance, I hurried off to the nearest police station which was at Château d'Eau. I identified myself and gave orders that Emilie was to be arrested and kept incommunicado until the next day.

Then, accompanied by two agents, I returned to Mère Bariole's and arrested Caffin while he was still in bed.

'What's this?' he exclaimed, half-asleep. 'You're not running me in, are you?'

'Don't blame me if someone has grassed on you.'

'Well, well, Jules. You don't say. This won't bring you any luck.'

'Are you simple or what? I have to do my duty, don't I?'

'Of course. But all the same, a friend is a friend.'

'Look! When I tell you that you're nicked, I mean it. Last night a load of lead fell off the back of a roof, didn't it?'

'So. Someone really has spilled the beans. It must have been that rascal Hotot. Give me five minutes with the Commissaire and I'll settle his account for him.'

The Commissaire arrived and listened gravely to everything Caffin said. As may be imagined, Hotot did not escape lightly. Linois and Bicêtre were arrested the same night, and all four of them were eventually sent to the galleys.

# NOTES

1. Godwin's preface to the 'Standard Novels' edition (1832) of *Fleetwood*
2. *A Study in Scarlet*, Chapter 7
3. *Caleb Williams*, Volume III, Chapter IX
4. *Les Vrais Mémoires de Vidocq* (Paris, Corrêa, 1950)
5. *Gaboriau: Father of the Detective Novel* (*The National Review*, Dec. 1923)
6. *A Study in Scarlet*, Chapter 2
7. Sir Arthur Conan Doyle, *Memories and Adventures*, Chapter IX
8. *Words* (London, Hamish Hamilton, 1964)
9. *The Seven of Hearts* (Cassell, 1908). The Leblanc bibliography is a maze of different titles under which his books have appeared in translation
10. To illustrate this problem: this edition of *Arsène Lupin, gentleman-cambrioleur* goes by the title *The Exploits of Arsène Lupin*. Richardson's introduction is to the Bodley Head edition of 1960
11. *The Return of Arsène Lupin* (1933)
12. *813* (1910)
13. *Studies in the Literature of Sherlock Holmes*
14. Between 1909 and 1911 there are, apparently, three English titles: *The Fair-Haired Lady*, *Arsène Lupin versus Holmlock Shears*, and *The Arrest of Arsène Lupin*
15. *The Eight Strokes of the Clock* (1922)
16. *Jim Barnett Intervenes* (1928)
17. Quoted in *Le Roman Policier* by Boileau-Narcejac (Paris, Payot, 1964) p. 130
18. Recently collected and edited by Peter Haining under the title *The Gaston Leroux Bedside Companion* (London, Victor Gollancz, 1980)
19. *The Mystery of the Yellow Room*, Chapter XVIII
20. Interview in *The Sunday Times*, 16 May 1982
21. *Le Cas Simenon* (Paris, 1950; tr. *The Art of Simenon*, 1952)

# SOURCES

1. Emile Gaboriau: *Le Petit Vieux des Batignolles* (1876). Newly translated by T. J. Hale.
2. Maurice Leblanc: *The Seven of Hearts* (Macmillan Publishing Co, Inc, 1908). Translated by Alexander Teixeira de Mattos.
3. Maurice Leblanc: *Jim Barnett Intervenes* (Mills and Boon, 1928). Translated by Alexander Teixeira de Mattos.
4. Gaston Leroux: *The Gaston Leroux Bedside Companion* (Victor Gollancz Ltd). Translated by Mildred Gleason Prochet.
5. Georges Simenon: *Les Nouvelles Enquêtes de Maigret* (Editions Gallimard, 1944). Newly translated by T. J. Hale.
6. Jacques Decrest: *Six Bras en L'Air* (No. 1 *Le Labyrinthe*, 1943). Newly translated by T. J. Hale.
7,8. Pierre Véry: *Cinéma, Cyanure et Compagnie (Librairie des Champs-Elysées, Le Masque* No. 468, 1954). Newly translated by T. J. Hale.
9. Jypé Carraud: *Les Cinq Plages de Stanislas Perceneige (Editions La Bruyère*, Collection *La Cagoule*, 1949). Newly translated by T. J. Hale.
10. Léo Malet: published in Ellery Queen's *Mystère-Magazine*, April 1952. Newly translated by T. J. Hale.

Appendix Eugène-François Vidocq: *Les Vrais Mémoires de Vidocq* edited by Jean Savant (Paris, Corrêa, 1950). Newly translated by T. J. Hale.